Our Sporting Times

Our Sporting Times

David Miller

Foreword by Will Carling

PAVILION

First published in Great Britain in 1996 by
PAVILION BOOKS LIMITED
26 Upper Ground, London SE1 9PD

Introduction and 'His Words Live After Him' copyright © David Miller 1996
Other extracts © The Times 1996
Foreword © Will Carling

Designed by Neil Palfreyman

A CIP catalogue record for this book is available from the British Library

ISBN 1 85793 880 1

Typeset in 11/12 Stempel Garamond
Printed and bound in Great Britain by Hartnolls, Bodmin

2 4 6 8 10 9 7 5 3 1

This book may be ordered by post direct from the publisher.
Please contact the Marketing Department.
But try your bookshop first.

CONTENTS

1986

Seeking out the liberals on both sides of the South African fence
How Terry Venables transformed Barcelona
Brazil and France duel in the sun
Maradona's 'hand of God' is not the whole story
Argentina deservedly defeat West Germany
Times man up to his armpits in the Solent
Jahangir grinds Norman into submission
The search for Oxbridge's lost elite
Winning is a family affair for Steffi Graf
Cash's victory against all the odds
Historic last final at Kooyong

1987

Deposed captain Gower reflects on his future
Gliding on the epic Australian scale
Reflections on MCC's bi-centenary
Momentous first Ryder Cup triumph in America

1988

Zurbriggen's aggression-free innocence
Katarina Witt an incorrigible flirt
Peter Young earns his pint
Lyle wins Britain's first Green Jacket at Augusta
How Tinling judged the lines
Modern pentathlon bronze for Britain
Courage alone not enough for toiling Thompson
The unrivalled Oriental courtesy of the Koreans
Germany, and Becker, come from behind in Davis Cup

1989

Amiable Bruno outclassed by Tyson
The horror of the Hillsborough disaster
The emergence of Monica Seles
Christ Evert: feminine yet tough
Constructing a city of peace in Hiroshima

1990

How Balestre drives the Grant Prix circus
What rowing owes to the Boat Race
Floyd inconsolable as Faldo retains title
Peter Blake's romance around the world
Fireball cricket in the Caribbean
England stretch Germany in cautious semi-final
Buchwald shuts out Maradona from World Cup final
Poles honour the heroes of Solidarity
Geoffrey Green, sportswriter unique in his time

1991

The amateur meteors who drew 100,000 to Wembley
Woosnam denies Olazabal to win thrilling Masters
Lendl's torment extended by another year
Becker sub-standard against rising Stich
Pan-American Games a credit to Cuba's people, not its system
Lewis takes his place alongside Owens
America's triumph benefits Ryder Cup
South African sport in the hands of three wise men

1992

Mansell thwarted by wheel failure and brilliance of Senna
Taylor's muddled tactics fail

Navratilova, and tennis, have cause for complaint against Seles
Redgrave and Pinsent toy with the opposition
Boulmerka strives for the liberation of Muslim women
Lewis, a British heavyweight challenger with genuine credentials
Re-integrated South Africa returns to Twickenham

1993

Senna appeals for F1 regulations to be changed
Parreira optimistic for revival of Brazilian fantasy
Ruthless Cambridge complete ultimate Boat Race humiliation
Bobby Jones: 'You play the ball as it lies'
US golfers strangely untroubled by Langer's Masters victory
England's unnecessary elimination from World Cup
Leconte's genius eclipsed by power of Becker
A letter to Arthur Ashe's daughter Camera, aged six
Martinez withers under Graf's onslaught
Atherton exudes leadership

1994

Busby's immense qualities as a manager
Total mastery of Torvill and Dean
Fairy-tale opening to Winter Olympics
Dan Jansen's world record in last-chance race
Bayul collapses in moment of triumph
A letter to sports enthusiast John Major
England help to make Ambrose look unplayable
Ayrton Senna dies at Imola
The tactical limitations of a hero fly-half
Impending exit of Navratilova exposes the flaws
Maradona, the boy from the back-streets of Buenos Aires
No shot the incomparable Hoad could not play
Germans' disbelief in World Cup capitulation
Baggio misses penalty to give Brazil fourth Cup
How Mikhail Bobrov helped to save St Petersburg

Tshwete calls for patience in South Africa's sporting race
Can Ma produce male athletes as successful as his women?
Why the brilliant Clough would have been bad for England
The rise and rise of Gerry Francis
Johan Cruyff's intellect on and off the field

1995

Stanley Matthews, a sorcerer beyond description
Why the Boat Race is different
Spurs steal victory in classic cup-tie
Jack Rowell's chain of command
Scotland's cynical cheating brings no reward
Foreman reprieved by judges' disgraceful verdict
A new storm to weather for Dennis Conner
Crenshaw's win is charged with emotion
Euphoria and symbolism at climax of rugby's World Cup
Sampras wins respect, Becker the hearts
Daly's Open victory is a fitting reward
Christie still erratic off the track
The world warms to modest Edwards
Ryder Cup again proves flagship to rest of sporting world
Atherton maturing as batsman and captain
Geoff Thompson's crusade against youth crime

FOREWORD

Having read through the amazing variety of significant sporting moments that have been threaded together through this book, it dawned on me that David Miller has what I perceive as the ideal job.

Having covered sport for forty years – although I'm sure I won't be thanked for mentioning it – David Miller has the rare ability to capture the essence, sometimes the sheer emotion, that comes across so powerfully when watching sport live. Very few manage even to see the crucial moments as they pass, let alone capture them, so it is a pleasure to write a foreword for a book that manages to do so repeatedly.

Sometimes sportsmen and women can get immersed in their own sports, their own problems and challenges, and convince themselves that no others could achieve such feats. Rugby has enjoyed a growing interest over the last seven or eight years and I, at times, have almost forgotten that other sporting events have taken place, and brilliant moments and achievements have passed me by. England has been involved in two World Cups and has achieved three Grand Slams, proud moments to remember, but as I travelled through this book, I realised how great some of the contests, matches and championships have been that I have failed to see.

I love sport, and always have. Above all, for some very strange reason, I love rugby, but I enjoy all sporting success for the surge of adrenaline and emotion it always provokes in me. So this book has been a great pleasure; a reminder and memento of sporting life that David Miller has excelled in capturing and bringing together in an enthralling volume.

WILL CARLING, 1996

INTRODUCTION

In April, 1962, I overheard Major Wilson Keys, the chairman of West Bromwich Albion and an England selector, say he would ensure that Johnny Byrne, the quicksilver forward of West Ham, would not go to the World Cup finals in Chile with the England squad. Byrne had punched a shot over the bar in a League match against West Bromwich, from which a penalty was missed. I felt Keys was going too far. I know now he was not.

The last thirty years of sport has seen the establishment of an eleventh commandment: no sportsman shall be denied the right to earn his living by any moral consideration implicit in the other ten. Many professional sportsmen, and indeed many in so-called senior amateur sport, have forgotten the basic reason for which money is charged at the gate: that the public voluntarily seeks entertainment. Too many contemporary sports performers, such as Linford Christie, are concerned only with their rights, rather than with their obligations towards their audiences.

Sport has been corrupted by politics, nationalism and money; and, particularly on account of the latter, by increasing violence, abuse of the laws, and resort to drugs. Much beauty remains. The heritage of Weekes, Worrall, Walcott and Sobers may have been tarnished by intimidatory West Indian bowling, but we have had the sublime batting of Richards and Lara. The legend of Matthews, di Stefano and Pele may have been abused by a thousand brutal, expedient defenders, but Romario, Juninho, Bergkamp and Kanchelskis are there to remind us that soccer remains the king of games. Memories of Obolensky and Barry John may at times be obliterated by New Zealand or South African rugby thuggery, yet Lynagh, Campese, Lomu and Mertens can lift 80,000 from their seats.

Sport at its pinnacle is foremost about glory, and nowhere does the dictionary definition of that word mention winning, only honourable fame. More often than not it is the quality of the loser which determines the fame of the performance of the winner. We have only to think of the Masters victories of Woosnam against Olazabal or Couples against Floyd, of Graf's against Sanchez Vicario at Wimbledon, of Coe's against Ovett in Moscow.

Without rigorous, fair discipline sport becomes meaningless; indeed, is no longer sport. It is not surprising if public confidence and interest decline when the public cannot be certain that what they are paying to watch is *bona fide*. The most elementary mistake so many professionals have made is to suppose that winning is everything, an idea imported from the Americans with chewing gum and almost as objectionable. Many Americans have forgotten the example of their own legendary golfer, Bobby Jones. Danny Blanchflower, inimitable captain of Tottenham Hotspur during the club's most famous days of all, maintained that football was, fundamentally, about glory, above and beyond any other kind of reward. Sport at its pinnacle must, by definition, be admired by everybody, not merely by those aligned behind the winners. If you want to understand glory and the way it reaches out to ordinary people, observe the response by Brazilians to the late Ayrton Senna or to their world football champions. Victory must carry that special, rare quality that causes everyone to celebrate.

How wrong we were, those of us who, thirty years or more ago, yearned for and advocated a brave new world of sport dominated by professional attitudes. How gravely misguided we have been proved. Away with amateur fogies, we cried. Down with the dogmas of our privileged grandfathers; forward with pragmatism and efficiency. But the professionals blew it. What we got was rampant expediency: millionaires such as Greg Norman attempting to manipulate even more millions. Without education, culture or experience, the professionals, granted self-determination, quickly learnt the price of everything but little understood the older, traditional values. Rightly and belatedly freed from social servility and financial restraint, the professionals have in less than half a century almost wrecked many of the sporting traditions and standards fashioned over the previous century. Some say sport must adjust to changing social attitudes. I question that.

Sport, that mystic alchemy, microcosm of life's big-dipper, has not lost its capacity to inspire the individual or enchant the crowd, to motivate a Zatopek, a Klammer or a Warne, to produce harmony near to perfection in Redgrave and Pinsent or the emotional will-power of a Dan Jansen.

Yet to have championed, as I did in 1960, the abolition of football's maximum wage in England – that monument to proprietorial Victorian injustice which humbled the genius of a Matthews, Carter, Lawton or Wright with a clerk's wages – today carries the guilt of handing firecrackers to five-year-olds. We now have footballers of only moderate ability earning £6,000 a week and still behaving as though they were drunken bricklayers.

To have helped push the All England Club towards leading tennis out of the shamateur world of moral witch-hunts which haunted Gonzales, Hoad and Laver, into the present era of million-dollar mugging, of foul-mouthed robots such as Courier, is to have destroyed simultaneously something of charm and worth.

To have closed for ever the odious separate gates for Players and Gentlemen at Lord's cricket ground, only then to have the Long Room overrun by the likes of Kerry Packer and a generation of umpire intimidators, ball-tamperers and cheating gamesmanship is to have created a fire more uncomfortable than the old social discrimination.

To have turned golf's dignified, uncluttered calendar of historic championships – when to watch Hogan and later Peter Thompson, Palmer or Nicklaus was to observe Zeus himself – into the interminable synthetic television world of unidentifiable 'Classic' monopoly money is the ultimate in showbiz dilution by dilation. And now the television moguls are trying to acquire 'ownership' of rugby, Union and League.

I do not think I am disciplinarian or patrician in attitude. Over two centuries ago my forebears founded the *Manchester Mercury*, one of the earliest newspapers and published in support of the liberal Whigs. In 1823 the *Mercury* was merged with the *Manchester Guardian*. The liberal attitude continued down our generations. So it all seemed quite simple to radicals back in the Fifties: the amalgamation of ideology and professionalism, of devoting every effort to winning without denigrating defeat, remaining gracious in victory, on the Wykehamist principle: 'Manners makyth man.' I grew up in a school, Charterhouse, where at that time even to wear a tracksuit was considered slightly professional, to warm up before a football match or even an athletic race was suspect, and to congratulate a goal-scorer was unpardonable. I competed as a junior in the British Empire Games at White City with starting blocks sawn from an old church pew, nailed to the cinder track through strips of Meccano. When, as captain of football, I requested the headmaster – Brian Young, later chairman of the Independent Television Authority, a former Oxford Blue for hurdles but a mite too godly for his own good – for permission to take a regular linesman to away matches for greater efficiency, I might as well have asked for a cocktail cabinet in the pavilion.

The master in charge of football, Anthony Wreford-Brown, whose father Charles had been a Corinthian centre-half and chairman of the FA, was an hereditary idealist who inspired us to run through the proverbial brick wall. To play with honour was the highest acclaim. Yet when I first encountered at university the professional mind, in the shape of our benign and brilliant coach, Bill Nicholson from Tottenham, and also the absurdity of the England selection committees, amateur (for whom I was for a while a contender) and professional, some of whom did not recognise players by half-time, I longed for the merging of the two codes.

The gap, however, was too great. The amateurs had forfeited their right to influence the professional game by turning their back on it eighty years before, simultaneously losing the advantage of mixed competition enjoyed by cricket; although, to be sure, it cannot be said that the traditional cricket establishment responded intelligently to the commercial era of the second half of the twentieth century. In football, the development of the professional game had long ago passed almost exclusively into the hands of tradesmen, more often concerned with personal prestige than sporting principles. How many outstanding chairmen of First Division clubs have there been since the Second World War? Perhaps three: Harold Hardman, former Olympian from 1912, of Manchester United; Denis Hill-Wood of Arsenal; and John Cobbold of Ipswich. They knew how to accept defeat as well as victory, Kipling's two imposters engraved on the entrance hall at the All England Club.

I am ashamed that my generation, lucky to have had a link with the glorious Thirties and to have experienced the vintage Fifties, the last of the untainted wine, has squandered the opportunity to help retain old values. Of course there have consistently been great events and great performers in all sports in the recent era, because talent develops spontaneously and always will, yet sport has continued to prosper only in spite of debilitating and growing cancer. Sport's opponents, such as Bernard Levin, my esteemed colleague on *The Times*, are able to write a shaming list of accusations against sport, all undeniable. Yet they are, in effect, accusing society, because sport will always be a mirror of the way we live. That is part of its fascination. If sport is seen in some instances to be rotten, then we should be turning our gaze upon ourselves. It is no coincidence that the exposure of financial irregularities by Nick Leeson of Barings Bank in Singapore and George Graham at Arsenal should occur almost simultaneously. The acts of violence by prominent footballers such as Cantona, Ince, Jones and Fashanu are no more than a reflection of greed and cynicism on the streets. The tolerance granted to such acts within the sporting arena would have invoked shame and horror in my youth. Today, it brings invitation to the Oxford Union.

George Orwell's sour pronouncement that international sport is an unfailing cause of ill will is an exaggeration. The football teams of Hungary and Brazil in the Fifties, of Aston Villa and the Corinthians in older times, of Brazil and Ajax today, have been the cause of international goodwill to which language and culture are no barrier. The tennis of Maria Bueno and Manuel Santana was an internationally appreciated aesthetic pleasure comparable to that of Fonteyn and Nureyev. The Olympic triumphs of Owens and Keino united the emotions of millions of free men, and Blankers-Koen in 1948 the minds of liberated women. The Olympic Games of Los Angeles, Seoul, Barcelona and Lillehammer, though by no means perfect, provided weeks of global unity at times of stress and tension in other fields. The climax of the men's and women's marathon races in Barcelona, between Hwang of Korea and Morishita of Japan, and Yegerova of Russia and Arimori of Japan respectively, were the stuff of Greek legend.

Yet my fear, and it is by no means exclusive, is that money, in conjunction with the two factors that primarily help generate it, television and sponsorship, will by the end of the century have erased from major spectator sport the little that remains of its example of integrity, honour and fair play. These are not the principles of nineteenth-century public school sport. A sense of honour is a basic human instinct. At the Ancient Olympics you were flogged for a false start. The lust for money today provokes cheating by the use of drugs, or simply the expediency of negative tactics or rule-breaking. The coincidental casualties from this commercial tendency are likely to be, I suspect, firstly team games, which depend for brilliance upon subordination of natural individual selfishness to the team ethic; secondly, the pre-eminence of the Western capitalist nations, as already witnessed in the most recent athletics World Championships; and thirdly, regularity in the achievement of record performances in measured sports because of over-competition. When sport becomes drenched with money, its standards perversely decline following an initial upsurge, and I think we can expect to see, as the twenty-first century approaches, more champions, both team and individual, emerging from such countries as Nigeria, China and the rest of the developing world where the hunger for identification remains the strongest motivation.

A question that will arise more than ever in the Nineties is that of 'who governs sport?': the varying battle of dinosaurs between the international tennis federation and the Association of Tennis Professionals; between FIFA and the rich clubs, between those clubs and individual players, all with their individual greed; between the international athletics federation and its competitors, and ultimately with the Olympic Games; between the rugby federation and the leading international players who inevitably demand a share of the megabucks being generated; between the leading golfers, backed by the International Management Group, and the traditional major tournaments, insatiable players wanting to turn millions into tens of millions, like the tennis players; and so on.

What is happening in all professional sports is that, while they have become more commercial, the governing bodies have mostly been outdistanced in business acumen by the street-smart agents, dealers and television negotiators. Only the bigger sports, internationally, have been able to afford to employ agencies to act on their behalf, and, even then, too many of them are prepared to sell their souls. The wider television sponsorship becomes, the more these power bases will seek to manipulate the governing bodies, many of whom are already on the run. The traditional administrators are in additional difficulty because their constitutions are out of date and legally vulnerable. For its own protection from every kind of exploitation, the world of sport needs an Independent Court of Arbitration, acknowledged and accepted by the civil courts, such as that established by the International Olympic Committee. The absence of such independence in disciplinary matters caused, for instance, the overturning of the Football Association's ten-year suspension of Don Revie, the England manager, for breach of contract, though the High Court judge declared the FA to be morally correct even if legally wrong.

Domestically, the reality is that much of British sport, on and off the field, is in a mess: competitively, administratively, morally. British organ-isation heads towards the twenty-first century in confusion: fragmented, arguing, jealous and left behind in the field of international leadership. Britain, which gave much of organised modern sport to the world, which formulated most of the rules, and where the Corinthian spirit epitomised attitudes that were universally admired, is a languishing power. 'International statesmanship has passed us by,' Lord Howell, the only effective Minister for Sport that Britain has had, observes. 'The British, the last bastion of ethics, seem not to have noticed that the train carrying everyone else has left the station,' Charlie Battle, an Anglophile lawyer from Georgia and live wire of Atlanta's Olympic Games Committee, says with evident disappointment.

The situation, on analysis, is even worse than might be supposed. The chief executive of the Football Association is heard to defend violent play in court. Gary Mabbutt, the Tottenham captain, is put out of the game for months by flagrant assault. Allan Lamb, the England batsman, ends up in court for voicing his opinion on abuse of the ball, under the regu-lations, by Pakistan. Will Carling, the England rugby captain, is threat-ened with reprisal, via the International Board, for similarly speaking out against New Zealand's cheating. Governing bodies stall, and the truth somehow becomes evil. Scotland cheat by abusing the laws in the attempt to prevent England winning the Grand Slam, and those scorned are the people who accuse them of cheating. The corruption of sport and its rules by money and sponsorship – both necessary lifelines – and by blind com-petitive expediency and neglectful officials, now threatens sport's funda-mental function, acknowledged by Pierre de Coubertin, founder of the Olympics: teaching us how to live our lives. We even have the once staunchly traditional *Daily Telegraph* telling us that sports champions should not be expected to be role models. The public will always see them as such. Not to expect this is moral surrender: as daft as saying teachers and policemen have only technical not social responsibility.

Introspective Britain, insecure at having lost an empire, is resentful that, after it dominated international federations and councils a genera-tion ago with leaders such as Sir Stanley Rous and Lord Burghley, and was the influential authority on rules in most Olympic events, never mind non-Olympic sports such as cricket and rugby, the scene is now dominated by Latins: Samaranch at the IOC, Havelange in football, Nebiolo in athletics, Acosta in volleyball, Vasquez Rana in the associa-tion of national Olympic committees. For all their limitations, their manipulations, these men have produced huge expansion, competitive and commercial, in their respective fields. They are not to be ignored. If they have been unchallenged by Britain, that is a reflection on the present anonymity of the British. The Princess Royal, a former president of inter-national equestrianism and a member of the International Olympic Committee, made ineffectual attempts at resistance from the periphery, restrained by her royal position. The rest of the world is no longer listening to Britain meekly shouting advice from the touchline. As Samaranch says: 'Britain has too many committees, too many voices. They have to regain their position. International sport needs them. They must open their minds to engaging more foreign coaches. Nobody questions that Britain was the birthplace of modern sport, but they cannot live by history.' As Jacques Rogge of Belgium, president of the European Association of National Olympic Committees and a potential successor to Samaranch, says: 'Your singularisation, as four countries, is both a traditional strength and a contemporary weakness.'

Gratuitious critical comment on foreign leaders by the British press has had no impact other than to help antagonise those leaders and push Britain further towards the fringe. Britain has a temperamental problem over leadership. We habitually mistrust, in all fields, powerful chief executives who might become dictators, and we lack departmental supervision and discipline, viz. Barings. We prefer instead figureheads, powerless leaders beneath whom operate a profusion of supposedly safe but indecisive committees. Hence Britain has been content to respect the Duke of Edinburgh and his daughter in prominent positions: he as president of the Central Council for Physical Recreation, she of the British Olympic Association, whereas in fact their royal restrictions prevent them being demonstrative public leaders (and I say that as a staunch monarchist). Their royal occupancy, domestically admired, blocks rather than assists Britain's return to authoritative international leadership, especially among the new world of Africa and Asia and the former colonies.

Prince Phillip's patronage of the CCPR has, historically, obstructed the creation of a single British sports body. He has backed the energetic Peter Lawson, former CCPR general secretary, in attempting to undermine the Sports Council, inheritor by royal charter of the national sports centres. 'The CCPR is totally ineffective,' Lord Howell reflects, having unavailingly attempted when minister to find a unifying formula. 'They turn up everywhere, and what do they do?' The CCPR is anachronistic: its Fair Play Charter and leadership training scheme are splendid, yet it has no direct authority in active sport, no power of censure.

It is shameful that almost half the British competitors at the 1992 Olympics returned in debt from their preparation, while Germany assisted 3,900 competitors beforehand with over £6,000 per annum each. 'It isn't all that easy to change a country's point of view,' Craig Reedie, chairman of the BOA and in 1994 elected a member of the IOC, reflects. Sebastian Coe, former Sports Council vice chairman, is succinct. 'In any sport, with short-term failure you look at the performance. With long-term failure, you look at the administration.'

It is a regrettable fact of contemporary sport that while spectators nowadays know a little about many sports, through the coverage of television, they tend to have little specialist knowledge and are unaware of the quality of what they are watching. There has been a decline, too, during my forty years in journalism, in the quality of commentating in the written press, most notably in the tabloid section which reaches the greater audience. A result of this is the promotion of 'personality' figures such as Eddie Edwards, the myopic ski jumper, and Frank Bruno, an amiable but limited heavyweight; a promotion which bears no relation to performance. There is also an obsessive preference for failure and smear stories, which demonstrates the ignorance of editors, for all that the evidence of circulation reveals that most newspapers sell best when the stories relate to success and heroism. We see the concurrent phenomenon of non-performers who become the focus of media attention, such as the deplorable Vinnie Jones, and commentators who claim air and print time, such as Frances Edmonds, merely by being famous for being famous. The traditional, knowledgeable commentators such as Rex Alston are a breed of the past.

Yet sport will survive, in spite of all, because of the fundamental innocence that it shares with children. The wish to be skilful, to compete, to excel is a spontaneous emotion. Sport forms a natural extension and convenient stage for our normal desires. As with the rest of life, sport is dependent on rules and self-discipline, without which its structure collapses. The great rugby union debate seems to me to be missing the point. This should not be whether the game ought to have capitulated to professionalism – amateurism having long ago become irrelevant – but whether it can preserve its sporting ethos. What matters is that rugby, however categorised, is played within the rules in a generous spirit and penalises those who calculatedly err.

I make no excuse if the extracts reprinted here, by kind permission from *The Times*, predominantly concern those performers who embrace their sport with dignity and good humour.

ANOTHER BRITISH HOPE DESTROYED

Hagler's combinations outclass Sibson

11 February 1983 Worcester, Mass.

The destruction which took place inside the civic centre here on Friday night was symbolised by the blizzard which simultaneously outside was paralysing the whole of America's north-east coast – fine needles whipped horizontal by a 50 mile-an-hour wind which made it impossible to see and overwhelmed even the most robust snow-plough.

The spite and speed of Marvin Hagler's combination punching over six rounds of the world middleweight title bout had England's plucky but utterly outclassed challenger, Tony Sibson, from Leicester, temporarily blinded by the blood streaming from cuts above both eyes, unable to see the hail of blows and finally groping his way around the ring as helplessly as any pedestrian at the mercy of New England's most bitter night for 40 years.

In the aftermath of Hagler's comprehensive and largely predictable victory, more calculated and awesomely effective than when he took the title from Alan Minter with a third-round knockout in 1980, is left one hard fact and a pile of questions as high as the 10-foot drifts here.

After six defences of his undisputed tenure of the World Boxing Council and World Boxing Association titles, most critics consider that Hagler must be ranked with Carlos Monzon as second only to Sugar Ray Robinson in the history of the division. From a fatherless childhood in the Newark (New Jersey) ghetto, where mother and children had to sleep under the beds during the 1968 race riots to avoid the bullets coming through the window, Hagler today stands a supreme, dignified champion entitled to the good life which his exceptional boxing skills and dedication have earned him.

If it is true, as he claims in the publicity handouts, that his handlers, Pat and Goody Petronelli – former fighers who grew up in Brockton with Rocky Marciano and in whose gymnasium he sought sanctuary from the streets and a passport to liberty – never took a nickel from his early $50 contests, then it is reassuring that there are at least two souls in the twilight world of professional boxing who can one day face St Peter without having to use the ropes and hope for a favourable split decision.

For the moment there is not a cloud on Hagler's horizon, for such other challengers as Frank (The Animal) Fletcher, in line to meet him in two months' time, are hardly fit to climb into the ring with him. Glancing at the ringside and the handsome, unmarked features of Sugar Ray Leonard, the undefeated and now retired welterweight, one had to concede that it must be in Leonard's interest – since he was already the richest boxer alive – that he never was able to challenge Hagler. Surely not even Leonard's ringcraft could have neutralised the weight difference and Hagler's frightening range of punches?

For Sibson, however, all is uncertain as he flies south for a holiday in Florida, the pain in his face – which was restored to shape by 17 stitches – cushioned by the feel of £350,000, or what is left of it by the time his associates, as they are known, have had their share of the action. There are hardly two concurring opinions on his preparation for the contest, his inadquate performance on the night, or the course which he and his advisers should now follow, properly to exploit his obvious financial potential yet to protect his record for the time when the ageing Hagler must quit.

While it should be said that the venerable manager, Sam Burns, has had a significant influence since he took control over Sibson's career, it is undeniable that a natural boxer with a fountain of courage and strength arrived at the pinnacle of his sporting ambition here grossly under-prepared – not physically, but strategically and mentally.

Whether the responsibility lies with Burns, Ken Squires the trainer, or Mickey Duff, the promoter, who was also prominent in Sibson's corner, it does not matter: it was amateurish in the extreme to allow the challenger not to have sparring practice, specially against a southpaw with such renowned fast hands as Hagler. Sibson's friend and admirer, Kevin Finnegan, the former British middleweight, was so distraught at the apparent lack of guidance that he left the hall before the finish.

Hagler landed with his first four punches, almost unprecedented in a title bout; a right lead and two lightning lefts, delivered straight and inside Sibson's guard, cut his nose in the first exchange. Already we sensed that for the challenger each round survived was only an extension of the inevitable.

Had his timing been improved by sparring against a southpaw, then not only might he have avoided some of the early punishment but he would have been better equipped to land the one lucky blow which would have stood all forecasts on the head.

Sibson was to admit afterwards that it had taken two rounds 'to judge Hagler's distance'.

There was for me an air of latent doom in the pageant beforehand. After we had greeted past middleweight champions in Carmen Basilio (1957), Peul Pender (1960), Terry Downs (1961), Vito Antuofermo (1979) and Alan Minter (1980), the gladiators for the evening arrived – Sibson in scarlet robe and trunks, swathes of grease on his eyebrows and an evident new boy's anxiety in his restless glance which could not be disguised by much shadow-boxing and the occasional wink at friends in the audience, as much to reassure him as them.

When Hagler made his entry, in hooded white satin-lined magenta cape, he carried with him the assured calm of some celebrated musical soloist taking the stage, his expressionless gaze a mark of absolute confidence in the performance he was about to give. Suddenly the age difference looked not six years but 16, in the champion's favour.

In the second round Sibson, in spite of weathering some more stinging right leads, began to advance, forcing Hagler to back off, and as they passed each other, returning to their corners at the end of the round, the boy gave the man a hard look in the eye: but bravado only met with disdain. I made the round even; and also the next when Sibson, with that woodchopper's left arm coiled menacingly, countered bravely and briefly had his man on the ropes.

Within half a minute of the fifth the challenger's left eye was almost closed and, although he now landed his one significant left hook of the bout, a few moments later his left eye was severely split. The ringside doctor inspected the damage back on the stool, then withdrew. The sixth was thankfully the end, for there was always the danger that courage could carry the Englishman several rounds further into humiliation and trauma.

His press conference afterwards was a combination of honesty and confusion. The fact that he could smile through his torn features was the sign of a fighter who did not live for victory alone, both flaw and virtue, and conflicted with his assertion that his pride had been hurt. How much? 'I never feared the pain, it was his class that hurt me. I'm still the best but one. I moved up a class and could not cope, he made my mistakes look worse than anyone else would have done.'

The next morning there occurred a strange contradiction between Sibson and his manager. The boxer claimed that he wanted to be 'thrown to the wolves' in America to fight for bigger money and experience than he could get by going for the European title. Burns quickly butted in to say that he did not want him 'pressurised into anything stupid' and added that 'the boy is very precious to me'.

The fact is that Sibson is a naive and relatively innocent star capable of generating substantial rewards for himself and others in a sporting financial jungle. We shall await with interest to see what shape his career now takes, whom he meets and where. I am assured it is more likely to be in Europe. The overriding impression is that whatever he does the percentages would be decidedly more in his favour with an Angelo Dundee in his corner.

LEARNING HOW TO BE BRAVE

Training muscle and nerve in the Welsh mountains

8 March 1983 Plas y Brenin

Go into the staff room at 5 o'clock at Plas y Benin – two gallon teapot and sticky buns – and you could be in any school master's common room, until you discover that the unassuming folk around you have adventure pedigrees which put James Bond in the shade.

That fellow over there with a hole in his wet sock has canoed round Cape Horn, the one in the scruffy teeshirt has defeated the north face of the Eiger, and, oh, yes, the one over there in the pebble glasses has skied down Annapurna. The ordinary citizen can be a part of this rarified company for as little as £39 for a weekend's climbing course.

Plas y Brenin, in fact, is a centre of sporting excellence no less than Wimbledon or Lords, nestling under the skirt of Snowdon in the challenging beauty of the Ogwen Valley.

It is here, unobserved by David Coleman, where the air truly is as cool and clear as the mountain stream, where the opponents this week, next week, and for ever, are the wind and the swirling mists, the granite and the ice and snow, where the only cheering is the chattering waterfall or the mournful cry of the ewe, that a remarkable team of instructors is assembled by the Sports Council at their national centre for mountain activities.

Here, in inspirational surroundings, you may learn everything from merely how not to get lost when out hill-walking in places where only the hawk is at ease without an ordnance survey map, to the kind of esoteric technique which would take you up Everest if your mind did not freeze first: you may be an inner city schoolgirl, or a middle-aged executive, but whoever you are, Plas y Brenin will test your nerve and muscle more than your bank balance.

The instructors, unlike some of our contemporary professional sportsmen, have an almost uniform characteristic of modesty. Their vocational enthusiasm persuades them to work mostly a 12-hour six-day week for around £8,000 a year. A relaxed classlessness pervades the whole centre, with its accommodation for 60 students in cosy bunk beds, and robustly filling, punctually served, institutional food.

During the two days I was there, the five courses in progress – an average six students to a course – were classic ice and rock climbing; mountain leader training; mountain craft and hill walking; white-water, sea and surf canoeing; and a 10 week outdoor education course, undertaken by a Midlands maths master, two young women (one with a Cambridge science degree) still looking for a fulfilling career, and a refugee from the army. This last course, recognised by the Department of Education and Science, is designed for those intending to become instructors in the outward-bound tradition, and costs approximately £1,000. Many would say it was cheap for the qualification gained.

Initiative, independence, self-sufficiency, imagination: these are the disciplines emphasised, and are learned, for example, by river passaging in home-made rafts and canoes constructed from inner tubes and logs. And there is the night line – a quarter of a mile of rope up in the pine forest winding through icy streams, over rocks, down steep banks of sodden undergrowth, where the lichens hang like lace. The students must follow the rope hand over fist, totally blindfolded at the dead of night, to sharpen the sense of smell, touch and hearing. The night I went with them there was cold steady drizzle and it was so dark in the forest even unblindfolded that you could not see a man's face two feet away. The test is so disorientating that when the instructors looped the terminus of the rope back on to itself in a 20 foot circle, the students started retracing the course without knowing they were doing so. After a quick dinner they were due back out again equipped with nothing more than a sleeping bag and a sheet of plastic to bivouac for the night, individually and alone, women included.

John Disley, the former deputy chairman of the Sports Council, and on the management committee of the centre, says: 'We're the brand leaders in this field. What we do today, the local education authorities will be doing in a few years' time.

The next day I went with the canoe group to Anglesey in search of surf, on a glorious day when the colours of sky and mountainside, pines and snow-capped peaks were as intense as a canvas by Goya. Though the waves at Cable Bay were no more than three feet, they were sufficient to test the technique of the men in the care of Terry Storry, who initially learned his mountaineering when cliff and quarry climbing at Exeter University, and was more recently a member of the British expedition which canoed down the Bio Bio river in Chile.

'It's remarkable what that fellow can do', said a surveyor from Leamington, whose sport is normally limited to flat water canals, and who considered he was getting exceptional value for money from his £130 week, representing what must be a subsidy of at least 50 per cent by the Sports Council. 'Terry can control the canoe backwards, forwards, and sideways in the white water rapids, seemingly without effort, while we're concentrating on merely staying upright. The instruction here is vastly better than you'll find anywhere else'.

The Sports Council money is not wasted. Though Plas y Brenin last year cost £551,000 to maintain, partially offset by a course income of £263,000, almost everyone who attends is likely to be ploughing back their experience into scout groups, the TA, sea cadets, or private climbing, canoeing, skiing or orienteering clubs. It is an investment in expertise probably much more precise and measurable than, say, the facilities at the Crystal Palace national recreation centre. Alpine courses in climbing and skiing are included in the extensive curriculum.

The climbing spans everything from scrambling without ropes for the more enthusiastic hill walker, through rock climbing of the Derbyshire Peak, grit-stone type, to the most advanced mastery of vertical ice. There is a climbing training room with 16 feet walls which simulates the half-inch holds which may be all that rests between you and a 600 feet fall. Snowdonia and Scotland may lack the glaciers of the Alps, but the weather conditions can be just as severe, as you are constantly warned.

'We are working to high technical standards', says Mike Woolridge, one of the many temporary instructors who pass through the centre, some of them working for board and £10 per week. Included in the roll of experts who have contributed to Plas y Brenin's unrivalled reputation is Peter Boardman, killed in an attempt of Everest last year with Joe Tasker.

The quality of the centre is epitomised by its present director, John Barry, a squat, extrovert Irishman who, with Boardman, in 1977 made the first ascent of the south summit of the perilous 23,600 feet Himalayan peak, Gauri Sankar. Last year for recreation, Barry canoed across the Irish Sea – to keep his 68-year-old father company. Then he had to get back to the office, so his father made the return trip alone. Barry's recently published book *Cold Climbs* is an index of horrifying home-based ascents, for which you do not need a passport for the privilege of being scared out of your skin.

Barry earns rather less in a week than Kevin Keegan does in five minutes playing football, yet he and his colleagues have decidedly more to offer the young if only they can get to them. The Sports Council is working at it.

OXFORD GO OVERBOARD WITH POWERBOAT POLITICS

The controversy of Boris Rankov's sixth Boat Race appearance

10 March 1983

Oxford University seem likely to be cheating in the Boat Race on April 2 as surely as if they were powered by an outboard motor. What is alarming is less the effect of this on the outcome of the race, which we all know does not matter unless you are out there in one of the boats, than the fact that nobody at Oxford appears to recognise, let alone admit, that they might be cheating.

The 'motor' in question is a languid, gangling 28-year-old son of a Yugoslav, Boris Rankov, over whose eligibility for the race the ensuing unseemly squabble with Cambridge has reached levels of logical nonsense which exceed the imagination of Lewis Carroll. I hasten to stress that the most dignified act so far in the row – pronounce it how you will – namely Rankov's offer to withdraw, has been rejected by his own Blues committee.

I ought at the outset to declare, if not an allegiance, then an affiliation, having competed for Cambridge several times in other sports, and must also say that, while I have every sympathy for Cambridge on the principle involved, I have no time whatever for their Tweedledum threat to pull out of the race, which can only serve further to lower the tone of the argument and alienate their sponsors and lose public sympathy.

They *must* compete. Not to do so would be as futile as the well-intentioned but misguided withdrawal of the British middle-distance runner, Christine Benning, from the Moscow Olympics because of the reinstatement of convicted drug users. The histrionic gesture of withdrawal proves and solves nothing and only lends credibility to the trivial jibe of Oxford's coach, Dan Topolski, that Cambridge are 'looking for an excuse for another defeat'. But I am not concerned with Cambridge.

What is so indefensible about Oxford's position is its obvious expediency, the thin ice of its wholly academic argument and its palpable weakness on both morality and sportmanship. I feel sure that Charles Wordsworth, nephew of the poet and initiator of the first race in 1829, would agree.

The public, quite frankly, neither understand nor care about the subtleties of definition of *in statu pupillari*, which is at the basis of Cambridge's protest, and neither do I. What does matter is that if a great sporting event between those nineteenth-century fountains of organised amateur sport – rightly evaluated by the BBC as being on a par as a national event with Trooping the Colour, the FA Cup Final and the Derby and being one of the most entrenched free social spectacles of modern times – is disfigured by surrender to expediency, what hope is there for the rest? In 1983, do Oxford no longer acknowledge or have a conscience for the concept of *noblesse oblige?*

The facts are that Boris Rankov last year came out of retirement on Topolski's persuasion to establish an individual record fifth consecutive victory. 'I thought I could afford one more term', Rankov told me. Now he is back looking for a sixth win. Yet he is in his fifth postgraduate year, a junior fellow on the payroll of St Hugh's College, where he lectures part-time in Roman archaeology while preparing a thesis. In Cambridge terms, in anybody's terms, he is a don, a senior member of the university, no matter by what dexterity of words you try to twist the meaning of 'student'.

He was rowing for Oxford when Simon Harris, the Cambridge president and stroke who rowed a heroic losing race last year and is now being required to fire other people's bullets, was still almost in short pants at school in Maidenhead. Rankov is one of several postgraduates in the Oxford crew containing an assortment of Americans, Canadians and international championship medal winners. Cambridge have a file of correspondence unanswered by Oxford on the eligibility question which finally precipitated, far too late, the recent threat of withdrawal. The technical flaw in Cambridge's stance is that the eligibility agreement was reviewed in 1975 in their favour to admit a 29-year-old, David Sturge, who ultimately was excluded by glandular fever.

Yet any average disinterested bystander, that classic legal definition of impartiality, would agree that any Oxford v Cambridge contest, or indeed one between any two universities, is for students and that morally – whatever the financial flexibility of our benevolent education authorities which, for all I know, may permit the honest Boris to continue his obscure thesis for another 10 years – Rankov cannot be considered a student.

If nothing else, he is depriving a succession of the average three-year-degree students of the opportunity to participate in a unique experience and even in 1983 participation is still, or ought to be, the name of the game. It traduces more than a century of tradition if one must read for a Doctorate of Philosophy to have a chance of a Blue.

Of course, the shape of university life is changing. The intake of women freshers now exceeds 35 per cent and the increase of postgraduates further dilutes student density and the broad base of rowing and other sporting standards. Yet it merely underlines Oxford's attitude of expediency that there are dark rumours, not denied, of touting for foreign postgraduates at international rowing events. The average age of the Oxford crew is 25, of Cambridge 21.

I do not doubt that Ladbrokes, the sponsors who will have contributed £400,000 by 1986, are quietly delighted by the rumpus, given that this year they do not enjoy the public focus of sexual equality on the Tideway.* The apocryphal slogans scrawled on the Oxford crew's Transit van last year read: 'This boat is powered by S. Brown's knicker elastic'. For the present, rankling over Rankov will do nicely.

But the issue serves only to diminish Oxbridge sport. You really would suppose that men of intelligence could arrive at a fair and correct solution over a pink gin in the Leander Club. It is about time they started behaving like men instead of students.

* The previous inclusion by Oxford of a woman Cox, Sue Brown.

CORINTHIAN SUPERSTAR

Howard Baker, Chelsea goalkeeper and Olympic legend

16 March 1983 London

The oldest surviving member of the world's most exclusive football club still has a sparkle in his eye when he recalls one of his more extravagant and spectacular party pieces – kicking the lightbulbs out of chandeliers eight feet or so off the ground.

That sort of agility puts in the shade Duncan McKenzie's leaping over a Morris Mini; it is part of a legendary era. Sadly, a recent touch of 'flu means that Benjamin Howard Baker, said by some to be one of the greatest half dozen sportsmen of all time, will be sipping nostalgia in his north Wales home when 300 members and guests gather at Corinthian-Casuals' centenary dinner in London tomorrow.

Now in his ninety-second year, the dandy socialite of the Twenties, who was as well known to wine waiters and hall porters as Douglas Fairbanks, who played a record 176 matches for the Corinthians and kept goal 120 times for Chelsea and Everton, who held the British high jump record of 6ft 5ins for a remarkable 26 years from 1921 to 1947 and competed in two Olympics, remembers it all, like Chevalier in the song, as if it were yesterday.

As he gazes out on the sheltered east-facing conifers high up at the back of Colwyn Bay – with immaculately-tied bow tie of the Lawn Tennis Association of which he is a life councillor, and with silver hair only slightly thinned – he recalls those far-off days alongside such other illustrious sportsmen as Philip Noel-Baker, David (Lord) Burghley and, just before his time, C. B. Fry.

The president of Corinthians of São Paulo will be there tomorrow night to honour the cub which, in 15 foreign tours before the 1914–18 War, spread the gospel of the game to every corner of the globe and left in their wake a concept of sportsmanship which remains synonymous with their name to this day.

It was the Corinthians, who, when conceding a penalty, would leave the goal empty for their opponents to score unopposed. 'I would stand beside one of the goalposts while they tapped the ball in,' recalls HB.

It is worth remembering that the Corinthians were formed, in October 1882, with the purpose of playing only outside all competition and – more specifically – to bring together for gentlemanly practice, the best players in England after six defeats in seven years by Scotland.

It was not until after the First World War that the rules of the club were altered to allow it to enter the FA Cup. What days those were: historic encounters against Blackburn, Newcastle, Manchester, Millwall, West Bromwich Albion and Sheffield United.

In 1927 there were 56,000 at Crystal Palace to see Corinthian Casuals lose 3–1 to Newcastle while, three seasons later, for their second round replay with Millwall, there were 60,000 packed into Stamford Bridge.

HB admits that while the spirit of the Corinthians was without equal, he had the greatest pleasure from his appearances with Chelsea. This unashamed showman, six feet three inches then and even today an impressive figure, would enrage and delight spectators by bouncing the ball around the penalty area and over opponents heads basketball-style while the chairman, Gus Mears, bellowed instructions through a loud-hailer from the directors' box. 'I couldn't help being a little bit spectacular,' the old man admits mischievously.

He joined forces with the professionals who were battling, with his not inconsiderable assistance, for their £2 win bonus. He remembers vividly going as a youngster to Goodison Park to see C. B. Fry play for Portsmouth – 'or was it Southampton?' – and having his own dressing room and bath.

In those days, HB's own illustrious career with the Corinthians was notable for a boy who came from a far from affluent home and was outside the public school circle. Yet, by the end of his career, he would have the London Express stopped specially at his local station at Mossley Hill outside Liverpool to allow him to arrive home a little earlier.

He was well known for addressing the crowd behind the goal in regal terms and, on one occasion in Paris, prevented the opposing captain from leading his men off the field in protest at the referee's decision. International incidents were not unknown even then.

HB played three times for the England senior team, gained 10 amateur caps and, in 1925, took part in the Charity Shield when the Amateurs beat the Professionals 6–1.

Such was his reputation that Aston Villa tried hard, but in vain, to entice him as replacement for the great Sam Hardy. His father had insisted that he must play football in his own time and not the company's.

His exploits were headlines wherever he went. He only became a goal-keeper when an explosion while minesweeping in the Royal Naval Volunteer Reserve, off Start Point during the First World War, left him with a suspect ankle. He had already had an England trial at centre half.

Howard Baker remained a ferocious kicker and, on one occasion in the annual match against Queen's Park at Hampden, he twice booted the ball first bounce over the opposing goalkeeper's head. He regularly took penalties and, in a Cup tie against Bradford City, the spectators were star-tled to see the City goalkeeper advancing to have a discussion with HB before the kick was taken 'He was asking me not to hit the ball straight at him in case I should injure him', HB remembers.

Yet his prowess extended far beyond the soccer field. In the Olympics of 1912 and 1920 he competed in the high jump and the pentathlon. 'They were not affluent days for our athletes, I remember, and Bobby Bridge, one of our walkers, was disqualified by the Swedish judges on the first day in Stockholm and came up to me dejectedly in the evening, saying "The boogers have sent me home to save money". He was most upset.'

At Antwerp, in 1920, he was beaten by an inch by the American, Landon, in the high jump. He gained his revenge shortly afterwards when competing for the British Empire in the United States.

The following year, jumping at Huddersfield, he set the British record – and never jumped again. 'I didn't want to specialise, I had other things I wanted to do.' He was seven times the Amateur Athletic Association high jump champion and also won titles at hurdles, discus and javelin.

For diversion, he would go swimming 12 miles or so in the Mersey on a Sunday with J. B. Crossley, who was training for the cross-Channel swim. He represented Lancashire at tennis and played doubles at Wimbledon. He also represented his country at water polo and played cricket for Liverpool CC.

Three years ago, this remarkable man suffered a serious car accident which punctured a lung and severely damaged his back. It seemed he could not survive. Yet here he is, standing healthily at the door to wish you a pleasant journey home and to give his regards to all those at the dinner tomorrow. 'Tell them I remember it all with a lot of satisfaction and a lot of pride at having been one of them,' he said.

THE CASUALTY WHO CAME BACK TO CAPTIVATE BADMINTON

Virginia Holgate defies horrific injury

16 April 1983

Some time towards the end of this afternoon, a young woman whose family at one time had to sell off some of the household furniture to keep her in the saddle, will turn another page of the rare story which she hopes will reach a climax next year with an Olympic medal in Los Angeles.

It is on the anvil of the Badminton cross-country course, the Cresta Run of three-day eventing created by the renowned equestrian architect, Frank Weldon, that Olympic prospects and ambitions can be forged or broken. Virginia Holgate is one of that special breed of British horse-women who, on limited resources, contrive, with a recipe of courage and resolution and not a little skill, to match the best men around the world. Lucinda Green may be better known, but there could be no more popular winner to step forward and received the Whitbread Trophy from the Queen tomorrow than this modest girl who, a few years ago, suffered, and survived, a devastating accident.

Badminton, set in its parkland and pasture of stunning natural beauty, which for centuries has harmonised yeomanry and aristocracy, is not only a British institution which bridges most barriers, like the Grand National a week ago, but, among the vast majority of competitors, sets standards of modesty and sportsmanship which still find an echo in Olympic ideals. While Badminton itself surmounts the horizon of any horseman like Mont Blanc, it is no coincidence that for every successful rider the Olympics remain the pinnacle which combines achievement with that other quality which is not easily defined.

Though the medium of television may have familiarised a huge public with eventing, in the same way as it has with show jumping, it is still true that, as with almost every physical sport, the skills and hazards are flattened and sanitised by the small screen, to the point where considerable danger is as painless to the viewer as just another Starsky and Hutch car chase. The reality, in which horse and rider synchronise with the landscape in a challenge which knows few equals in sport, is something different.

Yesterday morning Miss Holgate was, like every competitor, awake with the birds and the barking dogs for a day which hardly allows a minute's relaxation – exercising her mount, Night Cap, preparing for the dressage event, then walking the four and a half miles, 33-obstacle cross-country course for the third time, memorizing every yard, the approach to every complex leap, until they are as familiar as tying her own cravat. The course alternates annually between clockwise and anti-clockwise, and there is no room for complacency.

It will be a severe test of the 10-year-old Night Cap, who will confront the course raw, never having competed around it in either direction, and now totally dependent on the rider to take the right line, to coax him into exactly the right propulsion. He is, she says, 'a perfect gentleman', willing to do anything he is asked – quite unlike her first-choice mount, Priceless, at present still sick from a rat-carried disease and a real character with a will of his own who, though highly experienced, can be 'an absolute toad if he wants to be'.

The quieter Night Cap will today demand a fractionally different technique to Priceless, with whom Miss Holgate was fourth last year. Her mother, who knows horses, confides: 'I don't know what makes the ultimate competitor. All I know is that Ginny, however brave she herself may be, will never ask the horse to do the impossible.'

This seemingly slight, blonde girl with a cheerful face which, beneath the smile, shows the strain of months and years of the most demanding competition, was first out two years ago to tackle a course in the European championships in Denmark which some knowledgeable observers had described as 'impossible'. She conquered it, came sixth, and Britain took the gold medal, as they did again in the world championships last year.

It is one of the bizarre aspects of the finances of British eventing that prominent riders such as Richard Meade and Princess Anne will today be spectators simply because they do not currently have a fit or sufficiently prepared horse. With hay now considerably more expensive than coal at £130 a ton, to maintain a string of event horses is beyond most private means, and Miss Holgate is in a position to be able to switch to Night Cap only through support received from British National Insurance. 'The public just does not realise the expense involved in maintaining horses, not just the feeding and transport, but substantial items like veterinary fees, which you never know when they're coming.' The financial hardship within British eventing is highlighted by the steady drain of some of the better horses being sold overseas.

Miss Holgate has ridden since she was two – for many years around the world following the Service life of her father, a Marine who was an outstanding rugby player but died two years ago, just when she was climbing back towards the international eminence she had achieved when winning the European junior championship.

Now that Miss Holgate is lying second after yesterday's dressage, the Whitbread Trophy is within her reach. Twice previously in three attempts she has had a clear round in the cross-country and memory has faded of that horrendous pre-Badminton fall six years ago when a spectator ran across the course, disconcerted her horse, Jason, and he somersaulted a jump, falling on her and fracturing her right arm in 20 places. There will be no room for such thoughts today, and indeed she has demonstrated resoundingly that her confidence is unimpaired.

SPORTING BOYCOTT REACHES LIMIT OF ITS EFFECTIVENESS

A look at the reality beneath apartheid

3 June 1983 Johannesburg

On a recent trip to South Africa to look at the extent of racial integration in sport and to discuss with many individuals, of all political persuasions, the question of the continuing international boycott, I went out to dinner one evening with a prominent coloured Springbok sportsman and his wife.

We were staying at the same hotel in Cape Town, and a receptionist recommended a certain restaurant. Unwittingly, we entered a different one, where we were shown to a table by a young waiter and sat down. Two minutes later he returned and asked us to leave.

Why, I asked? Because the manager said we must. Why? Because the restaurant did not have an international licence. Why did not the manager tell us himself? He was busy. The waiter was increasingly embarrassed, the more so when I insisted we would not leave unless the manager gave an explanation – which he grudgingly did: a thickset, elderly boorish man who feebly said he was hoping for a licence but right now we must go because he had 'several attorneys dining at another table'.

As we left, politely saying we hoped he knew somewhere quiet to go if and when the revolution arrived, three other diners who had overheard the exchange said to me that I did not understand the problem, that it was difficult to explain. I said I agreed that any satisfactory explanation was indeed difficult.

Fortunately, that is not the end of the story. We crossed the street to another restaurant, where we had an excellent meal, with service and attention which would have been a credit to Claridges, and as we left the waiter and the proprietor, both white, were waiting to ask for the autograph of the man who, if the International Olympic Committee would relent, is capable of winning an Olympic medal. They had recognised him, and not only congratulated him but invited him back 'whenever you can come, and bring your friends.'

Incidents such as this persuaded me on a social and political as well as a sporting basis that the South African argument needed re-examination, and I went there for the first time from a starting point of complete conviction that the boycott stance was morally correct; that the end – the amendment of the many hated segregation laws implementing apartheid – justified the means.

What became apparent were two unmistakable factors: that there is an approximate dividing line among whites, somewhere between the age of 30 and 40, separating the old 'superior white' attitude and the liberal thinking of a modern generation which is awake to morality and reality, and that if a bloody revolution is to be avoided, then the best interest of the non-white in South Africa will now be served by readmitting, if not all, then certainly some of the major sports such as football, athletics and boxing, into the international arena.

This interpretation of the present state of social evolution may be particularly relevant in the light of forthcoming events: the special meeting of MCC to discuss sending an official tour, the court case brought by the South African Athletic Union against the IAAf for illegal suspension, and the decision to be taken by a new president on next year's projected rugby tour by England.

The readmission of South Africa internationally, even on selected fronts only, would have the effect of altering that erroneous concept which the majority of the rest of the world has of an exclusively white orientated country. I believe that the outside world is now tending to look at the isolation issue from totally the wrong aspect – whether the white man has made sufficient concessions and compromises in a hated administration to be given back his ball, his much-prized privileged membership of various international clubs, rather than whether the black/coloured man can use the sporting platform to help create for his country a multiracial image such as Brazil's, which will internationally dignify his ethnic race, expand his self-respect and prestige, while internally accelerating social and political changes already in motion and ensuring they are irreversible.

This view will be said by the committed forces of the left to be naive; that the non-white can never achieve dignity and prestige while he is denied, outside sport, so many freedoms. To which one can only answer that other than by the bullet and the bomb the changes which the outside world, and liberal South African whites, demand for that country can only be achieved by evolutionary degrees; that the external sporting boycott has now reached the *absolute limit* of its political effectiveness and is about to become rapidly counter-productive in encouraging reactionary right-wing extremism by the Conservative and Afrikaaner Weerstandsbeweging (AWB) opposition parties to the National (increasingly liberal) government.

While it was apparent travelling to half a dozen different cities that some whites still speak with forked tongue; that they pay lip service to integration without actually believing in it; that they now grudgingly acknowledge the inhumanities they could equally well have seen 25 years ago without the encouragement of external pressure, it is abundantly obvious, too, that double standards exist in the United Nations-backed left wing lobby which is determined that South Africa shall be excluded everywhere at all cost. What could be more hypocritical than the stand of the French government banning the rugby tour, while permitting the government supported Renault team to compete in the South African Grand Prix?

When I interviewed Hassan Howa, the former secretary of the South African Council of Sport and a militant opponent now of all cricket tours, he was quick to point out that many of the greatest sportsmen in history, Owens, Louis, Pele, Ali and Sobers, could never have emerged had they been born in South Africa. Not in the past certainly, but now they could: and what force of argument, what international identity could be exerted for the oppressed majority by the sporting South African equivalent of a Lech Walesa. It is now difficult to avoid the conclusion that, within sport, the racialism in South Africa is exhibited among non-whites.

Additional problems for sport are twofold: that the majority of those foreigners who seek to get South Africa readmitted are either of a conspiciously right wing allegiance, such as John Carlisle and his friends in the Freedom in Sport organisation, or are professionally orientated with a vested interest in the financial potential of the South African market.

It is stretching credibility to suppose that they are all deeply and sincerely concerned with the welfare of the Johannesburg diamond mine dormitory-dwelling labourer who sees his family in his homeland for a few weeks in the year, or with the one black child who dies of malnutrition every 15 minutes. Though I grant them the possibility that they may be.

There is unfortunately no chance, now and in the future, to separate sport and politics. It suits the political left to focus on white South Africa contravention of human rights as a counterbalance to the extremism of Eastern Europe, Central Africa and elsewhere, and they are vastly more successful in practice, for no other country is scrutinised to the same degree for sporting acceptance or rejection. Yet the outside world – the

IOC which refuses to send a commission of investigation, having promised to do so if South Africa withdrew its request at the Baden-Baden congress for readmission – is not aware of the extent to which the present government is trying to move progressively left.

A white Stellenbosch University-educated economist said to me on a flight from Durban: 'We on the liberal, middle ground would like the government to have moved much farther and faster, but had they done so, the reaction from the extreme right would have become dangerous. One of these days, the black man is going to run this country.'

The Pretoria Council may have closed the city parks in the worst imaginable piece of public relations, but the fact is that South Africa has had black presidents in its non-racial football and cricket administrations, a black vice-president in athletics, which is rather more than you can imagine happening in England for some years to come. The Botha government is committed to spending £300m on sport over the next five years, the majority of it to the benefit of non-whites – a practical demonstration of the shift in ideology which lies behind the projected presidential council embracing coloured and Asian prime ministers under an executive president.

Dr Danie Craven, for almost 30 years the leader of South African rugby, has survived attempts by the secret Broederbond society to dominate rugby, because his international contacts became crucial after isolation – though the Broederbond still attempt to influence the choice of captain. Craven, who personally apologised to Basil d'Oliveira when he was banned by Prime Minister Vorster, has battled to embrace all races in rugby.

But Craven believes the onus is now on England to rationalize world opinion on South African sport, if all the changes that have been made to the advantage of the non-white are not to be wasted. 'We in sport have thrown open all the doors, fought our government and now the people who should be on our side are fighting against us. If I let my emotions out, I would hate England for the way she has turned, but I'm proud of my English background. Everywhere I go, people are waiting for England to give the lead, but they won't wait for ever. The English influence is still there, but where is the leadership?'

A MANAGER NOT DRIVEN BY THE MONEY MOTIVE

Bill Nicholson, for whom loyalty and a search for style were second nature

19 August 1983

With Tommy Trinder busily proclaiming, some 22 years ago, that he would pay Johnny Haynes £100 week following the abolition of the maximum wage, Bill Nicholson asked Danny Blanchflower into his office at White Hart Lane. He suggested a wage of £68 a week to the captain of possibly the most entertaining team in the history of British club football.

Under the leadership of these two men, Spurs produced football between 1960 and 1963 the like of which we may not see again, consolidating the club's reputation for creative, intellegent play; begun by Arthur Rowe – who persuaded his directors to outbid Arsenal for Blanchflower by £2,000 specifically to make him captain – and maintained today by Keith Burkinshaw. With a new season about to start under the ever-darkening clouds of excessive television (now live), hooliganism and anti-entertainment tactics, Spurs remain an oasis of optimism. It used to be said that trying to stop Tottenham was like trying to catch sparrows, and happily that is still to some extent true.

When Nicholson offered Blanchflower that relatively modest wage, he patiently explained that he had devised a salary scale of £3,000 a year for the less famous players, rising to £3,400 for the stars, such as Mackay, White and Jones. Greaves was then yet to arrive from Chelsea via Milan. The rational offer, and its equally rational acceptance, was typical of both men. Money was never their motive in the quest for the unattainable, perfection in a team sport; unlike one of our more brash contemporary managers who, word has it, the other day told an American club he would buy a player from them if they first paid *him* £20,000.

Blanchflower, who left Barnsley and then Aston Villa in search of the refinements of the short-ball game which he was to discover and help embroider at Tottenham, whose imaginative captaincy led Northern Ireland to the World Cup quarter-finals in 1958, has long ago stated that football is not about winning but about glory. He was at a small social gathering a few days ago among friends of Nicholson, who belatedly had his testimonial this Saturday at White Hart Lane, preceded by a curtain-raiser from the stars of the Sixties, including Jimmy Greaves. At this get-together, Blanchflower said: 'Bill and I wanted three things from the game: a good team; to play our own, entertaining way; and to be fair to all the people in the team. What distinguished Spurs at that time was style and, almost by definition, style is something which is brief and passing. It does not last. That is why I cannot in all honesty say that I think Liverpool have got great style, because they have gone on so long. Because of money, I believe the days of the great team sports are numbered.'

When illustrious men such as Matthews, and Busby and Ramsey have rightly been knighted for what they have given, and many lesser footballers have been honoured, right down to some of our present avaricious internationals, it is remarkable that no formal recognition has come the way of William Nicholson, 45 years with one club since he came to paint the grandstand roof as a 15-year-old apprentice player from Scarborough. 'Nick' represents an era of honesty, patience, devotion and selflessness which has almost gone, still apparent here and there in an occasional player such as Perryman or manager such as Jimmy Sirrel.

It is typical of 'Nick' that a large part of the money he may receive on Sunday is already spent on a party for 300 private guests. Would that, during his active career, the club, notoriously as financially careful off the field as the team was extravagant on it, had been half as generous to him. With his popular, effervescent, London-born wife, Darkie, he still lives where he always has, in the comfortable end-of-terrace house within earshot of the Tottenham roar, tending their allotment between times – a couple rich in contentment.

In the late forties and early fifties I shared a common, fondly remembered experience with Burkinshaw; he in Barnsley, I in London. It was watching the Spurs of Ramsey, Nicholson, Burgess and Baily with its close spun patterns, as regular as those of a weaver's loom. It was my further good fortune to come under Nicholson's influence at Cambridge, one of his first coaching appointments. How eagerly we would immerse ourselves, out on the training pitch and later over toast and honey round the gas fire in someone's digs, in his clear, precise, professional's approach to the game.

He did not make us conspicuously better players, because, at 20, we were too ancient dogs to learn new tricks; but how marvellously he simplified the game by telling us what not to do! Great player that Blanchflower was, he acknowledges the shared affinity with Nicholson of those amateurs 'because our only objective was a higher fulfilment from the game.'

The fee received from the FA by the aspiring young coach who would make a contribution to football no less significant than Busby's or Paisley's, barely covered his train fares to the Fens. He had no care then and, in the evenings, would move on to St Neots, returning home after midnight. Now, he does not really need the testimonial, other than in spirit, for it is a belated tribute to his exceptional years of service.

There is no thread of the club which did not come under his scrutiny. They say that when the reserve team trainer came to him to ask for new practice balls, though he might be engaged in the middle of buying Greaves he would demand to see the old balls, turn them over one by one, and say that this one and that one would do another six months. When a West End store delivered a wedding present which was one size larger than had been paid for, he insisted it be sent back.

What can be done to reverse the present state of rising greed and declining entertainment? At a luncheon given to him yesterday by the Football Writers' Association, Nicholson was in no doubt: 'The game today is too stereotyped, because there is more than one way to play it, but everything now is built on the same defensive principles. In my time, I could put on a practice session in which three defenders could hold up five attackers, but now no team is happy unless they have four defending against three. Almost all our practice was directed at attack; defending is comparatively easy.

'But the other problem is that schoolboys, instead of playing in the streets, which are now full of cars, with a little rubber ball, are playing with those big plastic balls, so that they never learn the skills. If I had my way there would be no eleven-a-side football in schools before the age of 12, to give them time to learn the game, and I would insist on a 35-yard offside line to give them more room in which to play. But it is not just schoolboys who need skills and coaching. We have some top-class internationals who don't know it all.'

Yet those who run the game, the moguls of FIFA and the place-men of the FA, seemingly remain indifferent to the decline. FIFA is obsessed with money, with World Cup deals which raise grave concern for probity; while the FA meekly accept FIFA's denial of any attempts to adjust the laws to foster entertainment. It is regrettable that Sir Harold Thompson, the former chairman of the FA, could for so long have remained so inert to the path professional soccer was taking when the wisdom of men like Rowe and Nicholson, who did so much to shape the halcyon years of Pegasus and Casuals, was so close at hand. When Bert Millichip, the present chairman, condones the payment by his club, West Bromwich, of a basic £60,000 a year to a no better-than-average full back, we can be sure he is unlikely to halt the waves.

ALONE WITH AMERICA'S SUNKEN PRIDE

Conner's single error brings historic defeat

27 September 1983 Newport, Rhode Island

As a mellow apricot sunset faded on a glorious afternoon, one hundred and thirty two years of sporting history came to a close here. A self-effacing Australian yacht designer, Ben Lexcen, had his revenge.

In a seventh race of an America's Cup final series of often bitter controversy, *Australia II*, Lexcen's radical new fin-keel creation, swept to a 41 second victory. The switchback of fortune throughout the race was as remarkable as anything that had happened here all summer, and the climax was a fitting conclusion to such an event.

At his fourth attempt, the Australian businessman, Alan Bond, from Perth, who went to Australia as a teenage schoolboy from Ealing, took the prize for which he had poured out millions of pounds.* Yet the real winner, it has to be said, was Lexcen, for it was the boat which won, the crew who almost failed it in a tournament in which 10 boats had consumed more money and effort than a World Cup soccer competition.

Twice on the first and fourth windward legs, the Australian helmsman John Bertrand went looking for wind, leaving the defending American, Dennis Conner, in *Liberty*, uncovered. Each time Conner, in the acknowledged slower boat, was able to profit from a wind shift in his favour and opened a half minute lead and then a full minute.

Each time *Australia II* pulled back, and on the fifth down wind leg it was Conner, who before the start of the series was thought to be unbeatable, who became stranded. *Australia II* entered the last windward leg now 21 seconds in front.

As all the years of domination by the New York Yacht Club through 25 previous unsuccessful challenges at last began to ebb away, Conner engaged Bertrand in a grim, vain tacking duel from behind, but now Bertrand had him nailed.

Even when Conner made a huge, pointless tack off-course a mile from the finish, Bertrand followed, then finally turned for a last triumphant dash for the line, and a winning gun from the New York Yacht Club committee boat *Black Knight* – the gun which means that in 1987 the Cup will be defended in Perth.

Conner, the baseline perfectionist and 1980 winner whose book was entitled 'No Excuse to Lose', crossed the line almost lost in a tumultous sea of spray and wake as hundreds of spectator craft surrounded the Australians.

Now the New York Yacht Club must perform the ultimate embarrassment – inviting Bond and Lexcen to the Big Apple to hand over the Cup, almost their exclusive justification for existence all these years.

* Mostly, it became evident, other people's.

28 September 1983

Around here it is rather as if Everest had been bought by a Japanese camera company. The belated public sportsmanship being exhibited by the slick, socially exclusive New York Yacht Club, as it handed over for the first time in 132 years the coveted America's Cup to ecstatic Australians at a Bellevue Avenue mansion, was in severe contrast to its private, even resentful, anguish.

When *Australia II*, with its remarkable fin-keel by an untutored designer, Ben Lexcen, came from a minute behind over the final two legs of the seventh and decisive race to win by 41 seconds, the men in peaked caps, blue blazers and white slacks lining the deck of the black-hulled committee boat *Black Knight* knew they were watching the most treasured bauble in the sporting world vanish before their eyes. Their *raison d'être* had vanished.

As Alan Bond's wildly rejoicing crew sailed past, the *Black Knight* gun which had signalled the finish of the race then fired a four-salvo salute while the members doffed their hats and bowed in acknowledgement to a beautiful, innovative boat and the crew which so nearly failed her. Their fists were no doubt clenched at losing a lead of three races to one, never mind that unbelievable switch on the fifth leg, when Dennis Conner's 57-second advantage evaporated on a mistaken downwind course.

When Conner, the 1980 champion in *Freedom* against Bond's third boat, *Australia I*, achieved that 3–1 lead, the crackling shortwave radios out on Rhode Island Sound picked up the talk between NYYC Commodores Robert Stone and Bob McCullough, and their helmsman.

'You sailed a terrific race,' said the men from the club.

'Thank you, sir,' replied Conner stiffly that day: Conner the unbeatable, who was in a seemingly impregnable position against the boat he *knew* was faster, but whose crew could not collectively match his vast professional experience. Yet on Monday night, when what the NYCC members had believed to be impossible had actually happened, it was Conner who had to shoulder the burden of America's loss.

As *Australia II* came late into harbour against the faint remains of a crimson evening sky, the night was a blur of fireworks and rockets and blinking helicopters. The floating dockside groaned under the weight of thousands of spectators whom Newport may never see again. Television lights flooded the quay, the US syndicate boats Liberty and Freedom formed a guard of honour for *Australia II*.

There on her towing launch, *Black Swan*, was the red-jacketed Conner, with a fixed, empty good loser's smile gazing up at the myriad of frenzied Australian faces. How different it had been a few hours before as the tanned Conner, looking like Al Jolson with his sun-creamed white lips, had confidently jockeyed his burgundy-coloured boat in the pre-start manoeuvres.

Now it was Conner, unaccompanied by any member of the NYYC, who walked alone through the car park, through the milling streets of hard-luck cries to the Armoury, where he faced the press, knowing he had blown a winning position.

'I'd like to stay for an hour of questions', he said when paying tribute to *Australia II*. But when a mass of camera, television and press men is witnessing a man with tears swelling his eyes as he says the United States has no cause to be ashamed of their performance, they do not press him with questions. They just let him put on his straw hat, accept a thin cheer, and disappear back into the bedlam outside.

The NYYC might have morally supported the man who surrendered its heritage, but seemingly did not have the guts. It was left to syndicate chairman Ed du Moulin to appear later and say Conner was still the best helmsman. The truth was he just did not have the best boat, and after months of relentless pressure, the man who never allowed a mistake had made a monumental one.

Back in New York, where the club was formed in 1844, and settled into its present mansion in 1901, those members not in Newport had been listening to a radio commentary in the bar with its red leather chairs and portraits of boats and skippers of long ago. The club has no television: it is that kind of club. No one knows what they thought as *Liberty's* lead disappeared by the start of the final leg.

Richard Thursby, a NYYC member, has said: 'There won't be more than a couple of days' mourning before we start thinking about how to win the damned thing back.' But now it is free to any club and syndicate in the US, never mind the rest of the world, to bid independently. The exclusiveness which the NYYC enjoyed for so long finally turned against it. Never was a US 12-metre permitted to compete against a foreign boat outside the America's Cup; so they never knew, for example, what all the six foreign challengers learnt: that *Australia II's* tall, slim rudder was also part of her tacking ability, and they copied it.

When Conner finally got into the water against Lexcen's Lightning, as it is known, he was raw to the exceptional qualities which *Victory '83* and the others had long since discovered. Ultimately, by the narrowest but for all that colossal margin, the man who gave every command on his boat made the singular error which neutralised the earlier ones by Bertrand. It was the right result.

HEROISM AS HIGH AS THE SEA IS DEEP

An extraordinary rescue in the lost southern ocean

11 January 1984

Long before one was introduced as a small boy to tales of Macartney, Meredith, Broadribb, C. B. Fry and Captain Webb, and the more modern sporting heroes, Matthews and Bradman, the emotional bedside stories were of men such as Scott and Oates, T. E. Lawrence and Mallory.

If the first drama to make me cry was Pigling Bland getting lost over the hills and far away, then the second was Captain Oates walking out from the doomed expeditionary tent into the Antarctic snow saying that he may be gone some time. Altruism could have as much honour as achievement, demonstrated on Everest by one of my school masters, Wilfred Noyce.

The mountains and oceans will always remain a special kind of challenge, and as the American writer, Paul Theroux, has recently observed, the British character is inherently shaped by the surrounding seas. Richard Broadhead is an example of maritime altruism *and* achievement.

Yesterday at the Earls Court Boat Show, that annual indoor anomaly which embraces fantasy and functionalism, the Salcombe adventurer was presented with the Yachtsman of the Year award. The yachting correspondents rightly considered his astonishing rescue of a Frenchman in the Southern ocean during the BOC single-handed round the world race last year superior to the *Victory '83* crew's pursuit of the America's Cup.

It is worth quoting from *The Ultimate Challenge*, the account by my colleague, Barry Pickthall, of this remarkable race, a passage where Broadhead describes those awesome conditions which Chichester, Rose and Knox-Johnston have conquered, yet which would freeze the mind and muscle of ordinary men. Hand steering downwind for 12 hours at a time in the Roaring Forties and screaming fifties, with the windspeed indicator permanently locked against its maximum 60 knots, Broadhead would later recount:

'Every 10 minutes or so, the seas (behind) rolled into vertical walls, huge and as high as the mast, and as the bow buried up to the forehatch, I just sat at the wheel holding on for grim death, looking almost vertically down the boat as she started to go over. Then as the wave broke, the bow came up and she surfed off at 30 knots with the whole deck under water. All I could see was the bloody wheel, and the mast and rigging standing up through the surf.'

The romance between life and death is a strangely motivating phenomenon. Guy Bernadin, another Frenchman who came fourth in Class II, would say of his experience of being washed out of the cockpit in ferocious seas from which he miraculously survived: 'It was the greatest moment in my life.' I know a doctor's wife to whom the same thing has happened in the North Sea.

What was different about Broadhead's race, in which he finished third over the 27,000 mile four-leg course behind the Frenchman, Phillippe Jeantot, in the expensively sponsored *Credit Agricole* and the South African, Bertie Reed, in *Altech Voortrekker*, was that two thirds of the way between Australia and Cape Horn he turned back more than 300 miles in *Perseverence of Medina*, without engine, in the bid to rescue Jacques de Roux from the stricken *Skoiern III*, thousands of miles from any other assistance. And found him.

It was an accomplishment as exceptional as the survival of Bligh and his men set adrift from the Bounty, in conditions considerably more severe; though it would not have been possible without the position-finding assistance of the Argus satellite navigation equipment fitted by BOC to each of the 17 boats, capable of tracing them every few hours to within less than half a mile.

De Roux, a submarine commander, had been 'pitch-poled', stern-over-bow, horrifyingly believing while upside down in darkness that he was going straight to the unfathomable bottom. *Skoiern* ultimately righted with a mere four inches of air as bouyancy remaining under the deck, and though de Roux pumped out after several hours, a hole in the hull sustained when cutting free the broken mast gave him only hours to remain afloat while permanently pumping.

It would take Broadhead maybe three days to get back into the headwind: could de Roux last? An incredible ad hoc combination of satellite information to the race organisers and ham radio operators Rob Koziomkowski in Newport, Rhode Island, and Matt Johnston in Owaka, New Zealand, guided Broadhead to an approximate rendezvous some 50 hours after the SOS alert (the falling mast missed de Roux's deck-mounted Argus disc by inches).

Broadhead is one of those cavalier, freelance roamers whom most of us secretly envy but few could emulate. Leaving Harrow at 16, he followed his whim to the Caribbean and then Australia for several years as Jack of any trade; then studied farming at Cirencester, and went off in unavailing search of land fortune in Brazil.

Yet childhood Cornish salt was in his blood. He bought a 43ft boat, sailed to Rio and back as a round-the-world qualifying race, then Antigua and back in search of sponsors. It was one of his several hundred letters of inquiry which aroused BOC to sponsor the whole race rather than him. Everything was sold in order to enter his former Max Aitken boat nicknamed Perspiration by its unsuccessful Admiral's Cup crew.

Broadhead has the same disarming charm of understatement as the land speed record breaker, Richard Noble. Discussing the rescue saga, he says it was apparent during radio contact the day before de Roux's SOS 'that he wasn't having much of a time'. You know the kind of situation: 120-foot waves, boat leaking, salt water boils, wet pillow, nobody to help make the tea and toast, in seas which the New Zealander, Dick McBride, calls 'two insecting lines of moving hills'.

Almost lightly, Broadhead relates that he was having to change head-sails, without roller reefing, several times an hour to reach de Roux as soon as possible, and was 'a bit tired, feeling the strain a little, when pushing the boat faster than when actually racing'. Yes, of course.

When, below deck talking on the radio, he in fact sailed straight past a despairing de Roux, who let off all his flares from a quarter of a mile away with the weather deteriorating again and darkness approaching, Broadhead admits: 'de Roux must have been a bit worried! When I came up, I stood up on the boom, and luckily just spotted his jury sail a mile or so away. If he had been in his life raft, I would never have seen him in those seas.'

Jumping between boats, the exhausted Frenchman was fortunate not to break both his legs between the colliding hulls – a reunion as historic as Stanley and Livingstone. An hour later, *Skoiern* went down. What was it like, in that Antarctic hell hole, before a French frigate took de Roux on board several days later? Broadhead reflects: 'I think it improved his English a bit.' You would expect so. I mean, they had something to talk about.

STARS IN THE OLYMPIC FIRMAMENT

Torvill and Dean captivate global Games audience

16 February 1984 Sarajevo

There is an overriding principle, in any professional plans for their future, between Christopher Dean and Jayne Torvill that they should remain true to the artistic integrity which makes them supreme amateur champions and such an idyllic young couple.

On St Valentine's morning Dean gave his partner an orchid. We cannot know of what it spoke, yet it was symbolic of the intensely shared creative brilliance which would win them the ice-dance Olympic gold medal that evening with an unprecedented 12 maximum marks from the nine judges. As with the greatest exponents of theatrical dance, the romance and tragedy of their *Bolero* rose above any question of personal affection, which there undoubtedly must be to have sustained nine years of mutual devotion.

So mentally tense was Dean that after a celebration party in the British section of the Village, which continued long after Princess Anne left at 1.30am, he was awake again after only two hours' sleep. Miss Torvill lay dreaming till late, when she was woken, characteristically of this city, by a chambermaid giving her flowers of personal appreciation. Downstairs, among dozens of telegrams, was one from the Queen: 'Many congratulations on a superb performance which we watched with great pleasure'.

If Torvill and Dean achieved the illusion of being in another world, somehow apart from the rest of the competitors, it was indeed so: a performance instinctive rather than conscious. 'We weren't with the audience last night, we were with each other,' Dean said yesterday morning, talking in that unassuming way which makes the vision of his choreography such an astonishment. He added: 'It was a sort of hypnotic trance, in which all the work you have done before comes out of you.'

They discreetly but insistently deny that they are likely at present to marry, yet admit they cannot contemplate working without each other, whether performing professionally or teaching. 'We could only coach as a couple,' Dean said, almost thinking aloud, smiling benignly and provocatively at a press gathering which was working up a soufflé of Mills and Boon confection.

Olympic champions often tell you that everything, thereafter, in their lives is an anticlimax. Torvill and Dean do not yet know where they are going, except that after the world championships in Ottawa in March, where they must surely win for the fourth year, they step off the kerb into an uncharted area of commerce.

There is no established ice-dance theatre, as opposed to the individual figure skating showmanship of the former gold medalists, John Curry and Robin Cousins, or the Americans Dorothy Hammill, Peggy Fleming, and Charlie Tickner, bronze medalist at Lake Placid.

It is said that Hammill, the gold medalist in 1976, can earn £15,000 a week, and Tickner more than half that: it is probable that Cousins, with his own Electric Ice company, which ran for 15 weeks at Victoria Palace last autumn and returns to Bristol soon, earns even more. It would be surprising if he had not taken more than a half a million pounds over four years, including his two and a half seasons worldwide with *Holiday on Ice*, and the US professional circus, Pro-Skate, at Madison Square Garden.

What is the market for Dean's more subtle, refined inspiration? It was noticeable that here in Sarajevo it took a week for the audience to switch on to what they were seeing, and in the original set pattern programme the mood was flat. Are Torvill and Dean in a sense too clever for the audience they already have, and the restricted physical circumstances of an ice rink too unsophisticated for the milieu to which they aspire?

Discussing their prospects, Cousins says: 'I was lucky. Most of the medallists in 1980 were eastern European, and everyone commercially was wanting me. This year, there are Scott Hamilton and Rosalyn Sumners. It has been said that the gold medal for Sumners is the difference between two million and two thousand dollars.

'Ice dancing is not on the Pro-Skate circuit, but it might pick up when Chris and Jayne are free of the regulations imposed by competitive dancing. The important thing for them is that they will not want to change their conception. I wouldn't want to, and they won't.'

Dean said yesterday that the ideal would be to establish an 'academy of ice dance' in Nottingham, or, more probably, in London, but in conjunction with commercial performances. 'I cannot see a school working out as a commercial concern. It is too expensive. At the moment, what happens after Ottawa is a full stop. We don't know the next paragraph.'

It is estimated that Nottinghamshire council have spent £53,000 sponsoring their two modest citizens over the past four years, and investment in projection for Nottingham which has been absurdly cheap. Yet Dean was quick to point out that sponsorship, the finance to be able to train in Germany, was not the most basic factor in producing champions.

'It is determination,' he insists. 'Whatever the sport, you have got to spend the time.' And Miss Torvill adds: 'Without sponsorship, maybe it would have taken longer.' There was a calm certainty in her tone which did not allow for the possibility they might not have become champions.

They admit that the Olympics have been the most arduous competition yet, because of rest days between each of the three programmes, with judges and press being present every time they practise.

We may deride a judging system which gives perfect marks even when Miss Torvill touches the ice with one hand, a system which is arbitrary and suspect in its results, as are other judged competitions such as dressage, diving, gymnastics and boxing. Yet no rival competitor, judge, journalist or spectator had had the slighest doubt this past week that the British couple are unique.

From the first moment of the *Bolero*, when they have risen from their knees off the ice, made two sinuous, erotic gestures of the hip, and then glide away in a sudden, ominous crouch loaded with dire premonition, they captivated an audience of millions. 'I never saw them perform before like they did last night,' said Marie Therese Kreiselmayer, their host at the Obersdorf rink in Germany, where they train. It was indeed a trance: whether it was sport really became irrelevant. It elevated the Olympics.

FIRST LADY OF THE NATIONAL

Jenny Pitman rides tall in a hard man's world

3 March 1984

The saying around the stables is that you are more sensitively cared for as a horse than a human under the eagle eye of Jenny Pitman. And she admits it. The senior lad at one famous stable, reflecting on her unique and spectacular impact upon National Hunt racing, observed knowingly: 'She sure is hard.'

The description would not offend Mrs Pitman. A senior handicapper is said almost to have ruptured a blood vessel recently when on the receiving end of her colourful opinion concerning the weight for one of her horses. In her days as a stable girl for her father, one of the hacks came to be known as Sodyer, from her comments on its wilfulness.

Yet this formidable woman, who will send out Corbiere perfectly prepared tomorrow to defend his Grand National title, possesses, beneath an exterior as unflinching as Maxim Gorky's grandmother, the gentle disposition of a nurse. In the words of my colleague, Michael Seely, she is 'a quite outstanding judge of what a horse can do: a traditional realist, which is a rare quality.'

For anyone unfamiliar with the racing world, Mrs Pitman's achievement of becoming the first woman in 144 years to train a National winner and within 12 months take the prized Cheltenham Gold Cup with Burrough Hill Lad, is equivalent to Rachael Flint going out to open against the West Indies with Gatting. In racing, women either muck out the stables or try to look as handsome as the horse in the winner's enclosure.

Tomorrow morning before 7.00 Jenny Pitman will have watched Corky, as the champion is known, and the jockey, Ben de Haan, have a short workout and will then walk the four-and-a-half-mile course to determine just how each ferocious fence should be approached in the prevailing conditions. Just get my horses and riders round safely, she will say to herself, and I'll give up swearing or smoking. . . . Please God, don't let any of them get hurt.

The astonishing thing about the woman who has conquered a man's world is that she is not all Amazon but an emotional mother and, when it happened, a miserably divorced wife; a girl who adored her father and grew up on a Leicestershire farm under his guidance knowing just what she must do to match the boys.

She has just published an autobiography, *Glorious Uncertainty*, which in a sense ought never to have been written. Her joint-author, Sue Gibson, and her publishers should have protected her from baring her soul, from revealing many intimacies of her stricken relationship with the former jockey, Richard Pitman, which would perhaps have been better unsaid. Yet she is so unfalteringly spontaneous and honest that she probably could not help herself, never mind the publishers' expectant rubbing of hands.

When I asked her at Cheltenham, just before Burrough Hill Lad fulfilled all her prophecies, whether she was pleased that the truth was out, like Nelson she said she could not tell a lie. 'If I tell the truth, then I always know what I've said. I'm incapable of handling half-truths. No, I'm *not* not glad it's published.'

You wonder, as time will eventually heal, if she will regret some hurtful asides about Richard's relationship with their sons; but he is mature enough still to be predicting fulsomely, as professional commentator, that Corky will win again tomorrow. She herself admits that when, still married, Richard was beaten in the National run-in on Crisp by Red Rum, she was too upset to talk about it for six months. They grew apart, she reflects, largely because he was a successful jockey while she was labouring, anonymously, to become a successful trainer.

Her life, and the book, are fascinating, an amalgam of determination, luck, joy and sorrow. 'I'm just an ordinary person,' she said at Cheltenham among an admiring crowd. 'And I think that's why some people seem to like me. The National victory hasn't changed me. I had no private education, no silver spoon. I'm glad there are people with money and I'm pleased to work for them. But I still don't like parties, or drinking, though I'll occasionally have a brandy if I'm really knackered.'

You can tell the kind of brave/afraid woman she is from the incident in 1982 when Lord Gulliver, a potential National entry, died of a heart attack during a training gallop while ridden by her sister, Mandy. In the grief of the moment the weeping Mandy was told to pull herself together. It was later in private that Jenny's own tears were released.

She rode at 14 months and won her first race at four. There was no gas, electricity or running water in her early childhood days at the farm. Kitchen sink taps, a radio . . . these were revelations to come. Working from dawn to dusk, she learnt every wrinkle of equestrian psychology, with working horses which could not be allowed to go lame; which is why she now laughingly agrees that she is gentler with horses than humans 'because the horses don't understand so well'.

Those were the days when lunch was a raw turnip in the fields and late at night under a lamp in the stable she would fall asleep in her father's lap after sharing a bowl of bread and milk. Yet this tomboy, who ceremoniously made herself a 'blood brother' with another stable lad, who preferred new wellies for Christmas rather than a doll, was a mean hockey player, a tearaway who scrumped apples daringly, and when she fractured her skull in a fall, refused to cry in front of nurses in hospital.

She hunted as a girl with the Quorn, rode point-to-point at 14, and fell head-over-heels at 18 for the promising young jockey at Bishop's Cleeve stable. 'I loved him so deeply I would have changed places when he was injured.' They married. She changed her religion to Catholicism. Two sons arrived quickly. Lord Cadogan helped them set up their own yard but life was still economically hard. Morover, 'I didn't understand Richard's riding pressures and he didn't recognise my training progress in point-to-points'.

She remembers going to apply for her trainer's licence at the Jockey Club, where the stewards on the other side of the polished table whispered in her presence, which in her country way she thought was rude.

Career and marriage moved in opposite directions until one Christmas, when separation and an appendicitis arrived almost the same day. Yet within four years she was training 28 winners in a season. And then there was Corky. The story of his progress from raw novice, through alarming injury to champion, is alone worth reading. Mrs Pitman is some lady.

RARE COURAGE IN THE HOME OF THE BRAVE

Phelps provides memorable climax to the modern pentathlon

3 August 1984 Los Angeles

If you want to find the genuine flavour of the Olympics, go and hunt down the hard men of the modern pentathlon, who have exceptional versatility and a sporting regard for each other's performance which is found nowhere so prominently, except, perhaps, in the decathlon. Taking the freeway south out of Los Angeles, and the mountain road to Coto de Caza, we are to see one of the most memorable climaxes of the Games, with a Swede and a Briton experiencing heroic failure.

After the morning's shooting, fourth of the five events which represent the transport and defence of the military courier – horse-back, the sword, swimming, the pistol and running over rough terrain – Masala, of Italy, holds a narrow lead of 26 points in more than 4,000 over Rasmuson of Sweden, and almost double that over Four (France) and Storm (US). These four, it seems, will decide the individual medals, for Massullo (Italy), Jung (Switzerland), Quesada (Spain), Faraj (Bahrain) and Phelps (GB) are between 190 and 240 points adrift, Richard Phelps having slumped from third place after the swimming, to ninth following a miserable morning, for him, with the pistol.

To gain even a bronze Phelps now has to run over a minute faster than Four and Storm for four kilometres over a treacherously sandy and hilly course under the baking sun. You would say, as the 52 competitors assemble in the horse-jumping ring from where the race will start, that it was an impossible margin to close in a 12 or 13 minute race, even if Phelps, a Gloucestershire metal merchant, is the best runner in the field, which he is.

The shape of this final event, ever since the Moscow Olympics, is that the leader after four events starts first, followed by each successive competitor on a handicap interval equivalent to the time margin by which he must, theoretically, run faster than the leader to have the same time – that is, eight seconds for Rasmuson, 15 seconds for Four, 16 seconds for Storm and one minute 19 seconds for Phelps, who must run at least one minute and five seconds faster than Four for the bronze. This dramatic switch in procedure, from the former reverse order of running, means that the first man across the line is necessarily the pentathlon winner.

The neat little Masala is away and out of sight up the first hill by the time the tall, lean ginger-haired Phelps is off in pursuit with his angular, slightly crouching, style. When we next catch a glimpse of the runners Phelps has already overtaken three of the eight in front.

The announcer tells a now hushed crowd that at the two-kilometre halfway mark, Masala still leads Rasmuson, but that Storm has overtaken Four to go third. At the three-kilometre mark, the announcer says: 'And now, Phelps of Britain is third.' What sensation is this? Has information out on the course got muddled, we wonder cautiously?

The crowd waits with breath held. The American journalist next to me is incredulous, and disbelieving. 'Masala and Rusmuson are coming down the hill approaching the arena', the announcer says. The crowd is on its feet, yelling its heart out for even that bronze.

Where is Storm? As the first two runners come into view it is Rasmuson, in his blue and yellow vest, who is desperately edging ahead by a yard or two on the outside of the curve, as they battle towards the arena, but just as they enter, he is seen to be tottering. His legs have gone, his lungs are on fire.

Masala, arms flailing, claws past him towards the line. Rasmuson staggers into the guiding rope, eyes glazed and head rolling, looking as if he will collapse. Somehow, he stays upright for a few more strides until he literally falls across the line to take the silver.

As this is happening, Phelps appears, neck and neck with Storm to a huge roar from the spectators. But Phelps, after one of the bravest imaginable runs, is also on the point of black-out. Storm raises a weak sprint and goes by in a haze of cheering, with Phelps just able to drag himself home before he collapses into the arms of Ron Bright, his manager. What gallant failure. What a finish for this enthusiastic gathering.

Yet the Englishman will come to fight again. 'I've got another two Olympics, I hope', he eventually says, after being unable to speak for almost half an hour.

Phelps is still weak, and barely able to stand as other men come to congratulate him. The whole mood of the arena is one of amiability among men who have spent all of themselves over four days side by side, including 10 hours of fencing on the second day. They know what each has given.

Bright says that by 1988 Phelps will be the best fencer in the competition, and that they will work hard on his shooting. He just wishes there was a bit more money around.

The British had three officials. The Italians, who took team and individual gold, had the support of a millionaire and the backing of 12 officials. What Phelps gave us is not made of money.

CUTTING SHORT THE SCEPTICS

*Coe's unique fight against illness to retain
Olympic crown*

13 August 1984 Los Angeles

Before John Walker and Sebastian Coe left the UCLA village for their respective finals on the last day of track and field events at the Coliseum, Walker, the 1,500 metres champion of 1976, privately apologised to Coe for his statement some time ago that no great athlete ever lasted at the top for more than two years, and added that he thought Coe would win.

Steve Cram, the world, European and Commonwealth champion at 1,500 metres during the two years of Coe's continual health problems, had said earlier in the Olympic fortnight that nobody would be able to last seven races over two distances in the abrasive acid and heat of Los Angeles' polluted air. Joachim Cruz, the 800 metres champion, has not: but after Coe had electrifyingly kicked clear from Cram in the last 120 metres of a record race, Cram was the first to pay tribute to a unique performer.

'I'm satisfied. I enjoyed the race. I couldn't do anything else,' he said. 'Seb was brilliant, I didn't think he'd have it in his legs. I'm pleased for him'. It is the recognition of the calibre of his performance by other athletes which will most gratify Coe, because a successful defence of the title, which he gained in Moscow, has not been achieved in this Blue Riband of Olympic events since before the First World War. It was the perfectly gauged race, run in a time which lowered Keino's 1968 Olympic record, the more remarkable because at this time last year Coe was in hospital with a serious blood disease and did not start training again until Christmas.

The unseen heroes of this victory, which had the American crowds out of their seats, are a bunch of anonymous Haringey club runners – John, Gary, Perry, and Dennis – whose selfless relay running ahead of Coe in training in the wretched winter months of January to March enabled him to recapture the endurance which would withstand the seven races.

The 800 metres series arrived, he says without any disrespect for Cruz's record-breaking run, two races too soon. It was those four two-lap races that gave him the sharpness for the 1,500 metres, and it was only following the first round of the longer race that he had, briefly, any discomfort.

There is no belittlement of Cram, the silver medal winner, in emphasising Coe's exceptional comeback to repeat his silver and gold in Moscow. No British runner at any distance has won more than two Olympic medals. Although a couple of months ago he was not sure of selection, he confided after Saturday's race that, so confident was he feeling during the development of tactics in the race, that he fastened onto Khalifa, Scott and Abascal when they successively led the field, and had to discipline himself not to make a break with 270 metres to go, but to bide his time. 'The Olympics is a competition to win, not to put at risk.'

For a variety of reasons Coe is more satisfied with his Los Angeles gold medal than with Moscow's, not least because his father, Peter Coe, putting an affectionate arm around him afterwards, would say with mock seriousness: 'I couldn't find a single thing wrong with that performance, except you didn't dip at the tape.' Several minutes after the semi-final, in which Seb had foolishly eased over the last 30 yards and two fast finishers had nearly passed him, Peter, close to retirement age, was still visibly trembling with anxiety, and said to a friend: 'If you see him first, thump him.'

What neither son nor father had revealed prior to the Olympics was that by mutual agreement they had for the last month separated: not as coach and athlete, not tactically, not temperamentally, not permanently, but simply to take away the stress caused by their differing personalities and concern for each other, so as not to jeopardise the effort.

Seb knew that in the emotional turmoil of the Olympics, which can make or break competitors, he had to be his own man mentally. Peter acknowledged that change in his son when, discussing the significance of Seb's sharp semi-final performance, he said: 'The person who knew better than I or any judge that he could win was himself.'

In the coming weeks Coe will run several 1,500 metre races and at least one 5,000 to explore his intended switch. His main target now is the European 5,000 metres at Stuttgart, in 1986. But before this season is out he would like to try to recapture the 1,500 world record, lost by Steve Ovett to Sydney Maree last season, then regained.

For Ovett, it was a sad conclusion to his Olympic career. His courageous, almost belligerent insistence on coming back from illness in the 800, against the wishes of his wife and some medical advisers, was doomed to failure, and he dropped out of the race shortly after the bell with a recurrence of his breathing difficulties. Both Coe and Cram commiserated with the world record holder afterwards. 'It was very brave of him to step out after the 800 and I hope he finds out what his problem is when he gets home,' Coe said.

Khalifa, of Sudan, set a fastish first lap of 58 seconds and down the back for the second time Scott suddenly jumped into the lead, Coe moving in behind Khalifa as they went around the third bend. Scott said later that he was determined to make it a fast race and not just a kickers' finish; but his boldness served only to assist Coe and condemn his own chances. Scott led for just over a lap, passing the 800 metres mark in 1.56.8, over 8 seconds faster than the split time in Moscow, but with a lap and a quarter to go Abascal, then Coe and Cram swept past Scott, with Ovett pulling through into fourth place at the bell.

Around the penultimate bend Ovett was obliged to drop out. Down the last back straight Abascal clung to his lead, but into the bend was passed by Coe and then Cram as the former held off the latter's challenge. Coming into the straight Coe kicked for a second time, then a third, and raced away from Cram, covering the last lap in 53.25, the last 300 in 39.32, the time the same as in Moscow. His mood as he crossed the line had not the same ecstatic relief, as four years ago, but the satisfaction was deeper. 'It was a coldly calculated race for me from start to finish,' Coe said. 'It was the best I'd felt for two years, and took me back to the form of 1981, which I've not touched since then.'

THE LONGEST TWENTY SECONDS

Freezing with the speed skiers in Scotland

23 March 1985 Glenshee

Melissa Dimino was just a slim ordinary sort of waitress from California . . . until the day she skied down a French mountain at 124.75 mph last year to become the fastest woman on earth independent of mechanical assistance. Speed skiing, she says, becomes addictive. It is easy to believe her.

If nothing else, it is a more cute way to earn £10,000 a year than being a waitress; always assuming, of course, that you can cope with the numbing fear of launching yourself down seemingly suicidal slopes. Miss Dimino enjoys it, and cannot for the present think of doing anything else. Prior to her first race a couple of years ago she had never skied competitively at any discipline. 'The fitness is more mental than physical.'

So for the past two days she and 50 other competitors have been waiting for the Scotch mist to clear on the top of Glas Maol at Glenshee to start the Smirnoff Flying Kilometre, the first ever World Cup skiing event in Scotland. It is undoubtedly an enthusiasts' sport: in swirling cloud the racers were up there packing down a fresh snowfall on the run which drops more acutely than any downhill. With a late start and difficult conditions, times were yesterday not exceptional.

Yet Franz Weber, the six times world champion who has dominated speed skiing for the last four years, thinks that Glenshee could be a really fast course in fine weather. A former Austrian junior downhiller with Wairather and Wirnsberger, he quit skiing to go to university in Geneva and became the European skateboard champion of 1977.

It was almost by accident that he became hooked on speed skiing in Switzerland. With his current world record of 129.82 mph he is one of the handful of skiers to have achieved that rare sensation of skiing on a permanent air cushion, which is reached at around 125.

'It's a marvellous feeling as the violent vibrations go and it suddenly becomes smooth' he says. 'You are, in effect, airborne, and the smallest turn of your streamlined helmet can alter your direction like the tailfin of an aeroplane'.

With acceleration of Concorde proportions, seven seconds to 120 mph, his is hardly an exaggeration, but it is only in recent years that the sport has, so to speak, gathered momentum. In 1979, shortly after Steve McKinney, elder brother of the current US alpiniste Tamara, had become the first to break the 200 kph barrier (124 mph), speed skiing was withdrawn as an official event of the international federation FIS because it was thought too dangerous. A professional group, International Speed Skiing, was formed: since when there have been no deaths.

McKinney is at Braemar this week, more for recreation than prizemoney, before he prepares for another of the more eccentric sport ventures. A previous leader of Himalayan expeditions, he has the first hang-gliding permit granted by Tibet for the north face of Everest. 'It's just about the only first remaining on Everest', he says. 'The north face has this wonderful ridge, and I had the idea the last time I was there and a condor was planing right past my tent. We shall spiral down on one of the world's oldest civilisations!'

Weber, with some 15 sponsorships, earns around £200,000 a year including prizemoney, not to mention the free loan of a symbolic Porsche wherever he happens to be skiing. They drove one up here for him from London. If he is the only man making such money, few would doubt he deserved it. In 1983 at Les Arcs he crashed at 125mph.

He skidded half a mile, fractured a kneecap, had 30 per cent friction burns, and could not feel his hands for a fortnight having tried to brake his fall – without gloves. 'I had thought gloves reduced my speed, but not any more. The important thing was to get back on the slopes. Four weeks later I competed at Silverton in Colorado. I was so anxious I couldn't talk, but I managed to have a sleep in a tent while I waited to start at 14,600 feet – and broke the record.'

John Clark, who has the British record at 121 mph, is a former international downhiller who coaches the British women's alpine team. In his first race in borrowed gear two years ago he reached 113, and was invited to join Weber in the Smirnoff team.

'The difference from downhill is the intensity,' says the young Scot. 'It's the longest 20 seconds you can ever experience, your perception of time changes, there is so much to do'. Like Miss Dimino, he thinks the mental factor is critical: she crashed at the end of her record run and realised afterwards that her concentration had excluded the runout following the time zone. 'It taught me so much,' she says.

Clark thinks that the sport's appeal is that the speeds are simpler to understand than the split seconds by which Alpine competitions are measured. 'The more you're in trouble, the more you must attack the line, you have to know at the start exactly what you're going to do. I'm looking forward to reaching the smooth phase'.

Before the violent vibrations begin at about 115, the competitor has to lock into a stable crouch, hands held together in front, knee bent inwards so that the skis are on the inside edge. It has to be a natural sequence, Clark says. 'I never have thought of fear once I start,' Weber said 'When I finish the elation is so great that sometimes I am crying.'

SELF-HELP FUELS THE EAST GERMAN POWER-HOUSE

An investigation of communist sporting success

17 April 1985 East Berlin

There were chrysanthemums in a flowerpot in the middle of the crisp chequered tablecloth. The dark mat-tiled floor was as spotless as a hospital matron's pinny. 'What would you like?' a smiling waitress inquired within moments of my taking a seat: wine was 65p a carafe, and beer 25p. The eight lanes of the ten-pin bowling hall vibrated with the unending thud-and-clatter of six-handed matches, and the scores blinked on individual computer screens. A hum of conversation conveyed an aura of contented well-being.

This was East Berlin's unrivalled Sports and Recreation Centre, a palace of leisure built four years ago in the industrial working-class district of Prenzlauerberg, with half a dozen swimming pools, two ice rinks, sauna, gymnasium and restaurants. None of the facilities cost more than 50p an hour, except bowling at about 75p a head. The place was packed with people aged from five to 75.

A myth exists outside the German Democratic Republic that they possess some kind of miracle machine by which world eminence has been achieved in sport: a technical, laboratory-orientated masterstroke of organisation which coerces and manipulates compulsory volunteers towards ever greater performance in the hallowed name of Marxism. How else could this small nation of 17 million or so dominate world sporting events?*

It needs no more than a week to discover that, while bureaucracy and science undoubtedly exploit and enhance every possible potential, the secret of East Germany's disproportionate triumphs is to be found quite simply in the character, created over several centuries, of a people who in 1945 inherited a pile of rubble and desolation. It may suit the alignment of Western thinking to interpret East Germany's success in political terms, but the miracle lies as much in the soul and the inclination of the people as in the political system that moulds and directs some of their actions. It is an echo of the post-war material miracle of West Germany, a triumph of the ethic of self-help favoured by the Thatcher Government.

Communist Germany does not deny the bourgeois nineteenth century foundations of much of sport. De Coubertin's recommendation that beyond the Olympic Games it is more important that everyone partakes of the advantages of Olympic culture in the modest setting of daily existence is widely quoted. Of 60 museums, six are devoted to sport and its history. Also quoted is the humanist Christopher Friedrich GutsMuths (1759–1829) whose *Gymnastics for the Young*, published in 1793, proclaimed that 'all children should benefit from gymnastics'. It should be remembered that 100,000 sportsmen took part in 1922 in Leipzig's first-ever Workers' Gymnastics and Sports Festival.

It would be an exaggeration to say that the 40-year post-war ascent has been the work of one man, but certainly the inspiration and energy for thousands of officials and competitors stemmed from Manfred Ewald, the president of their Olympic committee. He was born in 1926; his father belonged to the anti-Fascist Communist underground, and Ewald was nearly executed in 1944. At 22 he was leader of the Free German Youth organisation; at 28 he became Minister of Sport though it was not until three years later, in 1952, that serious competitive sport re-started. So powerful did the Sports Ministry (DTSB) become that they could in effect give instructions to the Government.

Partly through initially limited financial circumstances, partly through the character of the people, sport was a fertile ground on which to help rebuild the pride of the nation. Article 18 of the new constitution guaranteed the right to sport for any individual: all stadiums became public and the use of facilities at the present 102,000 sports clubs is free. That figure includes 10,000 factory, or 'enterprise', sports clubs as they are known.

The statistics of the pyramid base of East German sport are astonishing, including 3.4 million club members (20.6 per cent of the population); 245,000 trained coaches; 329 stadiums; 196 indoor swimming pools (98 per cent, compared with under 50 per cent in Britain, of the population can swim); 9,918 outdoor sports grounds; 5,397 sports halls; 332 ski jumps; 1,668 athletic hostels; all supported by a 1984 government budget of £122 million. That is four times the British government's sports grant, as is the East German arts budget of £400 million. Anyone injured in sport receives free medical treatment. Travel to and from competition is free.

Such breadth of involvement could not conceivably be a State imposition, however much a central system makes it all possible. The national enthusiasm for sport is epitomised by the biennial Spartakiad games. From the merest villages, millions take part in the preliminary events, culminating in a final of 10,000 competitors in four times the number of competitions to be found at an Olympic Games. Television substantially covers such sports as rowing and canoeing. There is almost no family without a Spartakiad medal.

It was political exclusion in the early post-war years from the then Western-orientated sporting world that helped motivate the population. Barred from the 1952 Olympics, East Germany were admitted in 1956 in a joint team with West Germany. This produced controversy between Federal and Democratic states on who should provide the *chef de mission*. West Germany, never contemplating their neighbour's eventual rise, insisted it should be decided by who provided the more competitors, following joint eliminating trials. 'We realised that if *we* could have the majority, with Manfred Ewald leading the opening ceremony march, then West Germany would pull out,' says Klaus Huhn, a prominent sports journalist and founder of the esteemed Berlin-Prague cycle race. 'That was our main motivation.'

Wolfgang Behrendt became East Germany's first gold medallist, winning the bantamweight boxing in Melbourne. By 1964, in Tokyo, the Communists had the larger German contingent; a year later Avery Brundage, president of the IOC, accepted that there should be separate teams, though in Mexico the East Germans were still denied their own anthem. It was in Munich in 1972 that the 'miracle machine' ultimately unleashed its strength with 20 gold medals, 23 silver and 23 bronze. The same happened in the Winter Olympics, where they took a total of 14 medals, an astonishing performance for a country without Alpine slopes or the money to spend months abroad. To compensate, they had invented plastic slopes.

Initiative is the key. 'You cannot have success at the top if other areas are not working', says Norbert Rogalski, deputy director of education at the renowned Leipzig College of Physical Culture. 'For this reason, Government attention was directed at schools, working people and the armed forces. Officials from developing countries come to the college and ask how they can win medals. We say we can assist, but they have to develop the same system of a broad base, work hard, and the top level will appear. It took us 15 years. What can be said is that as a socialist country we're obliged to offer every scope to those with talent.'

Visiting the town of Zella Mehlis (population: 17,000) near the winter sports centre at Oberhof in the southern Thuringer Hills, I witnessed the degree of self-help through which talent emerges. The committee of the Robotron Club, sponsored by the local computer factory, met me in their tiny, home-built club house on a picturesque woodland hill: working men in their shirt-sleeves, as proud and dignified as if they were the New York Yacht Club. Round a glass of vodka or beer, they discussed their 1,530 spare-time members for bobsleighing, luge, skiing, football, handball, wrestling, table tennis, orienteering, tennis, fencing, swimming, gymnastics, wind surfing and forestry. Their specialities are Nordic skiing and wrestling. One of them told with a smile how he had taught Meinhard Nehmer, three times an Olympic bobsleigh gold medal winner.

'Last year, our sports men and women did 15 million hours of voluntary work,' said Klaus Eichler, the new young deputy to Ewald, when we met in Berlin at the DTSB. The Ministry has a personable and energetic successor to Ewald. 'The majority of our officials, trainers, referees and judges are voluntary, receiving a nominal 40 marks (£10) a month, enough to buy a bunch of flowers,' he said. Eichler believes that this voluntary force is part of the national strength, but that an expanding economy will have an effect on living standards and personal financial security which will give East Germans even more time and interest to maintain international sporting improvement. 'Increased education expands the desires for communication through sport,' he said. 'Our people now have 128 free days a year.'

* The full extent of official exploitation of banned drugs only became apparent with the fall of the Berlin Wall.

A WINNER WITHOUT THE KILLER INSTINCT

Gower the gentle iconoclast

29 August 1985

The public school, middle-class conventions of his upbringing have been carefully cloaked by David Gower with the classless contemporary mannerisms of a social cosmopolitan. Yet no one, including perhaps the man himself, is quite sure what is the real Gower.

The current England captain of cricket, who this morning in the 6th Test at the Oval hopes to guide his team to the winning of the Ashes, is a complex sportsman: known to all, yet truly known by few. Even the chairman of the selectors, Peter May, is said to find it difficult to communicate with him.

As a distantly viewed public figure, there is something of the politician David Owen about Gower. Able, intelligent, popular, there is flexibility in his nature, in seemingly wanting to be all things to all men, which leaves people unsure: gregarious yet private, personable yet emotionless, an ardent modern professional with the almost lazy aura of an old-fashioned amateur, a winner without the killer instinct.

His fascination with cats and leopards is perhaps indicative of his character. 'They have a serenity,' he says. So, occasionally unduly, does his leadership. There are times, watching him fielding at mid-off, when he appears to be observing the conflict rather than directing it. Yet after three Test series as a comparatively youthful, and somewhat reluctant captain, there is little doubt that he is maturing.

Ray Illingworth, the former England, Yorkshire and Leicestershire captain, under whose wing the schoolboy Gower entered first class cricket, says: 'He is undoubtedly improving, as shown by his handling of the last few overs of the one-day match against Australia at Lord's, and his judgement in the Trent Bridge Test. He would no doubt say he got the job a year or two earlier than he wanted it.'

Chosen at 27 to succeed Bob Willis last summer when almost simultaneously he had replaced Peter Willey as Leicestershire captain, Gower was prepared for the West Indies series at home to be gruelling. It was. England was overrun, but he felt they should have done better in the match at Lord's.

His own performance with the bat fell short; at least in part because of an early season infection, sustained in a finger injury against Derbyshire, which characteristically he at first declined to take seriously. A specialist has said that 15 years ago he could have died from it.

Ill for a month, he started playing again too soon, attempting to find form for the Tests, was never really fit, and after a brief holiday led the team in India, hardly a rest cure.

His batting remained, for him, sub-standard; and he was a less than diligent captain when England moved on to Australia for the superfluous one-day series. At times, too, he was touchy in handling the Press, resorting to the flippancy which is his self-defensive mechanism. An interviewer once wrote of him that 'he is so laid back he is almost comatose'.

Gentle iconoclasm has always been evident. At King's School, Canterbury, he was never a school monitor, yet when asked at 15, reprovingly, by his housemaster, what he thought he would be doing in ten years time, is said to have replied that he would be captain of England.

Berated as a teenager by Illingworth for the casualness of his dress, he once mockingly appeared at breakfast in a dinner jacket. He made an indifferent start as vice-captain to Willis in 1983–84, informal in dress and punctuality, but latterly as captain he has never put a foot wrong at such formalities as embassy receptions – before disappearing off to a disco.

Gower adapts, chameleon-like, to his circumstances, which adds to the enigma of who he is. He was born in Kent of a family with long colonial service, including a judge and an admiral, with traditions of duty from which he is clearly not immune.

Following a childhood partly spent in what was then Tanganyika, he returned to English preparatory school and thence to King's, achieved three A levels, failed Oxbridge, and went to read law at University College, London.

He has discreetly played down his background and speech: his mother has been quoted as saying that she long ago recognised that he had one accent with the family and another with friends. The everyman's voice of a Smiley.

The decision, when Leicestershire successfully approached Kent for his signature, to forgo a law degree for full time cricket, may well have accentuated the social ambivalence for someone who found it easy, and more acceptable, to conform to surroundings than conventions.

He quite enjoyed being regarded in the early 80s as one of the rebels, identifying with Botham; unconcerned that traditionalists at Lord's gritted their teeth if he appeared at nets in a T-shirt. He was of another world, another age, compared with the established figures of the MCC. 'He mixed very easily', Illingworth says. 'When he was young, without being cheeky he had the self-confidence to speak freely with the older professionals.'

If Gower was with them in spirit and ambition, he was still somehow not *of* them. The players, then and now, liked him and enjoyed playing with him, but he was largely reluctant to talk about cricket.

His articles for *Wisden Cricket Monthly* are as likely to refer to restaurants as to the game. He enjoys the good life, and will search for champagne at inflated prices in up-country India. His cultural tastes are as catholic as his behaviour: in the house near the Leicestershire ground where he lives with his girlfriend he is as likely to listen to Brahms as to rock, reads avidly and most days does the *Telegraph* crossword. Someone who knows him well says that, though he would not care to admit it, Gower does not consider his life ends with cricket.

Be that as it may, he is one of the most illustrious lights in the game. The secret of all games is timing. In tennis, the great players such as Perry, Hoad and McEnroe take the ball early. Great batsman often take it late. Maybe Gower does not take it as late as the famed Ranjitsinhji, but he is likened to the debonair Compton, and to the legendary Woolley, likewise a left hander from Kent with a similarly upright stance, who was the quintessence of style.

Hutton has said that Gower does not have Woolley's ability to demolish an attack, leaving the bowlers not knowing where or how to bowl. Yet Gower, admittedly on covered wickets, has scored 5,228 runs in 75 Tests so far compared with Woolley's 3,283 in 64.

The next five years will determine whether he is a good batsman or a great one. He is no ruthless accumulator, such as Boycott or Bradman, and is apt to try difficult shots regarded by some as irresponsible merely to prove he *can* play them.

'He was the greatest youngster anyone could have seen,' Illingworth says. 'A marvellous timer of the ball. He was tactically poor at first, weak at playing spin, but such was his timing he soon improved.'

In his first Test at Edgbaston against Pakistan in 1978 he memorably hooked his first ball for four, scored 58, and subsequently became the youngest Englishman since May, in 1951, to score a Test century. His 187 during eight hours for England against the West Indies in 1981 disproved that he cannot concentrate; as did his double century a fortnight ago.

Captaincy undoubtedly did not come as easily to him as does the game. There are those at Leicester who say the team looked more purposeful under Willey, yet this season Gower has several times shown himself ready to take a risk which Willey would have eschewed.

Mike Turner, the Leicestershire secretary, recalls that Illingworth, when captain of country and county at the age of 38, needed time to adjust after a Test match to the lower key of the county championship, and that Gower, ten years younger, is experiencing the same problem. Yet it must be doubted if England would have called upon him had he not already been made county captain, even if preferably he needed to have waited a year or two longer for both. Brearley, England's last outstanding captain, was, like Illingworth, in his 30s.

It seems unlikely that Australia, if unaided by the weather, can deny England at least the draw they need to take the series. A more searching examination of Gower's leadership will come in the West Indies this winter in an environment of sharper hostility than has been provided by the Australians. Will Gower be able to control, on and off the pitch, one of his predecessors as captain, the rogue elephant Botham, who was absent during the successful tour of India?

Gower has written of Botham that 'you seem to get the best out of him by letting him have his way when setting the field or bowling a spell.' That policy has not always proved strategic this summer, during which Botham has often been erratic.

With his growing influence, Gower is establishing within the England team a coterie of supporters and some of them, such as his admirable vice captain Gatting, would be happy to see a team ethic more vigorously imposed on the egocentric Botham. Can Gower, or indeed anyone, achieve that?

PROSPECT OF A FAIRER COUNTRY

Seeking out the liberals on both sides of the South African fence

22 April 1986 Cape Town

On the main highway out of Cape Town last week a Cape Coloured factory worker by the name of Solomon was trying to hitch a lift 450 miles north to the Transvaal border to bury his 86-year-old mother, who had died the day before. He had less than one rand (40p) in his pocket. A workers' rail pass is nine rand. He is paid fortnightly – and pay day was four days away. There was no question of an advance from his employer.

At the Western Transvaal Yacht Club, where they were staging one of the events of the recent South African Games, the elderly white steward confronted a small group of visitors: myself and four black Swazi fellow journalists. Grudgingly, and only after discovering that we were from the Press, did he allow us into the pavilion, saying to the Swazis: 'The results are over there – if you can understand them.'

The only hope for South Africa, as one of the more progressive white sports administrators said dispassionately of his own parents, is when this generation has died. Go to Witwatersand University and see the karate competitions, with wholly integrated audience, competitors and judges within a single non-racial federation, and you know that there is long-term hope.

Can time enough be gained in the face of justifiable township unrest and violence, of teenagers hell-bent on the destruction of the regime? The townships, with their degrading conditions, are no more all-violent than the whites are all-evil.

I drove through Soweto. The glances at a white were hostile and sullen but the children were eager to be photographed. Ron Pickering's anti-apartheid television film does not show us the areas of Soweto as middle-class as Cheadle or Esher. 'The majority of blacks do not want to fight. The problem is they no longer have control of their children,' Joe 'Ole Bones' Senakgomo, a former professional middleweight boxer who has lived all his life in a township, said.

When I went to a first division football match in Thokoza, one of four whites in a 15,000 crowd, and got a hard-boiled egg sandwich, bought at a snack stall, immovably stuck in my throat and could not breathe, the gateman was thoroughly good-natured and accommodatingly slapped me on the back.

At an ice skating gala there was an emotional moment that makes anyone, of whatever colour, grieve for the wrongs perpetrated by whites over three centuries. The Black Panthers, a coloured Cape Town group, performed in national costume to rhythmic music. The audience were mostly white. As the dance reached a crescendo they became gripped by the performance and finally burst into spontaneous applause which recognised no barriers. It was not a pretence.

South Africa is transparently not a fair country. We know there are continual humiliations of non-whites. Yet there are enough whites genuinely trying to achieve a peaceful revolution to deserve the opportunity to avoid a bloody revolution, even if the government's liberalisation is not moving fast enough.

Over the weekend the South African Sports Federations issued a statement demanding that the government abolish the remaining iniquities of the apartheid policy. The Mixed Marriage Act and the pass laws may be relaxed but the restrictions in education, the Group Areas Act and the Population Registration Act (recording colour) are still there.

Yet men such as Eddie Barlow, the former Test cricketer and adviser behind the Sports Federations' statement, are prepared to push and embarrass the government all they can in pursuit of national freedom of association which already exists in most sports. However, before South African sport can hope to reopen its attempt to regain international recognition, it needs a change of face at the top.

Long-standing officials such as Rudolf Opperman and Dennis McIldowie, veterans of the Olympic movement, Danie Craven in rugby and Joe Pamensky in cricket, who represent the old regime, must retire.

However much they have done for integration, they will not convince black Africa that they did not do so only because they had to.

FOOTBALL'S BRAIN IN SPAIN

How Terry Venables transformed Barcelona

7 May 1986 Barcelona

People in sport are apt to become suspicious of performers with more than average intelligence. They feel inadequate. Gene Tunney, the most literate of all world heavyweight champions, offended some American fight fans because he did not talk their language, and could discourse with Bernard Shaw. Throughout his luminous career in football, as a player, coach and manager, Terry Venables has been shouldering the same syndrome of received public opinion.

In the European Cup final in Seville tonight, Barcelona may provide the indelible proof, for remaining unbelievers, that he is no flash in the pan. There are, indeed, some fellow professionals who regard him, at 43, as possibly the best coach in the world today. By any standards he is unusual.

He collaborated on a television series, *Hazell*, and wrote a book, in his twenties, before he had ever seriously read one. The only child of a London docker and Welsh mother, he sang with Joe Loss at the Hammersmith Palais, performed in cabaret at the Stork Room, formed his own limited company at 18, won international caps at every level from schoolboy to senior professional, bought his own club (Queen's Park Rangers) by raising £1 million, won the Spanish league title with Barcelona at the first attempt, and has just signed a new one-year contract there that is thought to be worth £400,000.

'A lot of people seem to think I'm a slippery Cockney boy with a few jokes', he has said. 'It has taken one of the biggest clubs in the world to acknowledge what I can really do, my ability at coaching. I've always tried to come across as someone who can express himself and who has a sense of humour, but then some people label me "too clever by half". They used to say I improved lesser players but couldn't deal with stars. I came here and did it. Where's the next criticism?'

Many illustrious coaches have arrived, failed, and been sacked by Barcelona, a club which is a focal point of the Catalan capital at all social levels, arousing a passion and loyalty among its 120,000 regular supporters without equal anywhere. Big names from Argentina, West Germany and the Netherlands have been among those unable to bring Barcelona the European Cup, the prized trophy won six times by their arch-rivals, Real Madrid.

Sitting at a pavement café in Madrid during the World Cup finals of 1982, Venables and Bobby Robson, there to assist the England manager, Ron Greenwood, fell into a discussion on coaching appointments. Robson related how he had been approached by Barcelona but had turned them down because of the language difficulty. When Venables arrived back home he bought instructional Spanish language tapes. If anyone came for him, he would be prepared. In 1984, Barcelona did.

When Venables was a schoolboy in Dagenham, the teachers told his mother that he was always finished before everyone and looking out of the window. Dreaming of football. Too able for that, the teachers said. He had been hooked from the time, aged three, when an uncle brought home a small red water polo ball at the end of the war. 'Couldn't stop him', his father says. 'Captain of Dagenham schools, England schools, playing cricket, winning the schools cross-country.'

The boy developed an odd blend of East End humour and Welsh seriousness. While winning a variety of talent contests as a teenager, he delayed signing professional forms for Chelsea, for whom he had made his first team debut as an amateur at 17, in case Britain might select him for the Olympic games in Rome after playing for the England Amateur XI.

Soon he had become the fulcrum of an exciting young Chelsea side, winning promotion to the first division in 1963 and the League Cup two years later. Suddenly, he was controversially transferred by the manager, Tommy Docherty, to Spurs. 'We clashed', Venables admits. 'I was thrilled when Docherty arrived, and when he encouraged us to ask questions. I wanted to learn. Yet my questions were interpreted by him as a threat. I wasn't disrespectful.'

But smart, certainly. Venables, like his boyhood idol, Danny Blanchflower, wanted reasons, not instructions. His intelligence was already making some people in football uncomfortable. Inevitably, he became a representative to the union, the Professional Footballers' Association: not a barrack-room lawyer but a logical mind in a profession short of brains. How could a second division club demand, at a tribunal, a £250,000 fee for a player being paid £28 a week? 'Send for Terry' became a formula.

At Tottenham, where the famous Cup and League double-winning team of 1961 was on the wane, there were still some players with reputations to over-awe even the self-assured Venables: Mackay, Greaves, Jones, Gilzean. Five-a-side games in training were ruthlessly competitive.

On his first morning, Venables cleverly but unwisely shielded the ball with his body from Mackay. The Spurs captain took one pace back and kicked the newcomer in the crutch. Venables, in some pain, threw a punch.

The incident was soon forgotten. Tottenham players were used to such things. Yet Venables was to spend an often uncomfortable two years before moving to QPR, at ease with neither the team nor the demanding White Hart Lane crowd. 'He was always coming up with ideas about adapting our 4–2–4 formation,' Alan Mullery, then his midfield colleague, says. 'He and I had a rapport, but I don't think some of the others understood him, and I'm not sure Bill [Nicholson, the manager] did. Terry learned a fair amount about people, even if he didn't enjoy the football.' Venables reflects that it was a time in which he grew up.

'He played with knowledge', Nicholson says. 'Football's a game of habits, and his were efficient. He was a studious type of bloke. I didn't think he was unsuccessful, but the crowd wanted another Blanchflower.'

It had been at Chelsea that an important friendship had begun with the author Gordon Williams. Venables accepted his challenge to try writing. Williams likened his first effort, full of natural dialogue, to Damon Runyon. 'Who's he?', the footballer asked. Together they wrote a novel and a television series, and Venables was sorry to have to give up when he became manager-coach of Crystal Palace in 1976, succeeding Malcolm Allison in charge of a side dubbed 'the team of the Eighties'.

'Gordon was a wonderful influence', Venables says. 'I don't know if I could have done what I have without him. He provoked me mentally.' In three years, Venables took Palace from the third division to the first, leaving for QPR when he discovered that Ray Bloye, the Palace chairman, had gone behind his back to approach Howard Kendall and John Bond as possible replacements. (It is ironic that Venables should have recently received adverse publicity for his alleged involvement with Arsenal, which he denied but which caused Don Howe, the manager, likewise to resign.)

Guiding QPR to an FA Cup final and promotion to the first division, Venables had become the major shareholder in 1983, with plans for a public unlisted flotation to raise another £5 million. Barcelona's offer cut that short.

With his astute lieutenant Alan Harris, he proceeded to transform not merely a club that was an institution, but a system that was peculiarly, flamboyantly Spanish. Maradona of Argentina, the most gifted player in the world, criticised his arrival – and was sold to Naples. Archibald, unheralded, was bought from Spurs. Tactical intelligence was all. Venables and Harris sought to establish, as always, a style of play which was not dependent on how the opposition played, and to eliminate the Spanish players' compulsive inclination to show off.

'You cannot coach players to allow for the opposition when the opposition changes every week', Venables says. 'Barcelona were accustomed to coaches coming and going so regularly that they never acquired a settled system.'

While Venables was guiding an injury-plagued team to European victories over Juventus, the holders, and Göteborg (after being three goals down on the first leg), his marriage to a wife who had remained in England with a school-age daughter reached the point of amicable divorce. In the streets of Barcelona, they clamoured for him to remain.

Dave Sexton, one of the most respected and knowledgeable of English coaches, who instructed Venables as a boy, says: 'He is the most imaginative coach I've ever met, anywhere.'

Andres Varela, an experienced Spanish commentator, thinks Venables has revolutionised the club. 'What the public see and appreciate is discipline – not imposed German or Swiss discipline, but a free self-discipline which comes from the players, on the field, in training, in their personal lives. They are eleven playing for eleven.' Juan Antonio Samaranch, the president of the International Olympic Committee and Barcelona's senior sporting figure, has observed that his local club no longer has daily controversies with its players.

Whatever happens in Seville tonight, there should be no asking who, when the time comes, is the next manager of England – provided the Football Association are men enough not to feel intimidated by his intelligence.

CLASSIC TUSSLE ALMOST WITHOUT EQUAL

Brazil and France duel in the sun

23 June 1986 Guadalajara

It is doubtful if the first half-century of the World Cup saw a more eventful match than Saturday's quarter-final between France and Brazil. And the second half-century will be fortunate to see its equal. The two teams defied the ferocious temperature of 120 degrees in the Jalisco Stadium, and each other, to re-invigorate international football with a classic tussle which will be talked about for years.

Whether France can recover their mental and physical fibre in three days after such an epic to avenge the semi-final of 1982 when they meet West Germany again, keeps this competition in a state of fascinated anticipation.

Over two hours and a half, including the wretched necessity for the nevertheless spell-binding execution by penalty shoot-out, there were the dramatic qualities of many sports. No 15-round world title bout, nor match-play golf taken to the 19th nor five-set tennis final fluctuating on every point, nor Olympic race decided in the last few strides, nor Test won in the last over could have had more suspense.

It was one of those rare occasions which makes my occupation uniquely pleasurable, yet how to recapture the emotions, skills and courage which flowed back and forth across the sunlit pitch? I have not seen a better match in eight finals, nor one played in such a marvellous spirit: only one single mean foul, sheer desperation by Carlos, the Brazil goakeeper late in extra time, amid mutual generosity which put many teams here to shame. As in all great sporting moments, the quality of the losers contributed as much or more than that of the winners. How we grieve for Brazil: such a flourish, yet no reward other than admiration.

The match swung from end to end throughout, almost with the rapidity of ice hockey, and one knew not how the players sustained the momentum in their fifth match at altitude in three weeks. There were 16 scoring opportunities created by Brazil to 15 by France. In some matches there are none.

On Friday, Joao Saldanha, Brazil's former manager whose marvellous team of 1970 was taken over at the last moment by Mario Zagalo, insisted this team was better than four years ago. It was stronger defensively and more balanced, with Elzo, of Athletico Minas Gerais the foundation of the mid-field – 'the man who carries the piano', Saldanha said evocatively. What heroics were performed by Elzo and Branco for Brazil; by Bossis, Amoros and Fernandez for France, in the shadow of more famous reputations.

Brazil develop with every successive match, and if France, who provided thrilling performances against the Soviet Union and Italy, were their first opponents of quality, they unleashed within minutes all the traditional, instinctive touches which make Brazilian football so appealing: the enticement and the acceleration clear of a tackle by Junior, Careca and Muller which puts the opponents momentarily out of the game, the half-vollied trap-come-pass by Julio Cesar at the back or Socrates as the fulcrum of attack, which transforms apparent innocence into danger. Bossis, unexpectedly swapping sweeper/marker-roles with Battiston, was for half an hour or so being pounded by Careca as Junior and Socrates ceaselessly primed the guns like powder-monkeys. There is no team which can play as Brazil do when in the mood.

Suddenly France, the masters for four or five years of silken mid-field embroidery, were worried stiff by the shielded first-touch which was wrong-footing them. After 17 minutes, Brazil scored the most breathtaking goal of the finals yet, a ripple of passes between Socrates, Branco and Josimar, a first time exchange between Junior and Muller and a final thrust by Junior sending Careca through a striken French rearguard.

It was the first time France had been behind since they played the Soviet Union, and it stung them into response.

At last, in the 46th minute, France's rhythm clicked: Giresse, the oldest of 10 players in the match in their 30s, slipped another of them, Rocheteau, who was finding a new lease of speed, clear of on the right and his early low centre was deflected off Edinho; Stopyra's goalmouth dive confused Carlos, and the ball ran free as Platini stole through unnoticed, and with all the calm of a training stint in a deserted stadium tapped into the net.

The second half contained sufficient incidents for half a dozen matches. Zico replaced Muller with 17 minutes to go, and with almost his first touch sent Branco through on an overlap. Out rushed Bats, spread himself across Branco's path, missed the ball and hauled him down. Unwisely, Zico, not yet in tune, moved up to take the penalty. Behind Zico's back, Platini signalled to Bats's left and Bats took the hint to parry the shot. Brazil's chance to win in normal time had passed.

Extra time. We wilted in the shade in 90 degrees. On the touchline, the teams sank to the ground, grasping at ice pads and water. Would the tension continue?

Somehow it did. Both sides continued to hurl themselves at each other, but their legs were beginning to crumble. A last glorious pass by Platini, the most memorable of the match, sent Bellone clear, only for him to be manhandled off the ball a yard outside the area by Carlos. No foul given, no booking. A blunder by the sweat-soaked referee, Igna of Romania.

The whistle went. The unenvied penalty kickers assembled in the centre circle, drained and blank-faced like actors being asked to audition after running a marathon. Socrates had the first kick saved by Bats, and France were 3–2 up when Bellone, with moral justice, scored with a rebound off the post and back off Carlos's head. Platini skied his shot, to level the situation, but Josimar slammed against a post, and Fernandez, stoic, dependable Fernandez atoned for Platini's miss.

So now France must meet the West Germans to claim the place in the final which they deserve. It will be a better final if they do; and France have a score to settle with Schumacher.

The teams were:

BRAZIL: Carlos; Josimar, Edinho, J Cesar, Branco; Elzo, Socrates, Junior (sub: Silas), Alemao; Muller (sub: Zico), Careca.

FRANCE: J Bats; M Amoros, M Bossis, P Battiston, T Tusseau; L Fernandez, M Platini, A Giresse (sub: J-M Ferreri), J Tigana; Y Stopyra, D Rocheteau (sub: B Bellone).
Referee: I Igna (Romania).

ROBSON PAYS HEAVY PRICE FOR TIMID TACTICS

Maradona's 'hand of God' is not the whole story

23 June 1986 Mexico City

It is a stain upon the World Cup when its arguably most dangerous performer is accused of being a cheat. I do not hold with the accusation. The fact that Maradona's first goal, five minutes into the second half, was knocked past Shilton with his forearm as they went up together for Hodge's sliced clearance is counter-balanced by his second goal: an incomparable, solo gem which epitomised his talent.

As an argument that, but for Maradona's first goal, England might otherwise be in the semi-final, the controversy holds little substance. On the run of the game, there was no doubt that the right team won. England must question not so much Maradona's fortuitous goal as their own tactical approach. If you are organised specifically to stifle a single opponent, it is unrealistic to complain if on one of many occasions when he has you on the ropes he is given the benefit of an unfair decision.

Arguments can rage forever whether Maradona's intention was to use his arm, but he is not the only player to benefit in this competition from something illegal. Some critics called him a cheat at half-time on account of his regular tumbles when tackled. They are deliberately blurring an argument in which Maradona possesses most of the advantages.

No cheat commands the efforts of three and sometimes four men to try to halt him. This was often England's calculated response to the threat which his ability poses for any team. They closed around him like a gang of farm hands gingerly trying to grapple with a bull which has slipped his pen.

It was no more disturbing that Maradona handled the ball than it was, say, to see Fenwick apparently elbow Maradona in the face only nine minutes after he has been booked for a foul on him. Cheating takes various forms.

England can blame only the unfortunate referee on that first goal, and, dependent on his position, any referee might have been unsighted on what was undeniably a bad decision. It was far easier to determine that Maradona used his arm from high in the stand than is sometimes possible on the pitch, though England's manager is quite emphatic that he saw the foul. Maradona's arm was raised, but no higher than his head. Yet, to become obsessed with the decision, is to overlook all the other evidence which is relevant to England's defeat.

The unavoidable verdict is that England, by the admission of their own tactics until the time they were two behind, had not the nerve nor the ability to risk attacking a suspect defence which by the finish was having its inadequacies exposed by England's belated rally. The possibility of levelling or winning the match in the last 20 minutes might have been substantially greater had England been more positive in the first 20 minutes.

To keep nine men behind the ball, and achieve not a single co-ordinated penetration of the Argentinian penalty area in the first half, was as negative as Italy, a blatant policy of parking on a double yellow line. The risk is substantial, and requires defenders technically more nimble than those available to Bobby Robson. If he believed that stopping Argentina's attack was the first and essential priority, then such tactics are based on the admission that the opposition is more dangerous and skilful. To say that Argentina are nothing without Maradona is no more valid than to say that Australian cricket in the Thirties would have been nothing without Don Bradman. They exist: they must be accounted for.

England sought to do so with a system which was always stretched. An often square back four awaited Maradona's sorties like an Indian rural village not knowing when the tiger may strike next. Butcher, who is an acceptable defender in the context of the Football League, is out of his depth at the level of a World Cup quarter-final, an honest digger of potatoes. The England defence had extensive possession of the ball, yet seldom had any fluidity of positional change which might have opened up the Argentinian ranks.

The middle line was, frankly, little better. Reid was soon injured, again, and Hoddle never found his front runners. Steven and Hodge could not compete with Argentina's control. The flourish at the finish provided some hope, when Lineker at last was able to start running at defenders and Barnes finally made his World Cup debut. That was one of many decisions which needs some subsequent analysis.

POSITIVE WAY TO TAKE THE WORLD CUP

Argentina deservedly defeat West Germany

30 June 1986 Mexico City

Not a great final, until the last quarter of an hour when a combination of Argentina's fragility in defence and West Germany's habitual capacity to turn their back on the odds and come from behind gave the match its final flurry of anxieties and frenzied action. It was good for football that the team which throughout had placed their concentration upon playing football, upon being positive, should be the winners, and that they lived dangerously at times was all the better for the spectators.

It was a final distinguished, if by nothing else, by the performance of the Brazilian referee Filho, who kept the play closer to a correct interpretation of the laws than anyone, if I may be forgiven for saying so, since an Englishman in 1974, when Jack Taylor gave a penalty against the home team in the first minute and they still won. If we had had such diligence with the whistle, such an understanding of players' intent and what is and is not fair, we would have avoided that awful first hour in Madrid – with another Brazilian – while in 1978 Holland would probably have beaten Argentina, whose gamesmanship went unchecked by an Italian.

Not so now. Of the six bookings, five were for dissent or time wasting. Matthäus was booked after only 22 minutes when he hacked at Maradona's heels well after the ball had been despatched, and that served to restrain the Germans' latent capacity for intimidation. It was appropriate that Argentina should go in front in the next minute from a free kick, for the Germans were being a shade too confidently content to get 11 men behind the ball and hope that Argentina would eventually run dry of inspiration.

It was a match also notable for the errors of Schumacher, Germany's goalkeeper from Cologne, who likes to think himself the most professionally prepared, physically and mentally, in the game. He seriously misjudged the swing on Burruchaga's free kick which moved away as it dipped into the six-yard line, and was met unerringly by Joe Brown. On Argentina's second and third goals, Schumacher was strangely inert when drawn towards the ball first by Valdano cutting in from the left and then, in instant reply to Germany's equaliser, when Burruchaga swept in from the right. It was a rare trio of misjudgements.

Many critics have been saying that without Maradona, Argentina were relatively insignificant opposition. I had felt, since seeing them pace themselves through the first round, that they were likely to be able to adjust their game to produce what was necessary, certainly within the context of this competition. Germany, with their relentless marking, proved to be the most obdurate, but some marvellous, flowing first-time moves at close quarters between Burruchaga, Valdano, Maradona and Enrique thrilled the Azteca crowd and enticed Germany into committing repeated infringements, so that a succession of free kicks swung the tide against them.

Burruchaga was a delight, springing forward from midfield onto Maradona's promptings like a cat off a wall, to such effect that Maradona himself could most of the time be happy to play the subsidiary rule. Just now and then he would remind Germany that he was by a distance the outstanding performer of 1986.

Germany suffered to some extent from exactly the same problem as had England: getting so many men behind the ball demanded that extra pace and accuracy when they switched to counter-attack; and being currently without threatening forwards, they mostly could not find it. They were too dependent on Briegel's initiative in surges out of defence, but after the first half hour he became less and less significant. Argentina's one-touch was exacting a fearful strain on Germany's defensive running and covering.

Less than they did against England, Argentina only began to play for time after Rummenigge had stabbed the ball home at a corner with a quarter of an hour to go. For a reason which would not become apparent until the post match crescendo of victory had calmed, Brown, Argentina's sweeper, strangely stayed on the field in spite of a shoulder injury in the 52nd minute. He continued bravely to hold the fort with timely interceptions, yet was increasingly in pain and under pressure, and it seemed extraordinary that he should still be allowed to remain when Voller equalised. In that moment you would not have given Argentina an earthly to win in extra time: but Maradona and Burruchaga provided the instant answer with the final goal.

SILVER LINING TO SOME YEOMANLY SERVICE

Times man up to his armpits in the Solent

9 August 1986

Thursday was a mixed sort of day. The car wouldn't start because the battery was flat, which complicated an early breakfast interview with a chap from Royal Lymington before the day's fleet set off from Cowes. Round about lunchtime, a turbulent Solent, whipped by a Force 6, was lapping disconcertingly round my armpits somewhere near the Bramble Bank, halfway between Southampton and the island. At the time I was supposed to be in a boat. Such an occasion is termed 'broaching'. In the evening, my mind too genuinely a shade blown, I managed to put five gallons of derv in the car. It is not a diesel.

Not every cloud at Cowes this week, however, has been without a silver lining. The boat's skipper, who as commodore of the Royal Ocean Racing Club has an answer to such situations other than firing a flare, had us ship-shape in no time. A couple of his crew, who had been swimming about like castaways amid a chaos of ropes, spars, a horizontal mast and language fit to make Mrs Whitehouse emigrate, returned on board in immaculate order; little time was lost, a vertical profile was resumed, and on a spinnaker run at the end of 30 miles, *Yeoman XXVI* beat Tim Herring's *Backlash* for the Squadron's gun by a distance no farther than I could have thrown my full wellies.

I've seldom had as much fun without laughing. Admittedly, my sailing is more a matter of who gets up early to go and buy the bread in St Peter Port or Camaret, or unblocking the ship's loo with a wire coathanger. Not the least remarkable part of this Class I race was that the 86-year-old Sir Owen Aisher, a veritable old man of the sea, sat in the stern throughout, as upright as the Needles lighthouse, alongside his son Robin at the helm with no concession to age other than woolly gloves. When it was all over he had a beer and sailed back to Portsmouth.

Robin Aisher is one of the last of the top flight 'amateurs' of yachting, with enough knowledge and experience to have helmed his own boat in an Admiral's Cup. One of his contributions with the RORC has been the introduction of the Channel Handicap, a rating measurement which can be obtained by standard production family boats of, say, 30 feet for only £25 instead of the £500 or more necessary to have an international ocean rating. He believes that this will help offset the gap that is developing between the amateurs and the new breed of professional yachtsmen, which will increase even more with the advent of individual boat sponsorship.

Yeoman XXVI has almost as much technology below deck as a television broadcasting unit. All around above deck, electronic digital screens blink at you through the spray like an airport lounge indicator. A matter of some alarm is that the light displacement, a configuration of contemporary design, has so little bouyance for'ard that the broach was precipitated by the weight of two deck-hands on the bow preparing for a gybe. The nose went under as far back as the mast-step, the 45ft boat halted from 10 knots and slewed: the mast could have snapped. One of the crew observed later that he wasn't sure if he'd fancy the middle of the Atlantic in such a sensitive craft.

Few people can afford such complex gadgetry, and indeed the whole problem of yachting in Britain is how to overcome the public concept of its seeming financial and social exclusiveness. As was remarked this week by a club official with a conscience: 'The major clubs on the South coast are like social fortresses, with their guns pointing inland'. For a democratic expansion of yachting, the British have to move towards the pattern in France in the relationship with the local council. Mostly in Britain, in the edgy balance between 'town' and 'yachties', the council understandably tend to identify with 'town', and are grudgingly helpful. 'Sailing boats disfigure the jetty' one council contradictorily ruled on a mooring request.

Royal Lymington has a waiting list: but whereas potential social members wanting to dine have to wait, those wanting to sail are quickly admitted. Ten per cent of the 3,400 members are under 21, paying only £9 per annum. On Wednesday, the club is open to any child from seven to 16 in the town: and has been swamped by those anxious to avail themselves of the 15 Scow dinghies.

'Every club should be asking whether it is doing a good job for its community,' a chap from Lymington says, gratified that the club is now qualified as a Royal Yachting Association teaching establishment. 'So many youngsters would like to sail, but don't know how to start or haven't the means. They're like tennis players without rackets.'

Yachting, like golf, is strong on traditions of etiquette. It is imperative that this is not sacrificed in the breaching of social barriers. The natural tendency when a youngster who has just won a dinghy race appears in the bar in soaking clothes is to say 'get out' rather than 'well done'. It would be retrogressive if the yacht clubs were over-run: they need to become more cosmopolitan in outlook, but not unduly common in standards.

REVENGE COMES SWIFTLY FOR RECENTLY DEPOSED KING OF SQUASH

Jahangir grinds Norman into submission

26 November 1986 Zurich

The Pathan people of northern Pakistan, historic guardians of the Khyber Pass, do not accept defeat. The Russians are discovering this to their discomfort across the border in Afghanistan, as did the British, and as Ross Norman did in Zurich on Monday night. In the final of the Swiss Masters squash tournament, the World Open champion was ground into submission by Jahangir Khan.

'Revenge is in the nature of my people,' Jahangir said afterwards, with the kind of unassuming smile of someone giving his seat on the bus to an old lady. 'I needed to win this match far more than I needed to win the World Championship in Toulouse.' He had just done so in four sets, inflicting on the gritty New Zealander the full range of his remarkable talents which have for so long been unanswerable, even though he will only reach 23 next month.

The publicity which attended Norman's removal of the title which Jahangir had held for five years will, oddly, have been welcomed by Channel 4 television, which on Saturday screens their documentary on the unique family from 'Squash Village' – little Navakilley, home of some 2,000 tribespeople, 15 miles from the Khyber, where all the Khans, from Hashim onwards, have descended to the plains to torment the Australians, New Zealanders and British.

It was my happy fortune, as the scruffiest of insignificant club players, once to have had lessons from Nazrullah, Jahangir's late uncle; a gentle, tranquil man who would, without a glance, ricochet a shot off all four walls as mathematically as Steve Davis might pot it dead in a pocket on a snooker table. It was Naz who taught Jonah Barrington and it was this inimitable Khan dexterity which now had Norman, who is to squash what de Castella is to the marathon, clawing the air in vain in the third and fourth games.

'I had to play faster and more physically, and use more wrist than in Toulouse,' Jahangir said. "Ross doesn't like to be made to twist and turn, and this wore him down. I had needed that defeat long before, because it was good for me and good for squash. Ross likes to establish a rhythm, and I had to break this up tonight.'

Prior to Toulouse, Norman had taken no more than one game in half a dozen or so of their 30 meetings. The breakthrough came after Jahangir had ligament trouble in the Malaysian Open and, after a month's absence, lacked match practice. He also failed to adapt, as Norman did in Toulouse, to the behaviour of the fluorescent Merco ball. On Monday night a Dunlop ball was used and Jahangir, on his own admission, worked far harder.

I thought that one or two of the referee's decisions went unfairly against Norman. 'I know it was a lucky shot, but it was OK,' he called out as he scraped another drop shot off the boards only to hear 'not up' from the gallery.

The match lasted an hour and 40 minutes, of which the marvellous second game lasted 44 minutes. As the third and fourth games had run away from him, Norman baled demonically like a man in a leaking boat, but the water rose inexorably as Jahangir punched hole after hole with his angled, cut, volleys.

'The key to my being able to challenge him from now on is my condition,' Norman said. 'In last year's World Open, when he beat me in four games, I felt closer than I did tonight, even though that match was only one hour 28 minutes. I seemed a bit tired tonight. Every time I've been anywhere in the past couple of weeks, they've been opening a bottle of champagne. Most of my time not playing squash has been spent sleeping!'

He does not begrudge the demand on his time. Squash is not the magic roundabout of tennis. As No 2 in the rankings, and way ahead of the rest, Norman makes a modest income as a star of his sport. The Swiss Masters, top of the prize money tournaments with its BMW sponsorship, was worth just under £9,000 to the winner. Norman's world title, a tribute to his dedication only three years after a serious parachuting accident, will substantially increase his commercial endorsement value.

The interesting psychology of the relationship between the top two is that Norman has persuaded himself that Jahangir's more elaborate game requires Jahangir to be even fitter than Norman. Therefore, Norman's rationalisation follows that if he is super-humanly fit and more economic in style, that could be decisive.

Jahangir does not see it this way. He knows that, provided he can withstand a prolonged match, the wider complexity of stroke and touch should undermine Norman's economy.

'I must make him run,' Jahangir says with that languid smile. He does – and he did. Norman believes that if he can run long enough, and find equivalent mental strength, he can emulate Barrington's self-made proficiency. Those who doubted Norman have now reassessed. The new spice in the rivalry is important in sponsorship appeal. The Swiss, who have gone squash-crazy, were offering £120 to try to winkle a seat for the final.

WHO WILL REKINDLE THE CHARIOTS OF FIRE?

The search for Oxbridge's lost elite

9 December 1986

At Cambridge in the Fifties you could sit down to a three-shillings-and-sixpence (17p) lunch at the Hawks Club any day of the week among a group of international performers in half a dozen sports: a brains trust of table talk for which, gathered in a television studio today, Mark McCormack would demand a five-figure fee.

They included household names in major and lesser sports – May, Barber and Dexter from cricket, Marques, Mulligan and Arthur Smith from rugby, Marsh and Huddy (golf), Masser (rowing), Barrett and Warwick (tennis) Maitland and Cockett (hockey), Lyon and Broomfield (squash), Hildreth and Dunkley (athletics).

It was the same at Vincents Club in Oxford in the era of Cowdrey, Davidge, Brace and Derek Johnson. Pegasus, the joint football club, produced 21 amateur internationals including several, such as Tanner, Pawson and Pinner, who played for Division I league clubs.

Now, Oxbridge performance has declined relative to national standards, partly because overall national levels of ability have risen and partly because the structure of the student population has changed, with more women and less emphasis on sport.

Nowhere is the situation more critical than in cricket. The Test and County Cricket Board has recently warned Oxford and Cambridge that their first-class status may be at risk. In rugby, which during a century at Cambridge has produced 300 international players with some 1900 caps between them, Oxbridge now clings to its status by the increasing enlistment of post-graduates – which is also true of rowing at Boat Race level.

In today's varsity match at Twickenham, Oxford are relying on the scholarship schemes which attract international players with the academic qualifications to take further degree courses; soon Cambridge will be in the same position.

Although Cambridge could, from recent seasons, field an England line of backs, the total of 84 caps by 10 players between 1974 and 1984 compares badly with the 291 caps of 32 players in the previous ten years. The future worries Dr Alan Taylor, rugby senior treasurer at Oxford, who says: 'We could not hold our heads above water (in senior fixtures) if we relied on undergraduates.'

Five factors produced the decline, sufficient for a group of ex-Cambridge industrialists to have refused to help raise money for a projected £8 million sports centre at Cambridge unless there is a change in admissions policy.

The factors are: the end of National Service meant younger and physically less mature undergraduates; a changed admissions policy put less emphasis on sport; increased training at outside clubs lured undergraduates away from Oxbridge and into the clubs; a proportional rise in women students cut the available pool of sportsmen; and the decline of school sport meant fewer university entrants with a sporting background.

The trend produces a dilemma not merely for Oxbridge sport but, as a minority of Dons now recognise, for the fundamental attitude of the two universities towards their very function. Intellectual excellence must be the aim, but fewer than 20 per cent of undegraduates gain first-class degrees. The nationally available appointments for researchers and lectureships are diminishing: jobs must be found for the majority gaining second-class degrees.

Employers increasingly look for those with self-discipline, personality, gregariousness, and a sense of collective responsibility, as well as brains. Such characteristics are strongly evident in those with sporting achievement.

John Butterfield, distinguished physician, Master of Downing College and president of both rugby and cricket at Cambridge, says: 'I believe sportsmen make good citizens. What we are looking for (at Oxbridge) is leaders. It is valuable to know, from sport, the experience of losing.'

John Hopkins, Downing admissions tutor in Arts, says: 'There are half a dozen colleges (out of 30) who want people with energy, whatever they are doing.' And Dr Alan Tayler, St Catherines, Oxford: 'Below the level of distinguished scholars, what are our criteria? We want people who will benefit from the system, and go on to do something.'

Colin Kolbert, barrister and tutor of Magdalene, Cambridge: 'A poll would show that academic performance by Blues is above the university average. Those sent down have usually done nothing in *any* field. There are no unemployed Blues, but dozens of unemployed English firsts.'

Charles Wenden, fellow of All Souls, Oxford, with 30 years experience in international university sport, and Christopher Taylor, bursar of

Newnham, Cambridge, are emphatic: the maintenance of a high sporting profile is essential to Oxbridge public identification.

Many senior academics are indifferent, even hostile, to sport, resenting the lack of recognition they had as non-sporting students. Subconsciously, are they getting revenge? Wenden says: 'Maybe the attitude of the past 20 years (among tutors) has turned the corner.' Maybe not. Michael Risman, younger brother of Oxford's full back at Twickenham today, son of Bev, grandson of Gus, (both famous internationals) gained three As at A level; and Oxford rejected him. Cambridge, shrewdly, did not.

THE EXCEPTIONAL GIRL IN CONVENTIONAL SURROUNDINGS

Winning is a family affair for Steffi Graf

17 December 1986 Heidelberg

She has been called, in recent months of universal acclaim, *The Woman Borg*. The girl who will topple Martina Navratilova.

In her first tournament, for under-8s in Munich, an umpire called a point in favour of her opponent on a shot that was blatantly out. She cried in disbelief, and the tournament organiser told her father she would never be a player.

That was the last time Steffi Graf cried on court, though she has shed tears a few times after a match. 'Crying is normal and spontaneous, it is healing,' Peter Graf, her father says. He is also her coach. It is a parent-child relationship in competitive sport as unique, and at the present stage successful, as has been the father-son Coe partnership.

As with the Coes, the parent has been criticized for driving the child too severely, yet Steffi, like Sebastian, is emphatic that the intensity of the partnership is at her behest, under her direction and control. 'I need him, he's most important to me, but he wouldn't be so close if I didn't want it,' she says.

When she lost the Virginia Slims final to Navratilova recently, her eye tended to seek him out in the crowd, where he tries to sit anonymously. 'I don't need advice or coaching,' she says, 'just to know that he is there. It makes me feel comfortable, especially at the big meetings.' Some would say that the inherent strains in such a relationship when she is 17 – reflecting, possibly, an insecurity in the world outside tennis – will magnify as she matures, mentally and emotionally, over the next few years.

Yet to listen to the two of them talking, off duty so to speak, in the family home alongside the tennis and bowling club where all the winter practice takes place, is to believe the relationship is balanced and relaxed. The father seems protective rather than proprietorial. 'There are people who are jealous, who disapprove because I am father-coach-manager,' Peter Graf says. 'Yet I know what is right for her, I know her mentality and character.'

Earlier this year, Peter employed Pavel Slozil, the former Czechoslovak Davis Cup player, as full-time practice partner for his daughter. The intention is to modify her fundamental baseline game to include a more flexible, all-court serve-and-volley style which is imperative if she is to displace the seemingly impregnable Navratilova. Though she beat Navratilova in the German Open and lost a thrilling semi-final in the US Open after having three match points, she lost the Slims final in three straight sets.

Peter, an outstanding former club player, had intended to retreat but Steffi will not let him go. The day I called on her at Bruhl, outside Heidelberg, she was serving, again and again, from a bucket of 50 balls at Slozil, and from mid-court volleying his returns to the baseline corners. Formidable stuff. Yet she is, allegedly, a difficult person in training.

'I have to coach the coach,' Peter says with a smile. 'Pavel is still learning that Steffi is reluctant to talk during practice, that she just wants to concentrate and slam away the winners as she does in a match. He has to discover how to handle her.'

There is, indeed, a remarkable difference in her manner on and off court. Her focus, when playing, is absolute. I had arrived at Bruhl early and when she came off court she said, almost abruptly: 'Yes, we are meeting. At five.' An hour later, showered and relaxed, she was a slightly coy, smiling, relaxed schoolgirl, not the phenomenon who is the fourth prize money winner of the year ($455,000) third in the rankings and second in the Slims points table. Her ambition this year had been to win one tournament. She won eight.

When she was 10, she told the chief national coach, who had said she was too unemotional: 'Either I play or I laugh.' It is the self-generating discipline of which champions are made. 'I cannot smile when I play,' she says. 'The fun for me is in ending the point.' When she wants a laugh, she practices left-handed.

Her wish is not to be rich (which, relatively, she already is), or famous, but to master the game, to play it beautifully. Perfectly. 'I want to be a baseliner who can come to the net when it's necessary. To be able to do what *I* want on the court, what *I* feel like.'

Her personality is expressed through her racket, though she is not the impersonal, inscrutable machine that Borg was. She knows she has not a waiting mentality, that the match has to be played *her* way. That is why the silent winter weeks will be spent volleying against Slozil.

'I have to work at serve-and-volley. I don't really know as yet where to go. Against other volleyers, in the past, they have known I won't come in. If I did, I put more pressure on myself.' Now, she is strengthening the serve: slower swing, more snap. Taking risks. Navratilova does not hit passing shots that well, she knows.

Will she, like Borg, Austin, Jaeger, become prematurely burned out? No, her father says emphatically, because she wants to win points in six or seven strokes, not 30 or 40. And she does not have the spinal strain of a two-handed backhand. The intention is to keep the quality high and the tournaments low.

So far as it is possible to be normal in contemporary professional sport, Steffi seems pretty normal. Her parents, her younger brother Michael's humour, her two dogs: such conventional family surroundings should help.

A GRIPPING DAVIS CUP TIE ON GRASS

Cash's victory against all the odds

27 December 1986 Melbourne

Animal power and aggression against artistic refinement is perennially one of sport's most enthralling contests. The animal won here yesterday in a memorable opening match of the Davis Cup final, not so much because he was the superior tennis player but because he had the unyielding mental tenacity.

Pat Cash, by his own estimation, played his best ever match to beat Stefan Edberg, who at No. 4 in the world is ranked 21 places above him, by the slenderist of margins: a mere four games in 58 over three hours and 44 minutes, 13–11, 13–11, 6–4, for a critical and largely unexpected opening lead against Sweden in the competition sponsored by NEC.

Then Mikael Pernfors, an extrovert college boy at Georgia, playing only his fifth match on grass, levelled the tie with astonishing two-handed control of the ball in little more than an hour. He destroyed a stunned and outclassed Paul McNamee in embarrassing straight sets. What could Pernfors now achieve against Cash in Sunday's reverse singles?

It had been sometimes less than technically brilliant play between Cash and Edberg, but in this battle of young tigers, the Australian first string beat the Australian Open champion simply because he wanted victory more than his rival.

He played the handful of crucial points as though his country's name depended on it. It was symptomatic that he should close those two gruelling first sets each with an ace in a match which had only 13, eight of them from the winner. The other factor central to the outcome was that although Cash served 12 of the 25 double faults, he did so partially because he relentlessly went for his second service to keep the pressure on Edberg, whose confidence gradually slipped from him like the foliage of a dying tree.

'I don't usually play well in the Davis Cup,' the forlorn Edberg said afterwards. 'It might come in the future.' He has yet to win a major singles, and today's doubles will mightily test his equanimity.

The occasion yesterday was loaded with drama. A substantial portion of the crowd at Kooyong was Swedish, here to see whether or not their men win the trophy for the third year in succession in what may be the last Davis Cup final on grass, unless Britain should produce players capable of reaching this stage. The home of the Victoria LTA, having failed to build on its traditions in modern times, is to become redundant, replaced by a new Australian tennis headquarters adjacent to the Melbourne Cricket Ground, with an artificial surface yet to be decided.

A strong east wind that was simultaneously blowing the yachts from Sydney towards Hobart stiffened the flags, and the noisy Swedish chants took one back to the heady, patriotic days of 1958 during the World Cup in football when the Swedes were hosts and finalists. As the wind swirled the ball about in the midday sun, it seemed that Cash was caught in a whirlpool of doubts. In no time, he was 5–1 down with Edberg serving for the first set.

Yet at this moment Cash's animal instincts were to rescue him. Three days ago he was playing so poorly he had stormed off court during training and started practising his strokes on camera men. Now, about to be played out of sight, he held on like a clam.

When necessary, he scrambled. When possible, he whacked the ball fiercely. And after 35 minutes, with the same doubts and difficulties overtaking Edberg on his throw-ups and mid-court volleys, the match was level at 5–5. For another 12 games there was no break point. Edberg's game was the more fluent, though he hardly hit a decent backhand, but Cash's the more gritty. Edberg, you felt, would win if he could find his rhythm, for his were always the more ambitious shots with less margin.

Yet at 11–11 Edberg double-faulted and Cash hit three backhand passes and a lob to break service, and held his own service to love for the first set. In the second, the first break came as Cash led 9–8, but Edberg broke back. Two net-cords going against him on successive points saw Edberg go behind again 11–12, and Cash, looking like Maradona with the goal in sight, closed in.

Edberg's confidence was shredded: 48 games played in three hours, and two sets down. The authority of his play shrank, and though, all too late, he hit two sensational forehands to save Cash's first two match points, his gradually drooping chin had said it all. Cash had prepared for a month for this match, and he had his reward.

'To play for your country is far tougher than to play for yourself,' he said afterwards. 'The pressure of the Davis Cup makes you admire those who go to the line in the Olympics for sudden death, and win medals. A Wimbledon or US semi-final is nothing compared to the Davis Cup. I reckoned I was playing better than he was when I was 5–1 down, and after that it was a matter of just a point here, a point there – winning the right points at the right moment'.

Pernfors, the French Open finalist, returned service with such sting and variety that McNamee's game was dismantled: by the end of the first set he was missing the lines by yards rather than inches. Pernfors hit a succession of devastating two-handed backhand lobs; and also the stroke of the day, a cunningly sliced smash which hardly bounced and obliged the crowd to look twice to see where the ball was.

'He outclassed me,' McNamee said afterwards, staring emptily around the interview room. 'It will take me a while to get over this. I tried, I really did, to slow the game down, but he exploited my weaknesses.'

It will be long after Sunday's fifth-match encounter with Edberg, I suspect, that McNamee will recover. So if Australia are to regain the Cup they have to do it in today's doubles and tomorrow's first singles between Cash and Pernfors. It is tantalisingly evenly balanced.

FIGHTING CASH THE HERO

Historic last final at Kooyong

29 September 1986 Melbourne

As Neale Fraser, Australia's captain, said in friendly jest at the post-Davis Cup banquet: 'Where on earth did *he* come from?' Mikael Pernfors, yet another remarkably-gifted player to emerge from the rich forests of Swedish tennis, contrived to plot a momentous climax to the 1986 final with Australia, yet ultimately lost to a truly redoubtable competitor. It was an historic last final at Kooyong.

Bob Hawke, Australia's Prime Minister, may not be the race-form expert of international tennis, yet it was no inappropriate comparison when he suggested that Pernfors reminded us of Rosewall: the innocuous serve, the short-back-and-sides and modest physique, combined with a service return and with passing shots which would win prizes at Bisley.

The quality of any outstanding sporting winner is dependent, almost always, on the quality of the loser. For two sets Pernfors, aged 23, the United States national collegiate champion who has jumped in one season from 164 in the rankings to 11, played tennis as special as anyone present could remember.

Yet Pat Cash came back to beat him, memorably, 2–6, 4–6, 6–3, 6–4, 6–3 and thereby give Australia a winning 3–1 lead. On Saturday, Cash and John Fitzgerald had unexpectedly won the doubles in four sets against the recent Albert Hall winners, Anders Jarryd and Stefan Edberg, with Edberg once more a shadow of his normal self.

You may not like Cash. Indeed, there are plenty of Australians in this continent of rugged extroverts who would not choose him as a desert island companion. However, in this David Cup final – sponsored by NEC – Cash, at 21, has shown himself to be one of the sternest and most courageous competitors of this or any era.

No Australian in the history of the Cup has won a singles from two sets down. For almost an hour-and-a-half, Cash must have thought that Butch Cassidy and Sundance were together down the other end of the court. The shots went peppering past him – cross-court, down the lines, overhead – to leave him stunned. Six times he surrendered his service.

Cash's difficulties made Paul McNamee's embarrassment at his destruction on Friday less painful. 'Pernfors played the best tennis for two sets I have ever encountered,' Cash said afterwards. Mimicking Cash with his white Apache headband, Pernfors had set about his rival from the outset, breaking his opening service with two wicked lobs, and almost sprinting to change ends.

Within six games, at 2–4 down, Cash recognised the need for new tactics, staying back and frantically slow-balling to give Pernfors less pace off which to drive his stinging passes. To no avail. Pernfors again led 4–0 in the second set and should have taken it 6–2, but squandered two set points as he snatched at a successive, comparatively simple, forehand and backhand, dropping his own service on a double fault.

Cash was stalling all he could, keeping Pernfors waiting at the start of each point within legal limits. Inch by inch he edged back into the match. In the first and third games of the third set, Pernfors had break points on Cash's service but failed to take them, then lost his own service in the fourth game.

Cash was beginning to serve better, occasionally aceing; Pernfors to return less accurately. By sheer willpower, Cash kept forcing forward to the net whenever he could, grunting with the effort as he went for the low volleys under the pressure of Pernfors's top spin. He did not crack.

The tension among the 12,000 crowd was as sensitive as a primed mousetrap. A fault on first serve by either player would bring a spatter of applause just from nervousness. There was the expectation of a boxing hall, the chanting of a football stadium: yet all the while as well mannered as were the players. The emotion became almost unendurable in the critical seventh and eighth games of the fourth set.

With Cash leading 4–2, Pernfors survived two break-points and five deuces to hold on for 4–3, and then had Cash love–40 in the next game: three points for four-all. With unflinching concentration, Cash hammered down three first serves to reach deuce, and held the game. 'I didn't think about it,' he said, 'I just concentrated on my first serve. If you think about situations like that, you'd go nuts.' There were those among the spectators who were.

The final nail, as Pernfors ran out of strength, came at 2–2 and 30–all in the final set. How marvellously over three days Cash had played the key points! Now Pernfors volleyed deep to the forehand corner of the baseline, only for Cash to respond with a running forehand pass down the tramline which clipped the baseline. Next, still under pressure at the net from Pernfors's probing, he played a cruel stop-volley to break service for 3–2. It was effectively over.

As Pernfors served at 5–3 to save the match, to save the tie . . . to save the Cup which Sweden had held for two years, the tree leaves rustled in a gentle breeze under the cloudless sky of a perfect day. The crowd was gripped in silence at the climax of a great match. Cash came in like an ogre: a smash, a backhand volley at the net, another smash and he was the hero a nation needed to soothe the pain of simultaneous cricket ignominy.

'The Davis Cup means more sacrifice and more pain for less pay,' Cash said. 'But it's worth it. I would never have to be paid to be there.'

If that was a mood he had shared magnificently with Pernfors, it was something which, maybe through no fault of his own, had not touched Edberg, the world's No. 4. In the dead fifth match, he beat McNamee in straight sets; but his mental frailty, against Cash on Friday, and again in the doubles, had cost Sweden their title.

The scores were:

SINGLES: P Cash (Aus) beat S Edberg (Swe), 13–11, 13–11, 6–4; M Pernfors (Swe) bt P McNamee (Aus), 6–3, 6–1, 6–3; P Cash bt M Pernfors, 2–6, 4–6, 6–3, 6–4, 6–3. S Edberg (Swe) bt P McNamee, 10–8 6–4.
DOUBLES: P Cash–J Fitzgerald bt S Edberg–A Jarryd, 6–3, 6–4, 4–6, 6–1.

PRIDE IS THE SPUR

Deposed captain Gower reflects on his future

14 January 1987 Perth

The beauty of David Gower's batting, witnessed once more in England's first innings, has always been that it is primarily instinctive. The graceful, unmuscled sweep of the bat, the timing that comes from eye and wrist rather than shoulder and hips: such things cannot be taught. Yet it is a short step from playing by instinct to attempting to play from memory. For how much of this tour, one wonders, has Gower been switched on to autocue during an understandable post-captaincy period of disillusionment?

His tour average is average, in the mid-thirties, with 400 runs including one century and two fifties. Hardly your definitive Gower. How much had his demotion affected his appetite for the game, his power of concentration? Had he been on memory-computer?

'The hardest part, having stepped down,' he admitted, 'is not to let the mind wander, not to start thinking "what do I do now, where's the stimulus?" There's nothing like being captain, or even vice-captain, it adds to the responsibility you have to yourself as a player.'

He never has been, he says, an accumulation batsman, squirrelling away the runs with aggregate totals at the back of his mind, moving peg by peg, 500 by 500, up the statistics, Boycott-fashion.

'During the Australian tour of '79–'80 I had played reasonably well, hitting 98 not out at Sydney, but was dropped when I got back home and there was a lull in my career. On the '82–'83 tour, when I was vice-captain, I had a lot to prove and played some of my best cricket. The only thing wrong with my 70 at Perth was that I got out. I felt like I could score 200, or 800! I think it was the best I've ever played.'

Being naturally gifted in sport is both a virtue and a penance. Games players like Gower want to win because they cannot help it, not because they drive themselves to be better. It is part of the appeal and, in poorer times, of their failure. Freed from the responsibility of captaincy, Gower is not still calculating the tactics moment by moment with a captain's-eye view.

'You think about the match but your mind drifts,' he says. 'You switch off. You want either to be involved or not at all. Being on the selection committee is neither here nor there. You can be as authoritative as you like but the captain has the final say, they're his ideas on strategy. It's his show, he takes the responsibilities – though I don't know how much of that's being directed by Mickey Stewart (the team manager).' Being dropped as captain after one match last summer hurt Gower more, in retrospect, than at the time; that they no longer wanted him to carry the responsibility. Maybe, of course, he had not shown enough leadership, but the build-up of criticism of him and of the side offended him. 'To be told [I was out] wasn't fun, but it wasn't a shock when it came,' he says.

After a shoulder injury at Lord's, he returned to the side last summer at Edgbaston with an attitude of attack in his batting. There was no resentment against Gatting. He knew that he had to find a new point of mental focus.

'Of course an Ashes series keeps you going, there's your own pride and performance, but if you lose the will to do the job, then it's time to pack up,' he says. There have, he concedes, been days when he has felt pretty low on the tour, when he has not been positive: at the wrong end of the scale of aggression and concentration. It has worried him.

'At Melbourne, in the fourth Test, I badly needed to stay at the crease, to be positive – and I wasn't. It was disappointing, not so much to be out (for seven), but to have to admit I knew the probability before I reached the wicket. There's that feeling as you walk out, yes or no, something clicks as you pull on your gloves and hat, and the doubts disappear. Playing the first ball tells you immediately how you feel.'

After Melbourne, he had to stand back and take a long look at himself. To overhear people talking about retirement was stimulating! When cricket gave him so much, when he still enjoyed the game, to slide out now would be absurd. It was up to him.

'To keep enjoying it means to keep getting runs,' he said. 'To keep playing Test cricket, I have to be playing it well. If I can maintain concentration, I think I can still be good for some time to come. Two years, five years. I haven't a clue. But I'm eternally grateful to the game and I realise what I have to lose and also how much people appreciate what I can do.'

Maybe he was born 40 years too late; he should have played in an era when great players took their bat out of the bag, shook the dust off it and went out to bat without a care. Like Compton or Miller.

'In some ways,' he says with that wispy, almost furtive smile, 'it's been true. Without being arrogant, I wasn't bothered whether I did well. I thought "this is fun", and making runs was a bonus. I felt happier when I wasn't soul-searching. It was brave, self-confident stuff, believing no one could bowl me out. Then things altered. You began to feel tiredness. To lose your instinctiveness would diminish your talent.'

Gower's game has always been about talent, but he has always tried, he says, to make room for other things, not to be wholly cricket-orientated. 'If some people say "if he'd had a few less bottles of fizz and a few more nets, he'd have been better" they might be right!' he concedes. 'But it hasn't been a fluke, keeping an international career going nine years. It all depends how you want to lead your life.'

My colleague, John Woodcock, has written that he played like an angel on Sunday. It must be hoped that he had rediscovered that power of concentration.

MIND-FREEZE AT 2,000 FEET

Gliding on the epic Australian scale

15 January 1987 Benalla, Victoria

'Just pull that little yellow lever on the left,' the instructor behind me said matter-of-factly, 'and we're away.' 'Fine,' I replied casually, while swallowing with a dry tongue and wondering how I would find the nerve to move anything more than an eyeball.

We were at Benalla, in Northern Victoria, for the twentieth World Gliding Championships. Or rather, I should say, we were *above* Benalla. Some 2,000 feet above it, or twice the height of the Empire State building. Benalla, with its rural 9,000 population, was looking about as big as Trafalgar Square.

The alternatives confronting me certainly concentrated the mind, not to say temporarily froze the limbs of this first-timer. At that moment we were being towed in our two-seater glider by an old Piper Pawnee, a former crop-spraying plane, and leaping about as though on a sledge behind Red Rum at Aintree. If I pulled that yellow lever, we would peel off into nothingness, two men wedged into a transparent thermos flask, drifting about an azure, cloudless sky. I felt close to my maker.

Tremulously pulling the lever to release the tow line, and allow this aerial AA van up ahead of us to return to the airfield and tug some more competitors up into this opalesque, silent freedom, the thought briefly arose whether my building society would consider this a reasonable leisure pursuit. Reassuringly, I convinced myself that, of course, only racing was risky.

Only racing? We dived away to starboard in a steep bank, and suddenly I was looking at the parched terrain through the top of the little cockpit dome. Often when sailing I have longed to be a gull, but now I was not so sure. Yet within a minute or two, coming to terms with this profound experience, I was beginning to enjoy it.

The voice behind me was a great help. John Spura, a mechanic who emigrated to Australia from Europe, has been an instructor for five years or so. What would I like to see? he enquired, as if we were on top of a sightseeing double decker bus. As much as he could show me, I answered with totally hollow bravado. Although I had achieved some sort of temperamental equilibrium on behalf of our readers, I stopped short of accepting his offer to try the controls; still clutching my pen and notebook, I said I wanted to take notes. It must be said they were mostly taken by memory.

The privilege was to be experiencing the kind of conditions for gliding largely unknown other than in the great land masses of Southern Africa, Australia and America. Ingo Renner, a German–Australian and the current world open-class champion who will be defending his title when the racing starts on Sunday, thinks nothing of setting off on a day's 1,000 kilometre course.

In Britain, it is not uncommon for none of the competitors in a 250km event circuit to make it back to the finishing line, running out of lift and being forced to land out in a field: *aux vaches*, as the French say. In Australia, it is rare for the majority of competitors not to complete a 500 or 700km course. I was about to discover why.

The glider pilot's ability to stay airborne depends on finding upward currents of warmer air to provide lift. Thermals. In Western European climates, these may occasionally reach two or three knots, some two 200–300 feet lift per minute, rising off a stubble cornfield or large flat-roofed buildings.

With the dry earth's crust of much of Australia, conditions are ideal. Although the town of Benalla, where a new state gliding centre has recently been opened, has pleasant green parkland, a golf club and many thriving residential gardens, the surrounding bushland is as dry as a cheese biscuit. Visiting foreign gliders were being obliged to replace their steel tailplane skid-plates for brass ones, so as not to ignite the grass landing strip. Australia has more thermals than England has umbrellas.

Behind me, John Spura said he had spotted another glider spiralling upwards, and we ought to go and investigate. As in powered flight, once a glider is above a couple of thousand feet, there is little impression of speed. Even when the speedometer is registering 80 knots or so, you appear to be almost hovering.

Suddenly, as we approached the other glider, there was the sensation of being on the upward section of a big dipper: a huge thrust under one's seat. The variometer, which measures the rate of climb or fall, was reading between plus eight to 10 knots. In little more than 30 seconds, we climbed from 2,500ft to 3,300ft, two or three times the rate of climb of a small powered aircraft.

At the controls, John made the exclamations of someone who has just unwrapped a Christmas gift of rare vintage claret, and kept us in a rising left-handed corkscrew. I pressed my knees against the side of the cockpit, glanced uneasily at the violently rotating countryside beneath, and hoped that our Romanian model IS28–B2, with 7,000 hours on the clock, was well maintained.

As thermals reach upper, cooler air, they expand and slow until they reach a ceiling. Approaching 4,000ft my instructor levelled off, and then demonstrated 'dolphin' flying, by which you gain forward speed in a straight line and repeatedly lift the nose, dropping back towards the stalling speed of 38 knots, so as to maintain altitude as much as possible. Such a manoeuvre is fine, maybe, if you are at the controls, but for a passenger can induce the consternation of a cross-Channel trip to Boulogne in a force eight gale.

The skies and the horizons in Australia are prodigious. The air is so unpolluted you can see 50 or 60 miles even at lower altitudes. Around us, in the distance, were Mt Buller, the skiing resort, and the 4,000ft Buffalo Plateau. Gently, we cruised down to 1,000ft, entered the obligatory approach circuit of the airfield, coasted in over the rooftops, and after some 40 minutes bumped back onto earth.

John said I'd done well for a first trip, and I said I was more concerned that he had done well. The next day during practice an Australian and an Irishman collided in a thermal, though they landed unharmed. They do say it's a safe sport.

A GAME OF HUMAN POETRY

Reflections on MCC's bi-centenary

20 August 1987

Eloquence is heard, poetry is overheard, John Stuart Mill, the philosopher, said. Eloquence supposes an audience, but poetry is unconscious of the listener. MCC's bicentenary match celebrates a game which, more than any, abounds with poetry.

Cricket, of course, is not indifferent to an audience. How often has not Botham played to the gallery, though here is a man whose performance, in spite of himself, has poetry within its eloquence. The spontaneous players down the years have been born with an innate spirit of adventure, who conceded nothing to public expectation or demand, giving away their wicket with no thought of tomorrow.

Macartney, who would score a Test century before lunch; Woolley, who in consecutive innings at Lord's in 1921, against Gregory and McDonald, hit 95 and 93; Constantine, who at Sydney in 1930 took six for 45, including Bradman, Fairfax, McCabe and Kippax; Botham, who beat the Australians so memorably in 1981; they, together with such as Sobers and Miller and Viv Richards, made cricket a game of beauty.

In no other sport is it so true that style is the man. Compton, reproved as an apprentice for his technique by a diligent Middlesex coach, rejoined with impatience after another flurry of runs: 'Never mind the left leg, where was the ball?'

Constantine, one of the greatest of all-rounders, having rejected at 23 a career in law, said upon retirement: 'Had I plodded back to the lawyers' parchment den, I should perhaps have been wise and successful in interference, and never have known the ecstasy of fulfilment.'

Neville Cardus, who numbered Lord Birkenhead and Sir Thomas Beecham among personal friends, and as a critic acquired a profound knowledge of music, said: 'I have met far more interesting characters amongst the cricketers than amongst the musicians of England . . . No living English musician, critic or performer is half the work of art to look at and to experience as C. B. Fry. I would rather go into a pub with half a dozen north country cricket professionals than into all the studios or Athenaeum and Saville clubs in London. I have tried both, so I know.'

Cricket played spontaneously, not for national prestige or personal gain, is one of the purest activities invented by a man's mind, a synthesis of body and soul as moving as Louis Armstrong. Where lies the next 200 years of MCC, post-Packer, post-television, post-Pakistani condemnation of umpires?

If cricket has become by definition a game for cheats, it were better that it be buried now with dignity than descend into a formalised approval of the Artful Dodger. MCC, caught in the cross-fire of racial tensions, perhaps alone is capable of designing and preserving the future. But where are their leaders, and where the goodwill upon which they will depend?

Someone inquired of a colleague of W. G. Grace if it were true that the great man was a cheat. No, was the reply, he's far too clever for that.

The story goes that at Worcester against an opening pair, who had become entrenched on a hot and cloudless day, W. G. exclaimed to one of them: 'Just look at that flight of duck!'

The batsman stared unavailingly into the sky. 'Must have gone behind those trees,' W. G. murmured, and then, to his flagging bowler: 'A quick couple of half-volleys while his eye still has the glare of the sun.'

Thankfully, the distinction between gentlemen and players was removed, yet as an 11-year-old, with the privilege of having once been bowled at in a net at the Saffrons by Miller and Hassett, I never conceived of a difference. All cricketers were gentlemen. The day may come when none of them are. That must not be allowed to happen.

BALLESTEROS LEADS EUROPE HOME

Momentous first Ryder Cup triumph in America

29 September 1987 Columbus, Ohio

The Ryder Cup is already won. Historic. Memorable. Ballesteros, the inimitable, clinched it when he went 2-and-1 at the 17th against Strange, the unlikely Darcy having shortly before defeated Crenshaw on the last green. Three thousand supporters from Europe are euphoric.

The huge American crowd round the 18th green is trying to come to terms with defeat as they bask in the afternoon sunshine. As Ballesteros comes bowling down the last fairway in a swarm of wellwishers like some pied piper, it is difficult even for Europeans to believe it has happened.

Ballesteros is submerged beneath his congratulating colleagues. The last pair on the course, Brand and Sutton, appear on the horizon, level pegging: but who cares?

Wadkins, behind them, has hammered Brown 3 and 1. Tony Jacklin, once British and US Open champion simultaneously, surveys the scene. His eyes brim with tears. 'This is the greatest week of my life,' he says, quietly. And means it.

'I am so thrilled for Darcy,' he adds. Darcy, with that idiosyncratic Irish swing, is beaming, flush-faced, like a birthday boy overwhelmed with gifts. He does not quite know where to look, what to say. As he recoils from ceaseless back-slapping, he says: 'It was the 15th that did it. My drive hit the trees and rebounded back on to the fairway. I took a 3-iron over the water, a wedge up to the green, and holed the putt.' And he grins as though he has told you a secret: a secret watched by millions.

Brand and Sutton gracefully halve the hole and the match, and the party begins. The Ohio State University marching band, which had invigorated the opening ceremony, now gives the closing stages a swing. The European team catch the rhythm. Olazábal, the boy who has played like a man, does a solo tango, Darcy, Rivero, Torrance and Langer collect their national flags from a wildly cheering audience. Ballesteros drenches his colleagues to the skin with spray from a magnum of champagne.

And the American crowd stays rooted, sharing the satisfaction of the moment.

Formal presentation of the 27th series begins. With a wry smile, Jack Nicklaus leads out his superb team, beaten for the first time on American soil.

His soil; this masterpiece in golf architecture. Among the speeches, Lord Derby, president of the British PGA, pays tribute to Nicklaus having done so much to give golf its unimpeachable reputation, now splendidly upheld by the American team.

There is a standing ovation for Nicklaus, who, when his turn comes, admits: 'There is not a whole lot to say, you have seen a team which played superior golf . . . it is tough to lose, I think our players can only be better for it.'

Jacklin, who appears to need a microphone dais to lean upon to give him strength, suggests this victory could change the face of world golf. Twelve Americans view him silently, wondering if indeed a layer of the icing on their domestic cake may now go to visiting foreigners.

The day's drama, against a backcloth of unequal beauty, has floated for both teams like a drifting, child's balloon. One moment soaring sky-wards, the next about to land on a holly bush. The anxiety has been such that wives are following the matches; even great players assembling after the finish of their own match to follow their colleagues have barely dared to watch as vital putts are faced.

Down at the first green, at daybreak, a couple of old American grand-fathers had taken up their positions on shooting sticks, determined to shout their men home.

'Andy, Andy, you're the man. If you can't do it, no one can,' they yelled at Bean. Then Pohl, then Mize, and so on. Events would prove the Americans could not.

Ballesteros, so determined for three days to prove his stature to an American audience, remained buoyant and brilliant to the end. When he bunkered an approach and an American voice, unable to contain itself in glee, shouted: 'Yeaahh', Sevvy merely gave the man a huge grin: and holed out from the bunker.

After watching his first six men go through the ninth green, and finding the European position deteriorating from four up and four matches even at 11.30, to three up and three even by just after 1 o'clock, Jacklin races ahead to join the critical front three where Woosnam is one down to Bean, and Clark and Torrance are each level.

'Clark and Torrance have to hang on' he says aloud. They do. Clark wins the 18th to take the match, Torrance comes back from one down at the 17th to square the match. And Europe are on the way.

29 September 1987

America has just staged one of the most enthralling sporting events of all time: and has hardly noticed. Worse even than New York's *Post* and *Times*, which carried only nominal reports, one of yesterday's break-fast television sports newscasts did not even mention the cliffhanging, unique, 15–13 Ryder Cup defeat. It was thought more important to show pictures of empty National Football League stadiums, where the players earning an average $230,000 a year (about £140,000) are on strike.

The irony of such an attitude could not have been more pointed. Not only was the 27th Ryder Cup a stupendous competition fought at a summit of technique by 24 of the world's top players, but it was between millionaire money-earners playing for nothing but each other and their national pride.

It is my privilege as well as my job to be at many international events, yet I have witnessed no Wimbledon, no Olympic Games, no World Cup of football where for three days I lived, minute by minute from breakfast till teatime, in such suspense along with a crowd of 20,000. And all the time in a setting of enchanting natural beauty.

More than that, there is another aspect which the Americans do not fully appreciate, not only because of their baseball-football-basketball obsession: though in this they are in company with many others. It is that professional golf is almost the only major sport in which the players unwaveringly stick to the rules.

A unique part of the tournament has been not only America's first home defeat but, as always, the sight of famous players sitting, sometimes anonymously among the crowd, to watch and then encourage their colleagues following the conclusion of their own matches. In every way the Ryder Cup is the essence of sport, in the way we sometimes see it in Olympic relay races: which matter most to those running them.

The insular glory of an individual achievement, however great the satisfaction, does not have the enduring warmth of a team triumph. That is why, emotionally, Tony Jacklin values the last few days even more than his own victories, famous and rich though they made him.

It has been a revelation, in the European team, to see Lyle and Langer, Brand and Rivero playing together like brothers. To see Olazábal, the boy of 21 from San Sebastian, demonstrating the maturity of a 30-year-old, the way Ballesteros always promised he would. To watch Darcy, splendid, shy, self-effacing, from Delgany village outside Dublin, holing that downhill putt for the moment that wrote Darcy into history.

'T'lad should retoire temorrah,' a tipsy compatriot, one of hundreds who made the trip, happily suggested as a noisy evening swayed towards dawn at the Muirfield Village club. Darcy continued blinking and nodding and smiling. And Olazábal, himself drunk with fatigue more than champagne, would again mimic his Irish colleague's rolling head; and do another little Spanish rumba of personal celebration.

They have been, the Europeans, a fine bunch of characters. Doughty little Woosnam, promising he would bite the Americans' ankles, proceeding with Faldo to do it, and then promising to get drunk for a week. Disciplined, restrained, correct Langer, half smiling at the closing ceremony, having come back for his half with Nelson. Ebullient Torrance, rising once more when it mattered on the final day. And Ballesteros: the matinée idol he is, and playing like Apollo.

It always requires, it seems, a Pearl Harbour to wake up the Americans. The America's Cup defeat – almost equally memorable at Newport – galvanised them into action, and Muirfield Village 1987 will probably do the same. They went home muttering threats. 'The Ryder, it seems, is suddenly a major,' Dick Fenlon, columnist in the *Columbus Dispatch*, condescendingly wrote yesterday.

Those 12 Americans who lost knew that beforehand, and that is why they were smiling through clenched teeth as the trophy was handed over on that unforgettable, sunny September afternoon. As Lord Darby, president of the PGA, said, it will be a wonderful recollection to be able to say: 'I was there.'

GOLDEN GRATITUDE FOR SKIING GREATNESS

Zurbriggen's aggression-free innocence

17 February 1988 Calgary

Away from the Alpine precipices, he seems as though he could not punch his way out of the proverbial paper bag. You wonder where this shy, gentle young man from a Swiss mountain village finds the aggression to enable him to become the world's foremost racer. Can he really win five golds?

When Pirmin Zurbriggen arrived for his press conference almost two hours after his downhill triumph on Monday – predatory television and a standard drug test appointment having delayed him – he was still unable to believe it had really happened. He sat in the chair, clutching a bunch of carnations, and gazed around at this hoary swarm of scribes and photographers with the naïve, innocent eyes of a six-year-old.

Asked about his apparent lack of aggression, and its necessity in most racers, he stared uncomprehendingly into space for a moment, those fair curls and that reticent smile making him every Swiss mother's favourite son. 'I suppose that I have that kind of temperament,' he said haltingly, and not merely because he was speaking in English rather than his native *Schweizerdeutsch*. 'I'm a loner, I like being on my own. I have inside me this big dream . . . and when that feeling explodes . . . that's my expression.' The answer, like many, tails away into silence.

Yet, however inadequately, Zurbriggen's response is an indication of the unseen depths within this remarkable athlete, whose incomparable goat-like balance on impossibly treacherous slopes comes from ski-ing almost before he could run. Incidentally, it is alongside such childhood advantages of environment that the true level of Martin Bell's achievement in eighth place can be measured.

There is, I regret to say, instant scepticism among some sports journalists towards those occasional competitors who, in moments of triumph, say that it was due to God. There have been, it must be said, one or two medal-winners at Olympic Games who too glibly ascribed their success to the Almighty (or occasionally to Lenin).

When Zurbriggen, a religious man, closed his eyes and cast back his head in the instant that he realised he had surpassed the time of Peter Mueller, his great rival, there was a particular simplicity and gratitude in his face. 'I thanked God that I had won,' he said. 'I couldn't quite understand why it had happened for me, after all the pressures of the last few days.'

He admitted that what had worried him during the 15-minute wait between Mueller's run in first starting position and his in 14th was that the other racers were so much slower than Mueller. 'I knew that he had given a fantastic performance and that I must ski to my limit.

'I had watched Peter at the start and seen how perfectly he took the early difficult section and I knew then that it was going to be difficult to beat him. I had a good feeling, but I knew I must attack.'

He did so, not with quite the same hair-raising, daredevil assault of Franz Klammer at Innsbruck in 1976, but with a refinement of balance, line and control that was breathtaking: an inflatable on skis negotiating the near vertical rapids.

The downhill gold medal was the ultimate ambition, he said afterwards, never mind the discussion about his being the greatest-ever all-round skier, never mind the comparisons with Toni Sailer and Jean Claud Killy, who had each won three gold medals. He was doubtful about speculation that he would win five – the Combined event and Super G having been added to the slalom and giant slalom since the days of Killy in 1968.

'I'll be more relaxed now, after my gold medal. The others will be more nervous than me' he said. 'But everyone else is in good condition and it will be difficult. I know I can ski well in all events, and if I win others, it will be nice. But first was the downhill!'

Zurbriggen won the World Cup overall in 1984 and 1987, was second in 1985 and 1986, and leads this year, but many doubt that he can win five golds at these Winter Olympics. Max Julen, his friend and winner of the giant slalom in 1984, says it is impossible, that Zurbriggen could win the Super G and maybe giant slalom as well as the downhill, but never the slalom. Marc Biver, Zurbriggen's agent, thinks he might win three. In the world championship at Crans Montana last year, Zurbriggen won two golds, but Mueller took the downhill and Girardelli the Combined.

Alberto Tomba, of Italy, the most improved skier on the circuit, is waiting for him, someone suggested. Well, Tomba is strong and a favourite for the giant slalom and slalom, Zurbriggen answered. But you never know . . .

The downhill alone was, they say, worth a million dollars. Zurbriggen, who already has a million, is not concerned. 'The first thing was to ski well,' he said. 'My agent will look after the rest.' Zurbriggen did. Biver will.

GLAMOUR GIRL OF SEDUCTIVE CHARM

Katarina Witt an incorrigible flirt

18 February 1988 Calgary

They don't give gold medals for feminine sexuality in the Olympic Games, but women's figure skating can come close to it. The Olympic ideal owes much to Sonja Heinie of Norway, whose three victories in the Winter Olympics before the war led to a glittering career in Hollywood. With the doe-like eyes of Audrey Hepburn, a sensuous mouth and a dazzling smile, Katy Witt intends to make the most of her film star's figure.

'Every man prefers looking at a well-built woman to someone the shape of a rubber ball,' she says unashamedly. 'This sport promotes what is feminine. It is possible to be more womanly than in other sports. We can communicate something, and give happiness, and do this better as a woman.'

There is some resentment that the 22-year-old East German, three times world champion and Olympic winner in 1984, exploits her sexual appeal with the judges in this arbitrarily measured sport. She is an incorrigible flirt once she steps on the ice, and has been taught by Jutta Muller, her renowned coach, to select beforehand a male face in the audience and to play to him.

The women's programme does not begin until next Wednesday, but Witt had come to the auditorium at the main Press centre here in order to dispose of the many requests for interviews. As she walked through the door, pertly chic in mauve cord pants, smoke-grey sweater and lime shirt, she put her hand over her mouth in surprise at the sight of 350 journalists and a bank of television cameras.

She is studying dramatic art, and is retiring from skating after this year's world championships. Yet she is already a star.

She defends, not unexpectedly, the arbitrary standards. Subjective assessment, she says, cannot be changed, it is part of the Olympic Games in many sports. Every judge has different tastes. 'And we have to try to offer something that is acceptable for the majority – and that is difficult. But I enjoy the emphasis on artistry and costumes. The dress should enhance the music. When I wear the right costume, I feel much better. Why not?'

Why not, indeed?

Yet it is well advised that the International Skating Union will this summer discuss limitations on the brevity of women's costumes. We are reaching the point where some competitors are wearing little more than bikinis; which can present, unless the skaters are both perfectly proportioned and technically expert, an unattractive view.

This was particularly evident in Tuesday's free programme of the Pairs. While Canadian and American couples whirled yards of exposed female leg and buttock overhead, the elfin, child-like Ekaterina Gordeeva, a mere 16, and her Russian partner Serge Grinkov, the world champions, gave a bewitching exhibition of graceful, synchronised rhythm that needed no overt sexuality to impress the judges.

Witt is legitimately concerned with artistry; with achieving a more emotional interpretation of Bizet's *Carmen*, to which she and her rival Debi Thomas, of the United States, will both skate their free programme. Thomas defeated her for the world title in 1986, Witt regaining it last year.

They are less than friends. 'She dies, I don't,' Thomas says pointedly of their respective interpretations. Witt counters: 'You can skate, or interpret – the judges just decide which they prefer.'*

Witt acknowledges the self-discipline she has acquired, that Muller has counselled her in everything. Muller stresses that to achieve maximum performance the essential work is done when her pupils are still children.

Witt was selected, East German style, at five. She says her parents would not have had the money, in the capitalist West, to have enabled her to become a skater. On the other hand, in the state-controlled East, it is evident that they had little choice once the Karl Marx Stadt sports club had made its decision. Relaxation has been rare; though she was regularly to be found in Havana discotheques during the 1984 'reward' cruise to Cuba for the Olympic team.

She hates the complimentary figures, which are 30 per cent of the total, and does them only moderately. She and Muller would like the 'compulsories' abolished. It is the free programme, worth half the points, which, with the applause of the crowd, brings fulfilment. Katarina Witt was born for the stage as much as for the ice rink.

* In the final, Thomas died of nerves. Witt won.

WILL TO SUCCEED STRIKES A RESONANT NOTE

Peter Young earns his pint

19 February 1988 Calgary

Peter Young is a likely lad from Dagenham. A piano-tuner by trade. Does a bit of most sports. Running, rowing, spot of canoeing now and then, that kind of thing. Enjoys his pint.

The other day he was out here skiing. He says it is the best sport he's ever done. Cross-country. You know, where you seem to go more uphill than downhill, slog yourself silly till you're nearly sick. Fun for those who are fit, though.

The best bit was, he met the guv'nor, as he calls him. Juan Antonio, that fellow who runs the Olympics. Smashing bloke. Stayed to watch the whole race.

Mind you, a pity about that fourth place. Just another seven-tenths of a second faster over five kilometres and he'd have had the bronze. Medals? Well, he doesn't want to sound flash, but he's got a load back home, from bits and pieces. An Olympic exhibition medal would have been nice. Still, mustn't grumble. It is a good life. Specially when you are blind.

Peter lost his sight when he was two years old. At blind school, he wasn't particularly musical, but decided on piano tuning because it gave him freedom. He could be his own boss. He laughs. 'It is just a question of hearing,' he says. 'You don't really have to know G from C.'

He travels by public transport. Finding his way to clients' addresses isn't difficult from the Tube or bus station, if he has proper directions. House numbers can be tricky. If they're figures, he is okay. 'But if they are painted, I am in trouble.'

He is 32 now, got married a couple of years ago. Kathy works at the Midland Bank. He met her at the ice skating rink.

A while back, one day when he was running, the Blind Sports Federation said there was some skiing at Beitostolen in Norway. That's a bit keen, he thought; downhill and all that. Anyroad, why not give it a go.

It turned out to be cross-country and that was where he met Jan

Knutsen. Jan's in ICI Chemicals, a sales rep. And was a volunteer guide: skiing a few yards in front, shouting back instructions and warnings, leading touch-shoulder round obstacles. They have been together as a pair since '83. Jan drops in at Dagenham when he is in London two or three times a year.

Peter's been to four Physically Handicapped Olympics. He was eighth in 1980, got the bronze with Jan in '84, and was fifth last month in Austria.

They finance themselves, though they occasionally manage some fund-raising: a bit of sponsored marathon running, say. Peter did three hours 40 minutes in 1983, the same year he took part in the Devizes-to-Westminster canoe race.

'If I didn't do this kind of thing,' he says, 'I'd get fat and lazy. But apart from a sense of fulfilment, it increases your spatial awareness, your mobility and reaction. You're sharper. It makes you feel that much damn better. Two hours of this, a shower, and you've earned a pint.'

The winner this week was Hans Aalien, of Norway, a computer scientist in the final stages of a master's degree at Oslo University. He's 29, and has been blind since birth. He has been skiing for 14 years. Arne Homb is his guide.

They ski once or twice a week, and have run together a lot. But Hans is going to have to get a new guide for running. He is now too fast for Arne. Receiving the gold medal from Samaranch, hearing the Norwegian anthem: that was good.

'I beat Hans skiing once,' Peter reflects, as he gets changed for the evening party.

A GENTLE TOUCH IN VICTORY

Lyle wins Britain's first Green Jacket at Augusta

12 April 1988 Augusta

The jargon of golf these days, when you have just watched your chances plummet through the floorboards, is that you have to 'regroup'. It is a word that sounds straight out of West Point or Sandhurst. Patton or Westmoreland would approve it.

When Sandy Lyle arrived, with an eight-under-par two-stroke lead over Mark Calcavecchia, at what is regarded as the definitive phase of the Augusta National course, and proceeded to drop one shot at the 11th and then, plopping into the water off the shoulder of the green, two at the short 12th, his expression was not so much 'amen' as a mortal, blood-curdling 'aaarrghh'. There were not a few uncontrolled whoopees from the home crowd.

Calcavecchia, playing a hole in front, watched his putt roll round the rim and drop for a birdie at the par-five 13th to go six-under. Coming up behind, Lyle then bunkered his approach, came out to 20ft and missed the first putt to take a five.

It was a particular pleasure to walk this final round on what was to be a historic afternoon, with Herbert Warren Wind, veteran correspondent of the *New Yorker*, to whom Amen Corner owes its name. At this stage we were waiting, fascinated, as were the millions watching on television as well as the thousands thronging the course, for Lyle to 'regroup'. And seemingly it was not happening.

It is difficult to read the mood of this tall, unblinking but slightly shy-looking Englishman from Shropshire, whose parents' Glaswegian blood affiliates him to Scotland. He could be playing an artisans' evening four-ball. It is a characteristic which makes him both so likeable and, maybe, so good. He is said to be unflappable.

We had seen the steadiness in the outward half. Starting the day six-under, Lyle birdied the second and also, with a 20-yard chip from among the crowd at the back of the green, the fourth. There were brilliant recoveries at the seventh and ninth.

Driving into trees at the seventh, a brave short-iron high through the foliage found a bunker; a wedge reached the green, and a curling 12-footer saved the par. Off the fairway again at the ninth, a glorious seven-iron rolled to within two feet for a birdie three, to turn two up. He was, someone observed, just about to reach the 'wall' to which marathon runners fearingly refer.

And thence, via disasters, to the 14th, where Lyle has a par four. Craig Stadler, ahead of Calcavecchia, has now joined the hunt, going six-under with a birdie at the 15th; but as Lyle approaches the 15th, Stadler is already retreating from the 16th with a one-over-par four.

As Lyle gazes down at the 15th green, from where his drive rests comfortably on the ridge, observing Calcavecchia remain six-under, Herb Wind voices the thought that the next couple of strokes will probably determine whether or not Lyle will be champion. Lyle is in range for a possible eagle; and is still in range of a birdie when his approach runs just off the back of the green.

Yet when he arrives, to appreciative applause from the now immense crowd, his shoulders seemingly slump, a suggestion of resignation. It is to prove misleading. When his little chip grazes the hole, he slams his visor on the ground: though he will later say, in an admission of rare histrionics, that it had been 'putting on a show'.

Nevertheless, from seven feet past he misses the one back, takes par, and goes to the 16th still a stroke down on Calcavecchia. It is now that fortune rolls back towards the Scot.

His fine seven-iron to the short hole, that idyllic Azalea-decked arbour, rests some feet above the pin on a notoriously sloped green where in the past four days there have been few birdie twos. Lyle makes it: all square.

It is the most tranquil of late afternoons, the sun sinking from view, as Lyle reaches the 17th. A distant roar tells us Calcavecchia is on the 18th in two. As Lyle lines up his 20ft putt from the beard of the green, dwarfed by the pines standing sentinel around the back, the stillness among the thousands watching is that of a museum. He two-putts.

The rest, as they say, is history: the 18th fairway bunker, the seven-iron so cleanly hit it takes not a grain of sand, the backwards downhill roll towards the pin that is like a hand stretching out with a Nobel Prize, the final birdie putt.

A single historic stroke divides two men, but back in the interview room there is a marked cultural difference. When analysing his final round, Calcavecchia, though in no way boastful, uses the expressions 'great', 'real good', 'perfect', 'nice', 'so easy', 'my favourite', some 50 times in relation to his shots. American positive thinking.

The comes the fellow in the spanking new, august Augusta green, smiling an almost apologetic, satisfied smile. He had, he says with courtesy to accepted cliché, managed to regroup after the 12th: yet he remains immovably honest.

He declines to agree he is the best in the world, because 'there are a lot of other good players'. He would have to think about the possibilities of the grand slam.

The American Press are pleading with him, in effect, to shout yippee and he just will not. Calcavecchia has generously said his rival is 'real patient'. They had talked a bit beforehand. Sandy had given him all that English stuff. You win some, you lose some. Old chap. You know. 'I've never seen him doubt himself,' Calcavecchia said. 'I'm glad he's going home.'

Lyle has given himself, and certainly has given me, an afternoon of magical memories.

YOUTHFUL LOVE THAT FASHIONED A SPORT

How Tinling judged the lines

23 May 1988 Paris

Sixty years ago today the French tennis championships switched from their original site at Saint Cloud, and Stade Roland Garros opened with its first match: the then traditional curtain-raiser over two days between the French and English teams before the event proper began on Monday. It was, coincidentally, the moment that launched internationally the 17-year-old boy who was to become one of the most knowledgeable authorities, and the best friend, the game has perhaps had.

Incidentally, it is quite a year for tennis anniversaries: the hundredth of the Lawn Tennis Association, the 75th of the International Tennis Federation, the fiftieth since Suzanne Lenglen died, the twentieth for open tennis.

Teddy Tinling was a schoolboy with a bronchial weakness who was taken by his mother to the Riviera for the warmth and dry air. At the age of 13 he was given junior membership of the Nice club, and there he saw, and distantly was enraptured by, the legendary Lenglen. Until she died of leukaemia, in 1938, Tinling was a Suzanne groupie: and a youthful umpire, sharp of eye, to whom she became equally addicted.

Pierre Gillou, who was to become president of the International Lawn Tennis Federation (ILTF) – as it then still was – had seen Tinling officiating and invited him to Roland Garros. On the opening day he umpired for Betty Nuthall, the English No. 1, who defeated Jeanne Vaussard, the French No. 2, 6–3, 6–3. The following day Miss Nuthall, playing Marguerite Vroquedis, the French No. 1, and in the process of transferring from traditional women's underarm service to overhead, served 30 double faults . . . and still won.

'Marguerite and Tony Wilding, of New Zealand, the Wimbledon champion, were the first 'beautiful people' of tennis,' Tinling recalls. 'Marguerite played with a careless rapture that was bewildering and quite unmatched.'

Tinling has the score-sheet still, with every double-fault marked: and he continued to umpire throughout the championships of 1928 up to the women's quarter-final between Helen Wills and Cilly Aussem. Doubles were played throughout the first week, and singles only from the second weekend. 'Something worth thinking about once again,' Tinling observes, now the doyen of critics and, for the past 17 years, the director of international liaison for the Virginia Slims circuit of 57 tournaments.

In 1928 he encountered the first electronic scoreboard, a laborious system of clanking, revolving leaves operated by remote control from a knob beside the umpire's chair at Roland Garros: shortly to be improved upon at Wimbledon. French tennis was then in its prime, following the first victory in the Davis Cup the previous year. The stadium was named after a First World War aviator, killed when shot down for the second time, and a close friend of the financier of the new venture.

Lenglen never played at Roland Garros, having turned professional, though her benevolence towards the sickly English boy had helped establish what would be his life's work: including a 45-year spell as fashion couturier and tennis designer with all the controversy of his colourful creations for such high-profile ladies as Maria Bueno and Christ Evert. The V & A honoured him with his own exhibition two years ago.

In 1928, he survived on £1 a week and a gratefully received book of meal tickets from Colin Gregory, captain of the English team and later a Wimbledon chairman.

On one occasion, Tinling loaned 100 francs to Ludwig Salm, an Austrian of renowned ill manner on court. Expressing misgivings about his loan, Tinling was reprimanded by a friend: 'Ludi is a gentleman.' It was possible in those days for Salm to behave as badly as McEnroe on court yet remain socially acceptable because he was, off court, impeccably behaved. He was said to be on first-name terms with the Pope, his ancestors having been on the crusades.

Those were the days when life was splendid if you were on the right side of the tracks, though Tinling says: 'I always wanted to be astride the tracks – because there is such a great appeal on the wrong side.'

The Riviera in the Twenties, Paris itself, were paradise for the young Englishman. 'Riviera tournaments were in the gardens of luxury hotels,' Tinling recalls. 'It was the height of the Gatsby era. Laughter was the key, having fun was everything. It seemed that all the women were beautiful and all the men strong and handsome.'

Society emerged from the Ritz at midday to watch Suzanne for half-an-hour, then returned for cocktails. French sons called their mothers Madame. When he was 14, Tinling saw Lenglen dancing with Rudolph Valentino. 'My son is living in the South of France as a gigolo,' his father would bemoan.

His mother, however, found herself equally happy at home there. It was a bad day when the stakes for gambling in the casino were changed from gold coins to plastic chips. She never went back.

SPORTSMANSHIP SEEN IN SHARP RELIEF

Modern pentathlon bronze for Britain

23 September 1988 Seoul

If the Olympic Games are still about sportsmanship as much as about sport, then the modern pentathlon and the equestrian three-day event lie at the heart of things. In no other sport is there to be found more graciousness in defeat or modesty in victory.

In the space of six hours on opposite sides of the city, there were scenes of elation, fulfilment and dignity at the climax of the two events. Janos Martinek, of Hungary, in the pentathlon and Mark Todd, of New Zealand, in the three-day event, were individual winners instantly acclaimed by their rivals.

Both sports are threatened in the long term by the cost factor, measured against the relatively small number of participating countries. Yet de Coubertin believed them to be part of the kernel of the Games. As Todd said yesterday: 'Equestrianism belongs to the Games.'

The team winners were Hungary and West Germany respectively. For Britain it was a memorable day, with a bronze, by the merest whisker, in the pentathlon, and a team silver plus individual silver and bronze on horseback.

At the medal ceremony of the pentathlon there was the emotional yet characteristic moment when Joel Bouzou, last year's world champion of France, who had just been beaten for the team bronze by eight points or a mere three seconds in the cross-country, came over to the British team and said simply: 'Well done. You are fine sportsmen.'

The sun burned down strongly on this beautiful Olympic Park, the skyline of the surrounding hills a hazy outline, the throb of the city's traffic a distant hum. A small crowd was gathered around the little groups of exhausted athletes: the Italians extrovertly happy with their silver, the Hungarians quietly embracing each other with relief, the Brits, Richard Phelps, Dominic Mahony and Graham Brookhouse, standing around with the casual cheerfulness you find in the pub on Sunday morning.

For more than three-quarters of an hour they had had to wait for the official result from the judges; though the French pre-empted the announcement with a private calculation that their rivals had won by a fraction. Britain, starting the day fifth after four events and needing to overhaul the Soviet Union and France, had to thank the power of Brookhouse and the courage of Mahony.

Brookhouse ran the ninth fastest cross-country of the day to hold Ruer, the best of the French, to level points. Phelps ran marginally below his best, but was 7½ seconds faster than Bouzou: not enough, however, to get him closer than sixth individual place overall.

Mahony, with an injured knee, was a critical 14 seconds faster than Genard, the third Frenchman, over the hilly 4,000-metre course. Ron Bright, the jovial team manager who has been at eight Olympic Games as competitor or official, gave Mahony the tactical position with a kilometre to go, told him to run like hell if he could, and then himself fell headlong downhill rushing to get back to the finishing line. On a tough course, the Russians had caved in.

Bright, for better or worse, had taken the decision to include the injured Mahony in the team rather than Peter Hart, an outstanding rider and a faster runner. Bright admitted that Mahony's injury, costing him 100 points in the fencing, lost any hope of the team gold midway through the competition. Only the constant attention twice daily of Jenny Brown, one of the British physiotherapists, kept Mahony going for five days.

'I knew I wouldn't be able to go really fast, and I was almost grinding to a halt over the last 1,000 metres' Mahony said afterwards. 'I knew my role was to take 20 seconds out of Genard. Normally I'd mash him.

'Two weeks ago, I didn't even know if I'd be able to compete. I had a fitness test three days before we left home. The doctor thought I had 90 per cent no-chance. Ron took the decision to put me on the plane and to get me fit out here. In the fencing I didn't have mobility on the front foot, and couldn't lunge, and that cost me some wins. In the swimming (two days ago) by the end it was like dragging two elephants along behind me.

Modern pentathlon is, as Bright reflected while we waited for the result, a sport that needs five different psychological attitudes, contrasting forms of concentration. It is so much a philosophical sport, which is what makes the competitors friends as much as rivals. It is hoped that the present British team, sponsored by Minet and Racal, will stay in partnership.

Out at Seoul's new, panoramic equestrian park, there was a lack of atmosphere because the stands were half-empty, and because the Koreans are only just beginning to develop, and their public to understand, an unaccustomed sport. The host country, coached in Britain, did splendidly to finish in seventh place ahead of Italy, Japan and the United States.

Todd and Charisma, his little horse, are a rare pair indeed, and Charisma's victory gallop round the stadium with his rider after the individual medal ceremony was the clearest possible indication, ears pricked and head erect, of a horse's sense of occasion.

INVINCIBLE DECATHLON MAN BOWS OUT

Courage alone not enough for toiling Thompson

30 September 1988 Seoul

Daley Thompson is a wise old owl. Aged 30, he has been 12 years at the top in international decathlon competition, and although hampered here by a previously undisclosed thigh strain received a few days ago, he knew that the opposition was also off form.

So for two days he kept going, gambling that he might steal a medal. His fortitude helped produce a thrilling climax to the event yesterday despite the lowest scoring in an Olympic Games since 1972.

Thompson finished fourth, denied a bronze medal on the last event by a strong 1500 metres from Dave Steen, of Canada. The winner was Christian Schenk, of East Germany, aged 23 and a medical student, with a total of 8,488 points. Schenk had been fifth in last year's world championships. Torsten Voss, also of East Germany, and the winner then, was now second.

'If everyone else had been doing well, I would have dropped out,' Thompson said afterwards, his left thigh strapped like a burst waterpipe. 'I'm really upset. More so than in Rome last year.' In Rome he had finished ninth, also when injured.

The depth of his competitiveness, which has won him eight major championships, was doubly evident yesterday. After the high hurdles and discus he was still lying third overall, his overnight position. Then, on his first attempt at the pole vault, his pole snapped in two places on lift-off – a rare and unpredictable occurrence with a glassfibre pole. It damaged his left hand and inflicted the kind of emotional jolt upon the nerves which might finish a lesser man.

He shook himself like a half-drowned dog, cleared the bar at 4.70 metres at his second attempt, and went on to record 4.90 metres, which was below his best but enough to retain fourth place. Voss had now moved ahead of him, with Plaziat, of France, maintaining second position.

With a personal best in the javelin of 64.04 metres, Thompson heaved himself back to third, though around him other positions were fluctuating. Schenk and Voss were in front, but Plaziat, with a poor throw in his worst event, had fallen to seventh. The danger for Thompson now lay immediately behind.

Tim Bright, an American who cannot make up his mind whether to be a pole vaulter or a decathlete, had climbed higher and higher in the vault until he reached 5.70 metres. He had finished fourth in the Olympic pole vault trials, and his height yesterday would have placed him seventh in the open pole vault the day before.

Also threatening were Pavel Tarnovetski, of the Soviet Union, who was third in Rome, and Steen, now in eighth place and 120 points behind Thompson, but with a strong 1,500 metres potential.

Bright's prolonged vaulting on his own had thrown the schedule awry. The first round of the javelin throwers had concluded while Bright was attempting 5.80 metres. When Thompson and the rest finally got to the line for the last race at 9.20 p.m. the competition's second day had been running 13 hours. A full-scale dress rehearsal of the closing ceremony was being delayed.

The press and television ranks were still packed in hundreds, a testimony primarily to Thompson's reputation; never mind that, in his one blind spot of immaturity, he still treats the Press with ill-mannered discourtesy. He has latterly refused to speak to *The Times*, for instance, because my colleague, Pat Butcher, excluded Thompson – correctly, as it proved – from his medal forecasts.

But now, for all his injuries, he was running with characteristic guts. He slotted in at the back of the field alongside Bright, who needed to beat him by some 10 seconds to take the bronze, and 10 yards astern of Tarnovetski, who had to beat him by more. Way out ahead, Steen was the unknown factor.

On the final lap Thompson somehow managed to accelerate, left Bright and Tarnovetski behind, and had the thirteenth fastest time of 4min 45.11sec. But Steen, two years his junior, had recorded 4:23.20, the fourth-best time, and had taken the bronze behind Schenk and Voss.

Thompson limped away, a dispirited figure. 'I don't want to make excuses, but I have this little injury,' he said, trying to put on a brave face. Two defeats have dented his image of invincibility. There is no knowing how much a wife and child have reduced his competitive thirst, his incentive to train for countless hours each week.

'I'm going to continue – for another two or three years I reckon'. The voice was optimistic, yet seemed not to measure what will be required to come back. Schenk will get better while Thompson's snap in the explosive sprinting and jumping events has declined.

He has reached that point at which, even when fit, courage alone cannot carry him through. He can, however, look back upon a unique career. The recognition of that yesterday came with the handshakes from his rivals before they went their own ways off into the night.

A GOLD MEDAL FOR THE GAMES MASTERS

The unrivalled Oriental courtesy of the Koreans

3 October 1988 Seoul

As I walked away from the closing ceremony of the 1988 Olympic Games, just before the end, a haunting oriental chorale still drifting upwards into the night sky, I was more than ever in love with Korea. Confronted with the largest Games ever, they had been the perfect hosts. The debt which the Olympic movement owes them is immense.

The Koreans have the organisation of the Germans, the courtesy and culture of the Orient and the sense of money of the Americans. They can hardly fail. It is undoubtedly true that the Games always tend to bring out the best in a host nation, but few, if any, have given so much, and on such a scale, as have these remarkable people for the past two weeks: or, should I say, for the past seven years.

The worst had been expected. The International Olympic Committee and its president had been condemned for allowing the Games to go ahead here. Yet what has been achieved by a nation that 30 years ago was a bomb-site, and when it was awarded the Games in 1981 was a pariah to most socialist countries, is phenomenal.

The North Koreans did not terrorise us, the socialists did not boycott, the students threw only a handful of token petrol bombs. The only injuries we have are our telephone bills in a city where it costs almost as much to have a suit cleaned as to have it made. Even the Korean autumn has smiled upon us delightfully, someone pointing out that for the past two weeks it has been raining in Nagoya, the Japanese city to which Seoul was preferred.

The largest Games in history – in size, technology and publicity – have been an exceptional success. There has been a degree of friendship, from the level of foreign diplomacy down to local taxi drivers and shopkeepers, which may come to be seen as a milestone in social and political history. These Games may have had more influence than can yet be estimated.

There was a scandal which vibrated to the farthest corners of sport and throughout the population of Canada but which, in the long term, will, optimistically, prove to be a significant deterrent to others. It was nothing to do with Korea.

Considering some of the logistical problems, mostly accentuated through lack of language communication, the Koreans were more helpful, more accommodating than the hosts of any other Games I have attended. In spite of the intensity of security, I was admitted to the gymnastics hall when I had forgotten my accreditation card and was allowed into the regatta course competition area in a taxi without a private badge, on each occasion with careful scrutiny. I cannot imagine such understanding flexibility having taken place in Montreal, Moscow or Los Angeles.

The Games of Seoul provided competition facilities without parallel, setting a standard that Barcelona, or any other city, will find an immense challenge to equal. The Koreans advanced the public perception of the Games more than anybody since the West Germans in 1972.

The achievement of the South Korean team, finishing in fourth place in the medal table, could have one profound influence upon the future of the Games during the next 12 years. It is unlikely that China, which finished eleventh, would wish to stage the Games of 2000 if it could not expect to be the highest Asian medals winner. Japan, incidentally, finished fourteenth, and was hugely embarrassed by Korea in the judo competition, hitherto an exclusive Japanese domain. When you look around, and 80 per cent of the population seems to be under 35, the nation's potential is unlimited.

The friendship of these Games has overflowed. At the closing ceremony Arabs and Israelis walked round the track with total informality, side by side. Such anti-Americanism as there has been among the Koreans has been largely inspired by the NBC inquisitorial television coverage of boxing, a sore point since the blatant American bias of judging in 1984.

The closing ceremony was as colourful as the opening ceremony, tasteful and elegant. The Koreans have a cultural tradition in music and singing, in theatre and dance, which makes their ceremonial accomplishment no surprise. They welcomed us and bid us goodbye with such warmth that it is sad to be going.

At one stage in the closing ceremony it looked as if the uninhibited disorganisation among thousands of athletes in the arena – the worst offenders being the British – was going to get out of control, yet the Koreans handled the situation with a discretion that few would have managed under the eye of television. With competitors swarming around them, the ceremonial dancers smiled as benignly as ever.

The philosophical conception behind many of the Koreans' actions is such as to make Europeans feel humble. In what some might regard as a frivolous or shallow life spent following sport, this has for me been a fortnight of exceptional courtesy and co-operation: as Juan Antonio Samaranch said in his closing speech, the best and most unified of Games.

SWEDEN'S WILL TO WIN
IN DOUBT

Germany, and Becker, come from behind in Davis Cup

19 December 1988 Gothenburg

Stefan Edberg and Anders Jarryd and their captain, Hans Olsson, came to the interview room on Saturday and you would never have known whether they had won or lost. The fact that the Swedish doubles pair had just surrendered a two sets to love lead, and with it the Davis Cup, seemed to affect the trio no more than had they missed the bus to work. Swedish equanimity, in victory or defeat, is a phenomenon without parallel in the world of sport.

It can be said that acceptance of defeat in this matter offers a lesson, and a philosophy, which every over-stressed, emotional or aggressive competitor should seek to emulate. 'We have the right to lose,' Olsson said with a trace of defiance in the face of critics. 'To be runners-up is satisfactory.' Yet West Germany's victory, which to neutral foreign observers was a Christmas present to outstrip them all, inevitably raises questions about Sweden's will to win, or lack of it, which has been an embarrassment to fellow-countrymen.

This extraordinarily improbable result – a 3–0 winning margin for West Germany after the first two days, having trailed by two sets to love in two of the three matches – has pitched Swedish sport into a debate that will run and run.

Due credit must, of course, be given to West Germany: to the grit of Carl Uwe-Steeb for staying in an opening match with Mats Wilander that was 'impossible' to win, to Boris Becker for executing Edberg in the second singles with a repeat of his Masters-winning form, and to Eric Jelen for helping Becker to turn around an inexplicably forfeited doubles.

It may have been at times bizarre tennis, yet it generated a quite exceptional drama. Even hard-bitten, travel-weary tennis correspondents, whose palms had not been made to sweat in 10 years devoid of expectation, admitted that they were involuntarily drawn into an emotional web of unpredictability.

Undoubtedly the result is good for tennis, not to mention for the West Germans. It reversed the home defeat in Munich three years ago. Less certain is whether, as some claim, the result is good for Swedish tennis, on the grounds that it will shake them out of any complacency arising from almost habitual appearance in the final.

Three fundamental questions must be answered by the Swedes, which leave in their wake any virtue of being good losers. Did Wilander, Edberg and Jarryd lose because they were tired; because they did not care sufficiently; or because Olsson is a captain incapable of motivating his team and, critically, incapable of changing tactics in a losing position?

Undoubtedly Wilander, the world's No. 1 and triple Grand Slam title winner in 1988, is jaded, suffering from shin injuries. The controversy of defeat was given a further bitter twist yesterday when Sweden scratched from the fifth match of the final, on the grounds that Wilander, Kent Carlsson (thigh muscles) and Jarryd (shoulder) were all unfit to meet a German opponent.

The injuries were verified by Professor Bertil Stener, a medical consultant for the federation; and though the crowd booed Olsson, with unsavoury yet understandable frustration when he announced the decision to scratch, a fourth and final singles would have been as irrelevant to the final as Edberg's 6–4, 8–6 victory yesterday over Steeb.

Wilander's defeat, after leading Steeb 10–8, 6–1, can be explained by fatigue, and Edberg's, to a degree, by Becker's brilliance. The debate therefore narrows to whether Olsson was right in the first place to omit Carlsson from either singles position; and whether he should have been more instrumental in advising Edberg and Jarryd when their 6–3, 6–2 lead over Becker and Jelen began to disintegrate.

Edberg is ranked No. 5 in singles and Jarryd No. 1 in doubles in the world. For almost two sets, from 3–3 in the first, they were in a different league to Becker and Jelen on Saturday. For the only time in 12 service games, Edberg had break point against him in the opening game of the match, and he played throughout with a steadiness which might, the previous night, have given Becker more resistance. But with Jelen surrendering his service twice and Becker once, the Swedish pair, within one hour of the start, were on the brink of taking the final to a third day.

Now, however, there was a metamorphosis. Jelen vitally held his serve for 2–1 in the third set, and suddenly it was Jarryd whose nerve had gone. He held his serve for 2–2: just, after three break points. Becker was warned for throwing his racket after squandering the first of them. Jarryd's luck did not last. He could hardly throw up the ball for nerves, and lost his next six consecutive service games. Sweden had given away the match and the Cup by 3–6, 2–6, 7–5, 6–3, 6–2.

Never did Olsson seemingly offer more than avuncular encouragement. The situation cried out for variation: for Edberg to play 'tandem' on Jarryd's service, standing on the same side of court at the net to oblige the receiver to play the more difficult return down the line. Edberg did so on a mere two points.

The Swedes should have lobbed more often, should have done anything to disrupt the pattern. Instead, Jelen improved with every game, and Becker, whose mind seemed previously to have advanced already to Day 3, suddenly got the scent of victory and tigerishly went in pursuit of it.

Asked whether the Swedish temperament, personified by Borg and so often an advantage, was not sometimes a disadvantage, Edberg said: 'We have our own style, our own temperament. We played the way we always play. We can't change.'

Swedish newspapers have raised the question of whether Carl-Axel Hageskog, Jarryd's personal coach, should replace Olsson as captain. Hageskog was the Olympic team manager in Seoul, where Edberg and Jarryd won only a doubles bronze, as did Edberg in singles. It is doubtful whether Hageskog would alter national character. The Swedes either win because they are better. Or they lose. Besides, Olsson is valued by the players precisely because of his equanimity.

NEITHER NOBLE NOR UNLUCKY

Amiable Bruno outclassed by Tyson

27 February 1989 Las Vegas

I'm sorry, in a sense, for Frank Bruno. There is much more reason this morning, however, to be sorry for Mike Tyson, which may sound an odd thing to say about the man who has just emphatically re-established himself as undisputed world heavyweight champion. More than ever, though, I am sorry for boxing.

The best bout at the Las Vegas Hilton on Saturday evening was the WBC super-flyweight title contest between Azumah Nelson, of Ghana, and Mario Martinez, of Mexico, a minor classic in which Martinez, narrowly beaten by the champion a year ago, gave another courageous and skilful challenge before the fluctuating bout was stopped in favour of Nelson in the twelfth. The audience, gorged on the commercial hype and gambling on the imminent main event, hardly noticed these splendid contestants.

Do not be seduced into any feeling that Bruno was noble or unlucky. As a boxer, he is not worthy to be mentioned in the same breath as Tommy Farr or Henry Cooper. What he managed to achieve, as a no-hoper, was a dignified and brave exit that lasted, improbably, for five rounds in the course of a financial sting, following which he should retire richer and wiser.

Because Bruno was a European contender around whom tickets and television could be sold in a muddled heavyweight field, the commercial circus granted him a shot at the title. If Tyson had been an inch or so more accurate with the second right hander which put Bruno down in the first 18 seconds of the contest, it would probably have been all over within the first minute.

As it was, the combination of Tyson's slight rustiness after eight months out of the ring and Bruno's ability illegally to lock his left arm round Tyson's head and hang on for much of four rounds, extended an encounter which had only one possible outcome from the first bell.

Terry Lawless's main contribution was to have one hand permanently at the ready to fling in the towel the moment the rain of Tyson's fists became no longer acceptable.

Fortunately the referee, in the pulverising fifth round, acted even more swiftly than Lawless, and if the record will show that Bruno finished on his feet, that was only because the referee was holding him up against the ropes after Tyson had all but knocked his head off.

To Bruno's credit, he absorbed more punches than had been supposed possible; thanks in part to the referee's long-winded warning for an illegal punch on the back of Tyson's neck in the first round which gave Bruno another invaluable 12-second breather.

The background of the year-long on-off saga of this match is that Bruno and his handlers have made a killing from the mismatch – Jarvis Astaire and Mickey Duff looked uncommonly anxious during the moments beforehand – and Tyson has landed himself in the hands of one of the most objectionable men in the clouded history of this sport.

Watching Don King cavorting around Tyson this past week, manipulating Press conferences, gratuitously insulting people and patronising his new charge, has been to witness a formidable heavyweight champion becoming ensnared in surroundings which may ultimately prove more threatening to his stability as a man than those from which he has recently freed himself.

The failing marriage to Robin Givens may have been doomed from the start; but Tyson's additional abandonment of almost all the contacts with the Cus D'Amato stable, which had rescued him from being a hoodlum and made him into a champion, seem almost equally ill-advised.

King, his son Carl, and the multitude of handlers assembled around the champion under the presumptuous title 'Team Tyson' will consume a colossal slice of the champion's earnings; while the loss of his long-term trainer, Kevin Rooney, and his former manager, Bill Cayton, with whom a contract dispute continues, will diminish the forces of responsibility that served to keep an impulsive, emotional and aggressive boxer on the rails at least some of the time.

I fear that Tyson, who is almost unchallengable in the ring, yet clearly from Saturday's evidence against even a moderate opponent needs tactical advice, may not be able to marshall the enormous pressures which bear down on someone as famous, rich, and vulnerable as he is.

His immature vulgarity, in pretending to expose himself insultingly to Bruno on stage in public at the weigh-in, is just one small illustration of his instability. His lewdness in public is already regrettably well-documented.

When Tyson says, at his victory Press conference, that 'challengers with primitive skills are as good as dead', we wonder how many of those words may ultimately turn to become true of him.

For the moment, his consuming power, the quickness of his hands, the variety of his hooks and the stunning ferocity of his uppercuts were an arsenal which overwhelmed Bruno; who never had any objective beyond survival without serious injury in order that he may enjoy his rewards.

The injuries that may yet befall Tyson, outside the ring, are far more alarming in potential. Last week he told Johnny Tocco, father-confessor to so many fighters at his downtown gymnasium, that he had no friends he could trust. We have too often seen the mortality of heroes without friends.

The fate of heroes without respect for their public is even more in doubt. Tyson was reminded last week of the words of Jack Dempsey. 'A champion owes everybody something. He can never pay back for all the help he got for making him an idol.'

'INNOCENTS LYING CRUSHED ON THE GRASS'

The horror of the Hillsborough disaster

17 April 1989

With disbelieving eyes, we sat in the grandstand and watched almost 100 people die in front of us at an FA Cup semi-final.

For a whole hour or more, from the time the match was halted after six minutes by a policeman running on to the pitch to instruct the referee to remove the players, we were captive witnesses, and partly accomplices, to a tragedy that is a consequence of collective incompetence in the organisation of a sporting event.

Even as the game kicked off, circumstances were accelerating during a period of only a few minutes towards inescapable disaster, as a bedlam of people funnelled into a tunnel feeding the terrace behind the Liverpool goal: a tunnel from which there was no retreat backwards, and no safety valve at the front end. These were not hooligans, nor were they, as at Heysel, the victims of mindless rivalry. They died, innocent white figures prostrate on the green grass from whom the breath of life had been crushed, because of the fences built to restrain the mounting hooliganism of the past 25 years.

This was not like Heysel, where we watched incandescent Liverpool spectators charge at Italians, and drive them into a corner where a wall collapsed. The Heysel disaster arrived after a long and avoidable overture of threats on the terraces, and in its awfulness was quite quickly over.

The Hillsborough slaughter had a sudden, swift arrival; and then a drawn-out macabre climax that was initially unapparent to Nottingham Forest supporters at the opposite end. They began by booing what they supposed was Liverpool hooliganism, and was in fact mortal agony.

We watched them die because the south Yorkshire police, with tragically misguided good intention, opened the gates at the northern, Leppings Lane, end of Hillsborough stadium, thereby sending a torrent of spectators into an already dangerously overcrowded central terrace behind the goal.

We watched them die because police, in scheduling their control of an identical fixture to last year, were more concerned with traffic flow outside the ground before and afterwards – to have Forest at the larger southern Kop end near to the M1 – than with accommodation inside the ground.

Down at the front of the terrace, young people were crushed against barriers with a force exceeding half a tonne, yet for five or 10 minutes it looked no more, from 50 yards away, than another crowd becoming restive as the match began. Steel fences buckled as they died.

Down on the pitch, as I moved among the carnage after the game had been halted, I saw mature policemen, sweat-stained in shirt sleeves from their efforts to relieve the victims and to bring back to life the lifeless, crying unashamedly at the hopelessness of a disaster that had overwhelmed them.

We watched them die on this black Saturday because the ambulances which arrived were too few and already too late; because the firemen and police could not reach the majority of the victims being trampled on underfoot, on account of the high, so-called safety fence separating them from the pitch; and because Hillsborough, a modernised but still old-fashioned ground, had little if any of the necessary life-saving equipment.

One of the police, who had been vainly pumping on motionless chests and attempting the kiss of life, said despairingly: 'I had two of them just go on me as I tried. One of them seemed to start breathing again, but there was no oxygen available.'

Those who did not die, and were not either weeping at the loss of friends or limp with shock and pain, were angry. A group of them surrounded me, supposing me to be an official, and eventually had to be restrained by a policewoman as they made hysterical accusations to me against the FA and Sheffield Wednesday authorities for the disproportionate ticket allocation, and the police for opening the gates.

'They only care about the money,' a Liverpool spectator screamed at me, a man aged about 30 and tidily dressed but trembling with fear and frustration. 'They waved us through the gate, and there was already no bloody room in there. The police on the other side of the fence [by the pitch] were yelling at us to move back, but that was impossible. We were out of control. We are human. We've behaved ourselves ever since Heysel, but they go on treating us like animals.' Spectators in the three unaffected granstands sat through the drama as though watching some horror movie. Bobby Robson, the England team manager, twisted and turned in his director's-box seat in evident torment.

Yet anyone who saw the scenes immedand before the start of the match, outside at the Leppings Lane end, know that the police, including several on horseback, were rapidly losing control of a hoard of spectators aggressively pressing towards the turnstiles, with and without tickets.

No one wanted to take responsibility on this terrible day. Inquiries will be painfully revealing. Mr Peter Wright, the Chief Constable of South Yorkshire, was almost incoherent at the press conference after the full impact of the horror had become apparent. There was no evidence of any connection, he insisted, between the opening of the gates at the back and the pulverising of bodies at the front. It was a truth he simply could not bring himself to acknowledge.

Dr John Williams, a London University lecturer who has specialised in a study of crowd behaviour, had seen the near-impossible congestion in the street leading to B turnstile. Why, he asks, had the police not done more to reduce this surge?

As police and firemen and ground stewards still struggled to free the trapped and the dying from the terraces, some 15 minutes after the game had halted, I climbed to the steps of the police viewing turret.

From this position it must have been apparent, shortly before the start of the match, that congestion was already intolerable immediately behind the Liverpool goal. Why was there not closer radio co-ordination between police inside and those who took the decision to open the gates, so releasing a fresh river into a flooded arena?

The Chief Constable says there was danger to life in the mounting pressure that was building up outside. If the police could not control the crowd in the open, had they the right to believe the crisis would be solved by pouring people indiscriminantly into the stadium? No one can judge with hindsight what was the correct course in the minutes before disaster became unavoidable.

Those trying to cope, desperate and powerless police sergeants, waitresses from the stadium restaurant with pathetic jugs of fresh water moving tearfully from casualty to casualty, firemen who had never seen corpses on such a scale, were also suffering a day they will never forget.

SYSTEMATICALLY BREAKING THE MOULD

The emergence of Monica Seles in Paris

2 June 1989 Paris

The usual noise of tennis ball on racket strings is like the subtle plop of a pebble in water. When Monical Seles winds up her slim seven-stone frame for a two-handed drive, the impact can occasionally sound as though she were irately beating a carpet. The opponent is reduced to no more than a static spectator.

Seles, a Yugoslav who will not be 16 until December, was born in Novi Sad. She has an oval, porcelain-like face with pale, un-Serbian eyes and a cascade of hazel-coloured hair. You would suppose she more probably came from Hungary. In play, her expression is mostly furrowed concentration; off-court, charmingly without affectation, she cannot stop smiling.

She possesses a rare theatrical presence on court, playing spontaneously her own game, attuned to the crowd's response. 'I'm not mentally locked into the tennis, I'm conscious of the crowd, and they help me relax,' she said disarminlgy. 'It pleases me when the public are happy.' Such equanimity may take her far.

The tennis world waits with expectation to see whether this star in the making will develop into another Moffitt, Evert or Austin. Were Seles to maintain her development, Steffi Graf would not then rule the women's game uncontested for the unforeseeable future.

Tracy Austin, with that metronomic baseline game, was the youngest to appear at Wimbledon, aged 14½, in 1977. Chris Evert, another with computer judgement, played her first grand slam tournament at 16. Billie

Jean Moffitt was 17 when I first marvelled at her masculine low volleying at Beckenham, prior to her first Wimbledon, at which she won the doubles with Karen Hantze. What is the armoury of Seles, schooled for the past three years by Nick Bollettieri at Bradenton, Florida, and taking to her first grand slam event here like a duck to water?

She has raced through two rounds with almost embarrassing ease against two Americans, Ronni Reis and, yesterday, Stacey Martin, with a flow of ground strokes, struck tenaciously with an unconventional two-handed grip down both flanks, that are the product of perfect timing; taking the ball impressively early in the bounce. 'When she was still a small girl, she always had big shots,' her father, Karoly, said.

He attended a sports college, was a triple jump champion, and not only understands his daughter's innate talent for her sport, but clearly has a benign, affectionate relationship with her. Before moving from Yugoslavia specifically to join Bollettieri – who has coached Arias, Gottfried and, latterly, Agassi – Seles was wholly guided by her father, who is a cartoonist, and a man of sensitivity.

He studied her physiology as much as her technique, and utilised slow-motion analysis. He is particularly pleased that Bollettieri is not forcing his daughter, but taking a similarly patient line. In the past 18 months Seles has grown more than three inches, to nearly 5ft 8in, with the attendant risk that excessive competition could precipitate the same back problems that ended Austin's career. That is why her tournaments for the past two seasons have been strictly limited, with her bone formation being carefully monitored.

What makes her potential so exciting, quite apart from a recent victory over the declining Evert, is that she wants to develop during the next two seasons more of an all-court game, improving her volleying capability. She has a two-footed jump on service.

'Not that my service is weak, but I become nervous now and then [with it] in competition,' she says, with an unself-conscious giggle that is itself perhaps a sign of shyness in the public eye, and so in contrast with the assurance with which she terminates a rally.

'I'm still not playing in matches as I do in practice,' she said. In adjusting to the player's exposed existence, she shows a mixture of self-effacing politeness and bubbling confidence. 'My ambition is to have a serve-and-volley game,' she said; and in the background Karoly quietly added 'maybe next year.'

While wisely restraining the acceleration of her progress up to now, Seles's father encourages her to go out and hit the ball, to be uninhibited; to the extent that when practising with her 24-year-old brother, Zoltan, who is on a business-study course in Florida, she keeps breaking her rackets.

Her first grand slam event, she said, had not been more physically demanding; if anything easier. 'I feel fresher than last year,' she said. 'When I was so low [shorter] I had more of the court to cover. Maybe I'll feel it physically if I stay into the second week here.' If you're going to be a professional, she implied, you've got to get used to it. There is not the impression that she will be homesick when playing full time around the world and crying on the telephone to home. She admitted, however, that it was helpful at present to have her parents travelling with her.

Already it is Seles, and not her father, who decides, she said emphatically, which tournaments she will play. Karoly, though, is able to discuss with her the complexities and pressures of a ball game, the imponderables of outwitting an opponent, so different from his own relatively straightforward athletic sport.

Seles is alert to the dangers of the mental exclusivity of tennis. Her hobby in Novi Sad, 'where six months of the year you couldn't hit a ball,' was ice skating. 'I don't want to be a tennis robot,' she insisted. 'People say these years are the nicest of your life and to take care of them. There will be more and more worries later.'

More and more acclaim, too, if she continues as at present. And long may she remain as unassumingly good natured, a Slav–American version of the delightful Goolagong.

She has yet to experience the novelty of grass, but thinks all other surfaces are much the same. It is more than two years since she played on red clay – a young woman who takes things in her stride.

THE BEAUTY ON THE BASELINE GIVES HER FINAL FLOURISH

Christ Evert: feminine yet tough

5 September 1989 New York

Of the multitude of statistics that punctuate the 20-year career of Chris Evert – the Virginia Slims handbook selects a mere 21 of the dozens at hand – the most unusual is the one not mentioned: that she has been, simultaneously, one of the toughest and one of the most sporting competitors in the history of the game. And additionally, among women, one of the most feminine.

It is all the more remarkable because she has not been, like Margaret

Court and Virginia Wade or the more masculine Martina Navratilova, a muscular athlete. Less than fast about the court, she was precluded by nature from being a serve and volley exponent and instead has dominated the game all these years from the baseline, yet without ever being boring. Her metronomic accuracy has had its own beauty.

To that technical beauty has been added the graciousness of someone who never forgot that she was playing a game of chance as well as skill. When she came on court here on Sunday, serene in crushed strawberry pink skirt with a ribbon in her hair, it was difficult to remember that this was the women who seven times won the French title, six times the American, six times was in three grand slam finals in the same year, won at least one grand slam event in 13 consecutive years and leads all professionals with 157 individual titles.

She has cited in the past, as her three most significant matches, the 1970 victory over Court when she was still 15, the 1976 win at Wimbledon over Goolagong, and the 1985 French triumph over Navratilova. It might be said that the 1989 straight sets victory over Monica Seles on Sunday was, for sheer mental tenacity at the age of almost 35, the equal of anything.

Seles, the Yugoslav, aged 15, who belts the ball cross court two-handed from both flanks as though she were beating a carpet, may still have far to go but she presented inescapably a trial of emotional strength for the woman making her grand slam swansong. Many expected, after her victory over Evert at Houston, a Seles triumph; never mind that it was her first appearance in the Flushing Meadow concrete fishbowl, where the New York public comes to watch occasional tennis in between eating, outside, truckloads of junk food and buying designer sportswear.

Seles, trivially dismissed by some as nothing more than a hard hitter of the Bollettieri school with no tactical sense, is no more than a growing schoolgirl who, nevertheless, within four years will probably be challenging Graf. Evert herself half expected to lose, given her form up until a couple of days before.

'It was a huge match for me,' she said with that elegant, restrained manner that characterises her objective self-analysis. 'Usually, when I'm dreading a match, I'm a nervous wreck, but now I felt really calm. It took some of the pressure off because I was expected to lose. I played really well, the whole match, though I don't know where it came from. When I found myself leading 4–0, I began to be excited, and had to tell myself "don't".'

The following game was the key to Seles being crushed: on her own service, Evert had six consecutive break points against her, but held on to take the game with an authoritative forehand pass. Seles, still going for the revolver cross shots or unsportingly moon-balling defensive drives 10 feet over the net, was done for.

Interviewed a year or two ago by David Hemery for a book on sporting excellence, Evert said the four aspects of her career which most pleased her, were longevity of performance, consistency, a sporting attitude, and helping to promote the women's professional game.

Those who admire her, including younger players – who, some say, have been too impressed with that double-handed backhand – would do well to recognise that the foundation of those first two achievements was a toughness and single-mindedness which, as in all such sports men and women, is necessarily self-centred. At close quarters, it is not always endearing. Ice-maiden has been an apt epithet; even if, in between the tennis and a self-acknowledged moodiness, Evert has also been emotionally open and romantically inclined.

Her appearance in 32 grand slam finals is reflective, of course, as is the career of Navratilova, of the lack of depth in the women's game compared with the men's. While her duration in the top three in the world for 14 years, and prize money approaching $9 million (approximately £5.3 million), is testimony to her own exceptional qualities, it reveals that an outstanding woman has career and earning prospects that are disproportional to men of comparable ability. Graf is already confirming this, and Sánchez Vicario and Seles will probably do the same. Evert has been brilliant, attractive, personally dedicated, professionally responsible towards colleagues . . . and lucky. It is nice that perhaps the worst thing you can say about her is that her favourite film is *Sound of Music* and that she has seen it 15 times.

WHEN HISTORY FILLS THE ARENA

Constructing a city of peace in Hiroshima

2 November 1989 Hiroshima

There is little point in expecting sportsmen to carry the guilt, from other spheres, of their fathers. The majority of sportsmen, I have found, are without any deep sense of history, let alone a wider awareness of morality or shame. If sport does reflect life, too often it shows that life is without collective conscience.

Genocide, in any continent, does not make popular reading; it was different in Hiroshima yesterday.

When sport makes a conscious recognition of emotional, historic issues beyond its own self-interest – such as with Hillsborough and Heysel – it is unusual. The second largest and most popular sport on earth – volleyball – paid tribute to the estimated quarter of a million people who perished here in a city that then rose, all too literally, from the dead and, for another 10 years, from the dying.

The peace ceremony in Memorial Park, by those taking part in the seventh volleyball World Cup, was simple, unostentatious and chillingly unforgettable. At the conference centre next to the museum of the first atomic explosion of war, we had watched a film that records the immediate aftermath of that moment at breakfast time on August 6, 1945, when, in the middle of the rush-hour, life ended.

Young volleyball players who are barely old enough to remember Vietnam, never mind the instant here that changed history, sat in darkened silence as the sepia images flitted across the screen. The picture at first seemed like photographic stills until, occasionally, an arm or face, mutilated beyond recognition, would move or turn.

Afterwards, while a chorus of schoolchildren sang, we went outside and walked slowly to the cenotaph where the known names of some 150,000 lie recorded; Rubén Acosta, the international president of volleyball, and Yasutaka Matsudaira, of the Japanese federation, laid wreaths.

Around us in the park, carefree children threw grain to the pigeons, mothers rested in the sunshine, the distant traffic hummed and the Ohta River sidled down to the port. Acosta presented to Takeshi Araki, aged 71, the mayor of Hiroshima, a cheque towards the maintenance of the memorial dome. This is a former industrial exhibition hall that lay immediately below the epicentre, at 600 feet, of the 5,000°C ball of fire that fused bone with brick, and the blast from which, at 35 tons per square metre, reduced the dome to a pile of granite, leaving it lying like the ruins of Ephesus, tombstones of science among the grass. A hydrogen bomb would be 200 times worse.

At the instant of explosion, Akari, who studied law at Tokyo University, was personnel manager at the Mitsubishi industrial plant four kilometres from the centre, just beyond the radius of total destruction. He knew nothing of atomic fusion and believed an ordinary bomb had somehow ignited the atmospheric oxygen.

Himself a former volleyball player, he made it his life's work thereafter to construct a city of peace in which life might be preserved among nature's other gifts. He is one of those who contrived to bring the Asian Games to Hiroshima in 1994, a kind of proof of the spirit of the people. 'We want it to be a festival conducted in such a way that all the citizens can participate,' he said yesterday.

The ceremony left the competitors, indeed everyone present, almost without words. Bob Ctvrtlik, the captain of the United States's volleyball team and a Seoul gold medal winner, made a short speech on behalf of all the eight final nations; you could not say he spoke in penitence on behalf of another generation of Americans, for his own father defected from Czechoslovakia in 1947.

Besides, where does youth apportion the blame for the evils of those who came before them? By an irony, I had just been reading, during tedious flights, the 'sort of' autobiography of E. W. Swanton, *Sort of A Cricket Person*. Captured at the fall of Singapore, Swanton was a PoW working for several years on the Burma-Siam railway. The innocent who perished in Hiroshima involuntarily saved the lives of thousands more who would otherwise have died on the railway and in a continuing Pacific war.

'It was a moving and sad ceremony,' Ctvrtlik said afterwards, trying to relate, as were we all, his own existence to what he had just seen. 'We're just volleyball players, and all we can do is compete with all our heart and then shake hands and leave the game on the court.' Would that all games players were as mature.

I sat during the ceremony with Dr Horst Baacke, from East Berlin, president of the volleyball coaches' commission, who was taken prisoner on the Russian eastern front. He, too, could hardly speak afterwards.

'People mostly die slowly in war, not instantly, as in films,' he said. 'No war film was ever accurate. You cannot film the smell of war, burying your colleagues in a wood weeks after they died.'

A World Cup is not a time for morbidity. Yet every competitor who came to Hiroshima will be the wiser and better for the experience. I remember too well the day of the Israeli massacre in Munich, when the prevalent opinion among competitors, while the hours ticked by and the hostages' fate hung in the balance, was one of insularity: don't ask my view, I'm in tomorrow's semi-finals.

'We must hope mankind can learn the lesson that sport has much to offer in harmony between races and religions and even people you maybe don't much like,' Ctvrtlik said. Not all sports, sadly offer that lesson.

Rubén Acosta, at least, tried to bridge the gap.

ECCENTRIC, UNPREDICTABLE AND AUTOCRATIC

How Balestre drives the Grand Prix circus

28 February 1990 Paris

On a wall of Jean-Marie Balestre's stylish office, overlooking the Place de la Concorde, there is a huge mural portraying the ritual hunting of the Indian tiger, a moment before the kill. It is symbolic of the man behind the desk: emotionally obsessed with a desire for control, to assert personal authority over one of the most exotic, glamorous and dangerous of sports.

Balestre is simultaneously president of the French motor racing federation, of FISA, the international racing organisation, and of FIA, the overall governing body of international motoring. He exercises an almost unimpeded, autocratic control over the fourth richest sporting circus, behind only the Olympic Games, the World Cup of football, and international athletics (on account of its multiplicity of events). Yet Balestre, a confusion of passion, rationality and dictatorship, is hovering on the edge of crisis; not least within his own character.

He rules over a sport which is the publicity tool of an immense industrial empire. The president of Toyota recently claimed that, though second to General Motors in global production, Toyota could buy out GM in 48 hours if it wished. The commercial undercurrents are inestimable. In 12 years Balestre has built FISA's membership from 18 to 70. FIA, with 92 national associations, has allegedly 200 million affiliated members.

I came here to see Balestre aware of his Gallic eccentricity, his unpredictable nature; but unprepared for an hysterical outburst during the interview, in which he abusively chastised his Press attaché for more than a minute for discreetly passing him across the desk a sheet of information in the middle of an impassioned monologue, after which he buried his head in his hands in silence. Has he pushed himself, and his luck, too far?

Has he launched himself head-on into too many challenges to be able to maintain tolerance within the sport: against Mansell in Portugal last year, against Senna and McLaren in Tokyo and Adelaide, against

Monaco, Le Mans, the Paul Ricard circuit, the 1990 rally world championship, the appeals system itself?

In sport we have become used to monologues from the all-powerful leaders, though Samaranch and Havelange exercise a subtlety and discretion, a delegation of responsibility, that insulates them from some accusations of wielding excessive influence. Nebiolo, with his many athletic hats, has claimed that he cannot be held responsible for the actions of subordinates. Balestre, compulsive extrovert, acclaims all his responsibilities.

'I am a communications person,' he says, 'but unfortunately I'm not good when acting for myself. Sometimes a bit sharp. I have a lot of problems . . .' Indeed he has.

He came from journalism, in which, starting in 1938, he increased a fortnightly French motoring magazine's readership from 600 to 35,000, part of the foundation of a publishing conglomerate that now includes *Le Figaro*, *France Soir*, 50 radio stations and the French television Channel V. Making a name in karting, leaping from the French racing federation to be president of the Commission Sportive International, which he renamed FISA, and thence to the presidency of FIA, his career has been by turns charismatic and confrontational.

Balestre believes that it is his mission 'to maintain the credibility of sporting authority', yet his actions have strained that credibility to the limit. He fought, and won, the battle of the Seventies for authority against FOCA, the constructors' organisation; because, as he rightly says, 'Constructors are businessmen, not poets; it is not Bernie Ecclestone [the president of FOCA] who runs the show.' His own extrovert leadership, Balestre claims, is necessary for establishing sporting precedent over commercialism. It was necessary, he says, in a sport generating billions of investment, to override the old, amateurish European clique, to establish a global concept, to achieve professional administration: in safety, in stewardship, in commercial contracts. He, and Ecclestone, did that.

Yet the philosophy is frayed, the authority has become self-indulgent, involved in demands for apologies centred on personality. Mansell may have climbed down, for not seeing the black disqualification flag. Senna may have done the same, in the on-going row over his disqualification; though not, someone within Marlboro says, because of any pressure by them or Honda to persuade McLaren to lean on him.

The future is unsure, even if the Suzuka issue is not alone enough to unseat Balestre. Other factors collectively may be.

He denied to me emphatically that there was the risk of a breakaway by disillusioned Formula One teams, disturbed by random, arbitrary fines for pit-lane irregularities, for retrospective accusations of improper driving. Yet there is widespread alarm that on March 14, three days after this season's opening Formula One race at Phoenix, a plenary meeting of FIA has been called with the sole item on the agenda being an alteration of statutes to make race stewards' decisions final and not subject to appeal.

Motor racing, especially with the refined regulations regarding fuel and design, can never be similar to those sports, such as boxing, football and cricket, dependent on instant, final adjudication imperative to their traditional character. In every sport where there is no access to the 'pitch', such as horse racing, sailing and running, there must always be recourse where thought justifiable to a jury of appeal.

I suspect that Balestre seriously underestimates the prevailing mood. 'Everyone has a voice,' he says. 'We are all friends. I have been given executive responsibility, and if results are positive, I should be congratulated. If negative, I should be given the sack.' In the manner of Havelange and Nebiolo, he has accumulated an executive board of loyal supporters.

But the pressures are mounting. For all the present subjugation of Mansell, Senna and others, no one is happy with the adjustment of the rule book, almost without notice, that forbids complaint. No one doubts that the Le Mans dispute with the Automobile Club de L'Ouest is less about modifying a dangerous 430kph Mulsanne Straight than about proprietary interest.

A questioning eye is cast upon the switch of the French Grand Prix from Paul Ricard to Magny-Cours for three years without sufficient obvious reason; and upon the sudden, arbitrary readmission of Peugeot's Group B cars, previously excluded, to the 1990 rally world championship.

It so happens that Peugeot, co-ordinating with Dassault, the aircraft manufacturer, Michelin and Esso, has increased its staff by a third this year in a £10-million bid for the sports car championship.

The latest and most unnerving development for Balestre is the renewed accusation, highlighted by Pierre van Rossem, the Belgian financier, when last week relinquishing his control of the Onyx Formula One team, that Balestre was associated with the SS movement in the deportation of French colleagues. Balestre has always maintained this was a double agent front.

He may, of course, be able to allay that charge with another burst of emotional energy. He is a master of detail. His success in motor racing, he boasts, has been in management, 'in my dossiers, files and marketing, in dealing with realities, not dreams.'

Marketing himself may become more difficult than selling a sport which has 1.7 billion viewers every time Formula One drivers put their lives on the line, though even that commercial gold mine is in question. The contract with the European Broadcasting Union expires in December. Ecclestone is at odds with those nations not showing the races live. Luca di Montezemolo, executive chief of the Italian World Cup football organising committee and a member of the Ferrari board as well as a relation of the Fiat chief, Agnelli, is advising Ecclestone to cool it.

On reflection, you can understand why Balestre, who in many ways has done so much to elevate motor racing, may now sometimes want to hide his head in his hands.

A GALLANT LOSER
MAKES IT COME RIGHT

What rowing owes to the Boat Race

2 April 1990

There are losers: and heroic losers. In future histories of rowing's oldest event, the 1990 Boat Race will be remembered for the way Adam Wright, a comparatively novice stroke from Beccles in Suffolk, relentlessly drove Cambridge at Oxford's stern over the last three miles for the respective fourth and fifth fastest times ever rowed.

As Wright stood in stockinged feet on the shingle in front of the Mortlake boat house, still mentally numb from the Herculean effort, old men in light blue scarves came up and touched him on the shoulder in gratitude as much as in congratulation. Although he had been captain of boats at King Edward VI, Norwich, Wright had played rugby for his first two terms at Corpus Christi: a strong, natural athlete with a hidden talent for leadership. Mark Lees, Cambridge's coach, positioned him at stroke – his first time there – because he sensed this potential.

'It was one of the most courageous things I have ever seen,' Lees said afterwards. 'It was to do with mental strength, guts, and the influence of our sports psychologist, Brian Miller. We shouldn't have been in the race. Yet we never dropped below 36. They meant to win – and they rowed as though it were a 2,000 metres course, not four miles.'

So much for rank outsiders. Oxford were stretched to an extent never expected; and Beefeater, the sponsors, and BBC television are to be congratulated for ensuring the continuation of a race that, perversely for some in rowing, transcends the ordinary boundaries of sport. The Boat Race is unique because it gives us a close-up view of intense endeavour that is a part of the core of man's nature. Oxbridge admissions' tutors can ill afford to spurn this element of character.

The combination of a blissful spring afternoon and pre-race publicity produced crowds along the Tideway not seen in years and possibly on a par with the FA Cup Final. Searle, Oxford's president and No. 7 and one of Britain's youngest international medal winners, afterwards justified the hyperbole that surrounds these two national events on the grounds that the 18 competitors stepping into the boats at Putney are maybe even more dedicated than those who will run out at Wembley on May 12. And are amateur.

Here was a day when the mystique of the Boat Race will have touched the sensitivity of even the least knowledgeable sports followers. The small had frightened the mighty. Cambridge's performance, when outgunned by two stone per man and by every measurable yardstick of experience, bordered on the exceptional.

When they led at the start, against Oxford's advantage of the Middlesex bend, we momentarily believed the race might be about to join the succession of this year's sporting sensations in boxing, cricket and national hunt racing.

It was not to be. By the mile post, Oxford's immense crew were settled into a rhythm that carried all the inevitability of the chiming of Big Ben; and by Harrods, a length and a half up, they had usurped Cambridge's Surrey stream.

Yet now Wright and his men did the seemingly impossible. To Hammersmith Bridge they held their opponents, dropped only four seconds to Barnes Bridge, and were coming back at them at the finish. Let no one suggest that British rowing owes nothing to this race. Searle, whose ambitions extend to Barcelona in 1992, understandably said afterwards that he would rather win the Olympic Games. But as he sank his head onto his oar close to collapse at the finish, he and his crew knew they had just rowed a race that owed as much to the losers as to the winners.

They graciously recognised this, and after Lord Jenkins had presented the trophy, they were sincere hands that stretched out in friendly gesture towards the defeated eight. Beefeater have set a sympathetic style of sponsorship that others in this field should seek to emulate: though better provision should be made for photographers at the prize-giving, and the crews, in that pageantry before the start, should play their role properly in the wearing of their formal gear.

This was a great day for rowing, marred only by the sudden serious illness on the BBC Radio launch of the familiar Peter Jones, who died later that day.

MASTERS NICKED IN PLAY-OFF

Floyd inconsolable as Faldo retains title

10 April 1990 Augusta

'Well, that's it,' the man from the *Sunday Correspondent* said, turning his attention away from Nick Faldo in the direction of the likely winner, Ray Floyd.

There was an air of finality in this comment as Faldo gently clipped his ball out of the bunker at the back of the dreaded short 12th and saw it roll downhill 12 feet past the hole. The opinion in question was not one to be ignored, for the man is by way of being a known smart observer on such matters of probability. Moreover, at about the same time Floyd and Faldo were, as they would reveal later, arriving at much the same estimation themselves on the state of the Masters tournament.

When Jack Nicklaus, who has been regularly winning the event since many of those present, including Faldo, with whom he was playing, were boys, holed a 15ft putt on the same horrible 12th for a birdie two, the retreat of Faldo's chances was even more emphasised. And we were so busy watching Floyd, 100 yards away on the 11th, lip the hole with his first putt for a near 11-under par, that we nearly failed to notice Faldo's putt steal back up the 12th green slope for a priceless par three.

No single stroke can be said to win a tournament; but if any stroke enabled Faldo to retain his title, that was it. But for that, he would have been five strokes instead of four behind, with six holes to play, when minutes later Floyd emulated Nicklaus by scoring a birdie at the 12th.

Later, Floyd, almost inconsolable after what he called the most devastating moment in his career – the water-bound short iron to the second sudden-death hole, the 11th – would say: 'I didn't think I could lose [after the 12th]'. Faldo, reflecting on the four-stroke deficit at this stage, said: 'I knew I just somehow had to stick in there, that I was the last one who might now catch him.'

Stick he did. With the snowballing crowd's tremendous cheers, as they gathered behind the last four players, ringing in his ears as loudly for Nicklaus's birdie at the next hole as for the scoreboard news of Floyd's birdie one hole back, Faldo gave them cause for thought with the first of three birdies in four holes.

It is difficult to say what makes a great golfer because there are more complexities in golf than in almost any other sport. Cricket and football need balance, timing, eye and, sometimes, physical courage. A golfer has to manage five different categories of club, one of them, the putter, utterly different from the other four, playing stationary shots painstakingly calculated, with a billion people watching and waiting to say he is an idiot.

Faldo's enormous, and seemingly unshakable, strength, apart from excellent technique, including an agonisingly restyled swing, is that he appears to be able to play without noticing the other billion.

When he dropped two strokes at the opening hole – 'Got rid of all my bad shots at one go: bunkered drive, approach 40 yards short, weak chip, bad putt' – the chauvinistic crowd almost ignored the Englishman's presence for the next four or five holes; never mind that he was the holder and, with Nicklaus, had a birdie at the second, thanks to a fine short pitch to the front of the green.

He nearly scored a birdie at the third, with an approach to within 2½ft, his first putt running round the rim and out. He and Nicklaus were now level at six under, the crowd exuberantly over-reacting with raucous yells of 'Jack's having a real burn', and such like. Jack, however, took three putts at the long 5th to go five under, missed from six feet at the short 6th to go four under, but was still obliged to give the almost royal acknowledgement, half-raised hand, half a smile, as the pair approached each green to huge applause. For him.

Faldo stared ahead, focus narrow, unhearing, like O'Toole riding through the desert.

At the beautiful horticultural conjunction of the 6th and short 16th, they had to wind their way through what was almost like the Goodwood enclosure in August, past picnics and a thousand people disconcertingly crunching the ice from their Coke.

At the 7th, Nicklaus, having demolished a banana on the way down the fairway after driving into the crowd, played out into a bunker but raised the roof by holing his sand wedge for a birdie. Faldo, with a perfect approach, calmly did likewise. The ranking order was now Floyd nine under, Faldo seven, Nicklaus five.

The Augusta course is a miracle of gardening: its thousands of acres of weedless fairway as crisp as a fine toothbrush and far more true than today's Wembley, its frictionless greens as almost unplayable as sloping undulating tin trays. At the par-five 8th, the crowd as one man groaned 'It's short' at Nicklaus's little pitch on to the green; and watched it run 14 feet past.

Faldo was eight under when he holed from eight feet at the 9th, immediately surrendering the stroke when he bunkered his approach to the 10th, came out short and needed two putts. Floyd, coming up behind, scored a birdie at the 10th to go 10 under. And so to the 12th: ranking order now 11 under, seven, five.

After his perfect birdie at the 13th, Faldo arrived at the 15th green properly accepted by the crowd, reading the indelible scoreboard, as the only contender to Floyd. The banked grandstands gave him a standing ovation and he responded with a chipped third shot from just off the green to six feet for another birdie: nine under and in hard pursuit of their man. At the same hole, Floyd would miss his birdie by an inch from 10ft.

On to the short 16th and a birdie two; Nicklaus disintegrating hole by hole and going into the pond, to be four under. In the still evening, hushed as a church for every putt, the greens dappled in the lengthening shadows, it was like some vast cocktail party in a private garden.

Then to the penultimate drama. Floyd in the distance dropped a stroke at the par-four 17th just as Faldo was lining up his first putt at the back of the 18th. 'Fanny [his caddie] told me and I aimed for the safe two-putt,' Faldo said.

Floyd bunkered his 18th drive, went from there into the bunker right of the green, and came up the fairway in a pensive walk. To his great credit, his wedge to within 3½ feet in utter silence earned the play-off. 'To have lost without a play-off would have been even worse,' he said.

Down the 10th he and Faldo had to go once more, towards that vast crowd of eager vultures gleefully waiting for one dead body. Faldo's, they hoped.

It looked likely to be that way when he bunkered his second shot. Floyd stared up through the trees at the disappearing sunlight with a half smile. 'I'd hit two good shots and liked the line of my putt,' he would say afterwards. 'But I expected Faldo to come out well. And he did.' To four feet.

On to the 11th. 'It felt like a pretty good swing,' Floyd said of his ill-fated short iron into the brook, 'but I knew it was in the water as soon as it left the club.'

What pain sport can inflict on an individual. That old imposter with triumph: disaster. 'I don't think I've had anything affect me like this,' Floyd said.

Words are not something Faldo bothers with much. 'I just kept grinding away – mixed emotions, wondering whether the play-off was going to get its own back on me for last year, the four-foot putt at the 10th. Then, as we went down to the 11th, I was wondering: maybe this is my hole [as last year]'.

It was, and history was made, the boy who took up golf after watching Nicklaus on television in the Masters at Easter in 1971 becoming the only player to repeat Nicklaus's successive victories of a few years before.

THE QUIET MAN OF THE SEA

Peter Blake's romance around the world

12 April 1990 Fort Lauderdale, Florida

Never having sailed much more than 120 miles at a single stretch, I am not eligible to analyse results after five legs of the 33,000-mile Whitbread Round the World Race. What I do know, first hand, is that a reaching (wind broadside or behind) mizzen staysail can enchantingly transform a boat's performance, like a square-rig sail. Peter Blake, ocean racing's foremost sailor, is proving this with a vengeance.

The day-and-a-half overall lead which the New Zealander now has with *Steinlager 2* after five legs is due primarily to two factors: the two-mast ketch rig, which critically favours three of the leading yachts including *Fisher & Paykel* and *The Card*, and his experience of multi-hull technique which he has adapted to such effect on a mono-hull.

Blake, who at 41 is approaching double figures for circumnavigations with 400,000 miles logged during 20 years, is midway through a six-year, projected three-boat sponsorship with his New Zealand breweries group, Lion Nathan. *Steinlager 1*, a trimaran in which, hair-raisingly, he won the 7,500-mile Round Australia Race two years ago, not only gave him the most exciting sailing he has ever known. It taught him some radical new approaches to the big, 'maxi' mono-hulls.

On this race, Blake has almost abandoned the conventional use of down-wind spinnakers, aesthetically beautiful but cumbersome. Instead, sailing slightly off the line of the wind in a series of S-bends, and using a large headsail and massive 3,000 square-foot staysail – rigged amidship between mizzen and main mast – *Steinlager 2* is achieving a valuable two to three knots more than with a spinnaker.

'Without this, we possibly wouldn't be winning,' Blake says, sitting relaxed in a cafe on the dockside as the rest of the leaders of the fleet of 23 arrive at intervals of several hours. 'The design computers said it wouldn't work, because they had no experience of ketch rigs. And the trimaran taught me the benefit of keeping the boat light – changed the traditional way of sailing a mono-hull. In a multi-hull, the distribution of every kilo on board counts. *Steinlager 2* is the most uncluttered of all the big boats, in layout and crew. Everything is in the right place. There are still lots of things in this race that people haven't thought about.'

Blake is a thinking man. Although he is a national hero in a country obsessed with sailing, and is widely regarded as a fine leader, there is about him none of that expedient fanaticism or subdued frenzy that exists in such men as his America's Cup compatriot, Chris Dickson, or in Chay Blyth. Blake is in the gentlemanly Alec Rose mould, with the MBE for his services to the sport, and the romantic feel for the sea which he shares with his mentor, Robin Knox-Johnston; winner of the *Sunday Times* first single-handed round the world race in 1968.

Ashore, for the first time in weeks after sailing 5,475 miles up the coast of South America, Blake is worried about being short with his two young children and their comparatively casual land life following his existence of no more than two hours sleep at a time and, even then, always on duty.

Sailing almost since he could walk, Blake likes to travel from A to B, as opposed to sailing round the buoys, which is why the America's Cup never beckoned. He has done One Ton and Admirals' Cup events, but, 'I didn't like the nit-picking and back-stabbing that is part of the America's Cup at times,' he says.

His strategies are long-term; not, like one or two boats in the present race, calculating tactics by the hour rather than by the week, which led Rothman's, working by computer on the first leg with the chart folded, to find suddenly when they turned over that the Cape Verde Islands were obstructing their course to Punta de Este in Uruguay.

Yet Blake's attention to detail, the legacy of four previous Whitbreads, is as scrupulous as an America's Cup skipper's: regularly servicing the winches at sea, inspecting the sail seams, plus detailed planning of crew clothing and food stores. During night watches, winches are attended every minute, with no static cleating (fixing) of sail sheets. He dearly would like to win at the fifth attempt – after finishing second in the last two races, in 1981–82 in *Ceramco* and 1985–86 in *Lion* – but will not be heart-broken if he fails.

'These have been a fascinating few years, with room for some lateral thinking,' he says, with the mood of the true sportsman, for whom taking part is as important as winning. He has, you sense, the measure of his life, which, when not afloat, he lives at Emsworth in Hampshire. There is a steady thoroughness, typified by the feat, in 1981, of sailing *Ceramco* 3,700 miles from Ascension Island to Cape Town under jury (makeshift) rig after being dismasted, rather than retiring under engine to the nearest port.

With what seems to be a bizarre misjudgement, some other skippers, such as Lawrie Smith, have previously described Blake as not being a winner, but he shrugs off the criticism. 'Perhaps their view may change,' he says, without rancour. 'I don't think it's worth saying things that antagonise anyone.'

The romanticism in him yearns to build a radical, multi-hull Steinlager 3 that could emulate Verne's circumnavigation in 80 days. 'Maybe 80 is not practical,' he says on reflection. 'But 90? That would be something.' In his mind's eye, he is already celebrating with champagne at the Jules

Verne café in Paris, his young family around him: the last adventurer.*

Yet he recognises that the America's Cup judgement in New York later this month may precipitate a counter attraction for public interest and sponsorship in two years' time; that his dream might have to be shelved for more pragmatic involvement in a home-waters America's Cup challenge as administrative organiser. 'I'm not really qualified to skipper, but setting it up, that's a challenge,' he says.

For the moment, Blake is concentrating on the next and final leg of the Whitbread, aware that the only thing likely to prevent victory is breakage or a collision. Stage-racing is, in one sense, unfair: the first to arrive on one section has the most time to prepare for the next, and now he is busy making sure everything will be shipshape for the next departure.

'With 36 hours in hand, we can afford to be relaxed [on the final leg],' Blake says. 'We won't break the boat up by driving it too hard. We don't have to stress the boat or the crew. It's a nice feeling. If we get 10 miles behind, we don't have to panic. But I won't say we have won till we cross the line.'

Panic is the last thing you would expect of this man, who measures time not by the sound of hurrying feet, but by the subtle shift of the wind.

* In 1994 Blake and Robin Knox-Johnston achieved the remarkable non-stop circumnavigation time of 77 days, 22 hours, 17 minutes.

WHO WOULD WANT TO BE A MODERN TEST PLAYER?

Fireball cricket in the Caribbean

16 April 1990 Antigua

Forget the time-honoured expression 'It's not cricket'. The fact is that Test cricket itself is not any longer cricket. Allan Lamb, England's deputy captain, and Micky Stewart, the team manager, unequivocally say so.

The Test series finishing here is a different sport from what we used to know. It is designed out of expediency by the contemporary generation of players, approved out of convenience by the present generation of team managers, and tolerated reluctantly by the Test and County Cricket Board and International Cricket Council.

It is hustling and intimidatory. Not to mince words, it is often cheating. You may argue that some of the same things were said about Jardine and Larwood 60 years ago. The difference is that, then, most people deplored expediency.

Now many of them welcome it. And expect it. That's life, 1990.

The persistent bowling at batsmen's heads, the time-wasting slow overs, and all the other sharp practice that has become endemic is something we must live with, according to Lamb and Stewart.

'The game in England is based on social activity,' Stewart says. 'The first-class cricket which I first played was an extension of that. International cricket is nothing to do with that any more. It is a hugely competitive game, generating millions of dollars. It is nothing to do with the game it was: a nice game, a nice way of life.

'It is still a nice way of life but you have to be successful. If you don't score the right total, you're never in the game.'

England did not get the right total here, given the batting wicket; and they bowled indifferently and boringly on the first day of West Indies' first innings with unvaried pace that lacked real menace, allowing West Indies to build an almost unassailable position. None the less, Lamb, deputising for Gooch, echoes Stewart's sentiments. And takes them even further.

'If West Indies bowl only 11 overs an hour, we should do the same,' Lamb reasons. 'England have to become hard. If you can't stand 10 bouncers in 12 balls, you shouldn't be out there. We have to play the West Indies at their own game.

'The umpires should be pushed to the limit. They have a hard job, but that is where the control lies. It is not the players who should be blamed [for the way the game is].'

Lamb argues that the umpires should be much more prominent figures in the game, exercising discretionary, disciplinary power more often: even to the point, as in football, where two successive warnings for infringement of the rules would lead to a player's suspension from the following match.

In Barbados, Lamb recalls, he repeatedly complained to the umpires, claiming that Haynes was heavily banging the pitch with his bat, not in repair but deliberately to break up cracks and make them dusty in preparation for England's batsmen. The umpires, according to Lamb, refused to act.

What Stewart can justifiably claim satisfaction in is that he has produced a gritty team that, until the last couple of days, was competing on equal terms with the game's foremost side. Indeed, Stewart somewhat controversially claims that 'the West Indies is now the home of cricket'. He finds more cricket knowledge, he says, among ordinary people than he does among some professional staff and club cricketers at home. If that is so, it is the more a pity that Richards should be so childishly over-sensitive to criticism that he missed the start of play, when captain, because he was remonstrating with a writer.

The England manager is disappointed that people were surprised at England's preparation for the tour, the first time there has been such a professional approach.

Stewart and Lamb, however much some may disagree with their ethical approach, or lack of it, are caught in an impossible position. Public demand and media pressure have become an intolerable burden. The instant communication of television, expertly performed, from the West Indies, amplifies the pressure.

I am not sure I would want to be a Test player. Lamb and Stewart personify the contemporary game, though their point of view should not be summarily dismissed. Long ago I played football with Stewart and know him to be a sportsman. Time changes; and changes us. Today's players are prisoners of circumstance, of their era. They no more think that what is happening in the game is wrong than our great-great-grandfathers, pillars of Victorian propriety, thought that sending children up chimneys as sweeps was wrong.

Stewart claims that he and his opposite number, Clive Lloyd, have had discussions before and during the tour and are happy both with attitudes on the pitch and between the players off the pitch. Stewart denies that spectators are concerned with over-rate; though this is contrary to evidence in previous matches. What seems generally accepted, and expected, by players and public is that losing gracefully is not any more one of the options.

One of the best and worst days of my life has just passed. I have experienced an exquisite, lingering sunset here in the Leeward Islands, a liquid fireball sinking behind St Kitts and Montserrat, and illuminating a cloud formation as huge and unmoving as the Himalayas: and realise that what I have lived a part of my life believing in now no longer exists.

WORLD CUP OVERWHELMED BY FEAR OF DEFEAT

England stretch Germany in cautious semi-final

5 July 1990 Turin

England, whose World Cup passage this past month has been something of a lottery, were victims of one last night when they were beaten by penalties. It has been by far their best performance yet and they will feel disappointed in going out in such a way, especially after Waddle had hammered the ball against a post in the first half of extra time.

Yet Buchwald did likewise for West Germany in the 117th minute and, for all England's courage and running on the night, it has to be said that the Germans were fractionally the more positive team.

Only fractionally. That was the surprise, for Germany were the established favourites for the cup and their inability to distinguish themselves in their sixth match emphasised three aspects of the tournament: that there has been no outstanding team; that intense heat throughout the month has drained the strength of every player; and that England, finally finding a framework into which to fit their ability, became a team of some substance.

They began competition deep in criticism and departed with dignity; none more so than Shilton, who was magnificent at the effective end of a World Cup career spanning 17 years.

It was evident almost from the first kick that Germany were more afraid of England than England of them. The supposedly most-feared side in the finals was more restrained than in any match so far, and for the first 20 minutes England ran along on a tide of attacking, almost adventurous play. Here was the England we have been looking for these past six matches.

The exclusion of the injured Barnes and the introduction of Beardsley, as a forward midfield runner playing in behind Lineker, gave England shape and coherence. The man-to-man marking of Wright and Walker on Klinsmann and Völler, with Butcher as sweeper, allowed England's defence to look solid. Butcher, if anything, was sweeping in front of the back two markers. Völler was going to have difficulty to live up to his claim, during the first round, that he and Klinsmann were the most potent attacking force in the finals.

The Germans' tentativeness was unexpected. Clearly, they were caught by the same fear of defeat as Italy had been against Argentina. Brehme was reluctant to come forward and the general caution allowed Lineker to cause all sorts of problems as he moved sharply this way and that onto probing balls from Gascoigne, Waddle and Platt.

Waddle was coming out of his shell, releasing that ability which we know he has but had seen for only a brief spell in the first half against Belgium. Platt, running with zest, helped to keep forcing Germany's midfield trio of Hässler, Matthäus and Thon onto the retreat.

England's initiative was to last no more than 25 minutes or so; by the half hour they were standing back with ten and even 11 men behind the ball waiting for the World Cup to come to them. At last, the Germans started to move forward and threaten: Shilton had to make a particularly fine save from Augenthaler just before the interval.

Once again, as in previous matches and as in the European Cup semi-final in Munich, the German spectators were disgracefully engaged in racist chants towards coloured players: Parker and Walker of England. And this is the nation that is about to become one of the major economic powers of the world.

England's lapse into caution continued with the start of the second half. Wright passed back to Shilton almost from the halfway line. We were having a return of that unambitious play we had seen in the first round against Egypt and the Netherlands.

There was a brief break when Parker raced into the gap behind Germany's defence on the right and was only blocked inside the penalty area by a lunging Augenthaler. This was a temporary interruption to Germany's belatedly found momentum; Matthäus was slipping into his customary stride, with those fierce central thrusts at the heart of the opposing defence.

It was, therefore with the run of play that Germany took the lead, though they were a shade fortunate in the execution. Pearce clumsily felled Hässler and the industrious Parker, ironically too quick in the attempt to block the free kick by Brehme, deflected the ball high over Shilton.

If this was misfortune for England, they could not complain that it was against the run of events. They themselves needed fresh momentum, more support for Lineker and somebody who might make a scoring run from midfield: such as Platt. To this end, the manager sent out Steven in place of Butcher, strengthening attack at the risk of exposing the defence.

He was rewarded when Lineker equalised. As in 1986, Lineker has shown himself to be one of the most dangerous opportunists in the world when given support and now he was quick to punish the uncertainty between Kohler and Augenthaler on a high, dropping cross from Parker.

FINALISTS DEFILE THE GAME

Buchwald shuts out Maradona from World Cup final

9 July 1990 Rome

Once again Argentina has demeaned football. The deplorable World Cup final of 1990 will be remembered not for the way West Germany won it, mechanically and without style, but the manner in which Argentina lost it, disgracefully.

The nation which has so much to give the game in skill, winners in 1978 and 1986, now wore the sour, petulant face which we have also too often witnessed in the past. The only good thing that could be said about the match is that Brehme's penalty eight minutes from the end ensured that Argentina lost and that the watching sporting world would not have to endure more extra time or a penalty lottery.

This was the worst final ever played, worse than the first hour of 1982 between Germany and Italy, and the first in which anyone was sent off, Monzón and Dezotti, of Argentina, being dismissed by Codesal, the Mexican referee, who gave an alarmingly erratic performance. Codesal had missed the clearest of penalties against Argentina's goalkeeper, Goycoechea, after an hour; and when he sent off Dezotti a few minutes from the end for manhandling Kohler, the German defender, Codesal should have dismissed Kohler too for blatant time-wasting.

In Argentina's seven matches during the past four weeks, there have been eight players sent off: three of their own and five opponents. It is symptomatic of their performances that for the final they were missing four suspended players, Caniggia, Olarticoechea, Giusti and Batista. After the final whistle, the rugged Batista had to be restrained from molesting the referee.

As in 1966, following their display of wanton fouling against England in the quarter-final, Argentina should be censured by FIFA and severely fined. In front of billions of television viewers they have given an appalling example of the game.

Almost as objectionable as Argentina's behaviour was the orgiastic embracing of the whole German team, in a heap upon the ground, when Brehme scored the penalty for Lorenzo's foul on Völler; also Völler's grotesque gesturing following a second-half foul on Maradona, for which he was rightly booked for dissent, an offence similar to that for which he was sent off previously together with Rijkaard, of the Netherlands; and, last, the encouragement of hysterial reaction among the public by the organising committee's use of the giant television screens for the projection of frenzied close-ups of Franz Beckenbauer and others in the moments immediately succeeding victory.

The excessive scenes of celebration after the handing over of the cup, magnified almost more than the play itself, were a conspicuous contradiction of FIFA's campaign for fair play. The trophy for fair play was awarded to England, who had the fewest bookings and whose entertaining third-place match the night before with Italy put into perspective the wretchedness of last night's match.

With five players missing through suspension or injury, it was hardly surprising that so much of the match should be played in Argentina's half of the field as they attempted to hold off the forceful but too often unimaginative Germans. The deputy for Caniggia – who scored probably the most significant goal of the tournament when he eliminated Brazil in the second round – was wholly inadequate. Dezotti, who plays with Cremonese in the Italian second division, could take no advantage of the rare opportunities that were provided for him to cause danger to Germany's back line. Indeed, Dezotti was booked after only six minutes for a foul on Littbarski on the edge of his own penalty area.

If Argentina were to have had any hope, it had to arise from some spark of inspiration from Maradona, but this we never saw. Buchwald close-marked him throughout, never gave him more than a yard or two's space unless Maradona opted to go deeper than 20 yards into his own half. For most of the match the world's best player was a lonely spectator, unprovided and unsupported, and with that Argentina's chances died.

There was just one spell a few minutes before half-time when he did work clear of Buchwald but it came to nothing; a free kick flew too high and his marvellous pass into the path of Dezotti went unrewarded.

Germany had scored five of the 15 goals struck from outside the penalty area, and it looked as though this was what they needed now if Argentina were not to drag the game into extra time. The second half began with Littbarski beating three men on the edge of the penalty area and grazing the right-hand post with a drive off his wrong foot, and Berthold diving to meet Brehme's free kick five yards out but sending the ball over the bar.

There was just over an hour gone when Augenthaler, who has been a rather sluggish sweeper during this tournament, advanced into the penalty area, was challenged by Goycoechea and brought down. The referee vigorously waved on play. Now came Monzón's sending-off for a late, crude tackle on Klinsmann that caught him on the shin with upturned studs.

Brehme's penalty came almost as a relief, though Troglio was booked for protesting. Argentina threw everything into a last assault to protect their trophy and when Kohler tried to run away with the ball in his hands after a free kick it was hardly surprising, though inexcusable, that Dezotti flung him to the ground. Finally there was the depressing sight of Maradona being booked: what must sadly be his last contribution of note to the World Cup.

The teams were:

ARGENTINA (1–2–5–2): 12 S Goycoachea (Millonarios, Colombia); 20 J Simón (Boca Juniors); 18 J Serrízuala (River Plate), 19 O Ruggeri (Real Madrid; sub: 15 P Monzón, Independiente); 13 N Lorenzo (Bari), 17 R Senoni (Udinese), 4 J Basualdo (VfB Stuttgart), 7 J Burruchaga (Nantes: sub: 6 G Calderón, Paris Saint-Germain); 21 P Troglio (Lazio); 10 D Maradona (Naples), 9, G Dezotti (Cremonese).

WEST GERMANY (1–2–5–2): 1 B Higner (FC Cologne); 5 K Augenthaler (Bayern Munich); 4 J Kohler (Bayern Munich), 6 G Buchwald (VfB Stuttgart); 14 T Berthold (AS Roma; sub: 2 S Reuter, Bayern Munich), 8 T Hässler (Juventus), 10 L Matthäus (Internazionale), 7 P Littbarski (FC Cologne), 3 A Brehme (Internazionale); 9 R Völler (AS Roma), 18 J Klinsman (Internazionale).

Referee: E M Codesal (Mexico).

SOULFUL LONG-DISTANCE RUNNERS

Poles honour the heroes of Solidarity

16 August 1990 Gdansk

They gathered peacefully, in the gently falling rain, down at the shipyard by the notorious Gate 2, now festooned with flowers, where 20 years ago striking workers were mowed down by police and army guns.

Yesterday, on the tenth anniversary of the foundation of Solidarity in 1980, the people of this city, of the whole of the nation of Chopin, were remembering their heroes with a memorial half-marathon run from here to Gdynia, the adjacent Baltic port. The event was part of the Solidarity Games, the staging of a dozen sports as a symbolic, unaggressive recognition of Solidarity's triumphant revolution 'without a broken window-pane'.

There was no shouting, no feeling of vengeance, just an overwhelming, silent sense of freedom as the 1,100 runners gathered for the race. Mothers with prams, heralds of the new generation of hope, watched the jostling runners as they warmed up, in mute appreciation of the significance of the moment.

A cheer was heard. Lech Walesa, Poland's latter-day Wat Tyler, had arrived at the scene of a decade of proletarian heroism. There had been talk that he would run a short distance in the race; perhaps because he recently took part in a publicity motor race.

But Walesa is not these days built for running. He would fire the gun. Upon a word, the runners and the crowd moved from Gate 2 the short distance to the 70-foot-high memorial statue of three crosses, bound by an anchor at the top and forged by the shipyard workers, the base depicting the crafts of their trade. The three crosses represent the three uprisings of Polish workers: at Poznan in 1956 and in Gdansk and Gdynia in 1970 and 1980.

Even a foreigner was involuntarily near to tears as, unaccompanied, the national anthem was sung under a weeping sky; yet one more soulful moment of a people historically trapped in the nutcracker of middle Europe's political rivalries.

The start of the race was somewhat short on Olympic protocol. Television cameramen, runners and voyeurs jostled for a position with a view of the starter. Ultimately, the only evidence that the race had begun was that the man or woman in front of you was no longer standing on your toes.

With all the urgency of an English village cricket team taking the field after a long tea interval with too many home-baked cakes, the runners departed: representatives of half a dozen nations, including the United States, and almost 20 per cent of them women with, additionally, a significant number of handicapped competitors.

As the tail of the field disappeared, Walesa held an impromptu press conference on the steps of the Solidarity headquarters and accepted a bicentenary memento from *The Times* from which he would be able, he said gratefully, to drink his morning cup of coffee and think of the world's oldest daily newspaper.

The finishing line in Gdynia, 20 kilometres away, was poignantly sited, alongside the town hall where, during the 1980 uprising, many strikers were imprisoned and Janek Wisniewski, a leading Solidarity activist, was killed.

When the building was liberated the walls were found to be covered in blood. Outside, on the city square where the ancient trams rumble past, stands a wooden cross, a temporary memorial to Wisniewski and others that will be replaced by a monument similar to that in Gdansk.

The impact of the scene in Gydnia was its representation of the average: ordinary peole with ordinary lives harbouring simple ambitions, unostentatiously proud, resilient and, when necessary, defiant. Their response to historic change was to treat it with maturity.

The winners of yesterday's race were Marek Deputat for the men and Iza Zatorska for the women. Among the runners was Jacek Domanski, one of the actors in Andrzej Wajda's film *A Man Made of Iron*. Many incidentals around the finishing line seemed simple enough, but would have been unimaginable barely a year ago, such as the banner for the Polish navy's branch of Solidarity. It was a day of imperishable memories.

HIS WORDS LIVE AFTER HIM

Geoffrey Green, sportswriter unique in his time

6 September 1990*

Words can prove mightier, Vaclav Havel, playwright and president of Czechoslovakia, has said, than ten military divisions. Words can be said to be the source of our being, the very substance of the cosmic life-form we call man. Spirit, the human soul, our self-awareness, our ability to generalise and think in concepts, our capacity of knowing that we will die, and living in the spirit of that knowledge: surely all these are mediated or actually created by words? We have always, Havel says, believed in the power of words to change history.

Geoffrey Green, whom we remember today with affection and gratitude, had a special way with words, written or spoken. In writing for a newspaper world famous for its words, he may not have changed history, but for more than 30 years he added measurably to that newspaper's prestige. He was one of a tiny handful of sports journalists, during the first century of sports writing, on account of whose style, wit and sensitivity readers exclusively would buy a particular newspaper. If Geoffrey was exceptional in several respects, it was by his evocative, compassionate writing that he most made his mark. It is said in our trade that a good picture is worth a thousand words. Geoffrey was a contradiction to that theory, and his words live after him.

Recollections of him tend to be sentimental or superficial, sometimes irreverent. When he was not writing or broadcasting, and even occasionally when he was, he gave the impression of a casual, gifted, self-mocking amateur of the Twenties, of the era of Wodehouse, Scott Fitzgerald and Coward, cocktails and epigrammatic conversations. He and his brother Archie, happily here today, spent their early adult days sharing the same suit of tails, *de rigueur* for social events, exchanged over the length of the country by frantic telegram. Beyond the social carousel, however, there developed behind the then anonymous *Times* by-line a journalist with a professionalism and eye for detail that were fluent, instinctive, unostentatious . . . and the envy of colleagues.

Giving a copy of his weighty *History of the Football Association*, one of his many books, to John Hennessy, the sports editor of *The Times*, Geoffrey wrote on the title page. 'Not to be read at breakfast time . . . if at all.' Life, he liked to convey, with a deliberate camouflage of any problems or sorrows, was a continuous party. Every day was Christmas Day, though his gregariousness was born of a fear of loneliness. A feature of Geoffrey's charm was the making light of his troubles. Saddened by the separation of his parents in his adolescence, he would play jazz records, on a wind-up gramophone, on the landing outside his mother's bathroom. Jazz was his elixir: not many have helped Louis Armstrong to climb the walls into Pembroke College after midnight. His humour could be laconic. Of his father's financial fall from the grand existence of colonial India to a rented room over a sweetshop, he observed dryly, in his autobiography: 'From polo . . . to polo-mint.' It was characteristic, when his tiny daughter Ti asked him, looking out of a bedroom window, what were the two letter Hs standing on a rugby field, that he should identify them as Heaven and Hell, at the poles of life which was played in between. He could be domestically inattentive. Realising he had not for some time sent one of his godchildren a birthday present, he hurried to Hamleys and dispatched a bumper book of steam engines. His godson duly replied: 'Dear Uncle Geoffrey, thank you so much for the lovely book. However, I think you should know I am now nineteen and articled to a City accountancy firm.'

Geoffrey was not especially literary or academic after Cambridge – a notably failed teacher of scripture – but it was his ability to bring a sense of theatre to his reporting that earned him not only a wide and loyal readership but the attention of the professionals about whom he wrote. International footballers, cricketers and tennis players appreciated the wider social interpretation that Geoffrey gave to their ordinary, and sometimes extraordinary, technical skills and endeavour, and which they could not articulate. In 1956, he wrote from Wembley: 'Marshalls and scarlet Caesars have won their victories on land, but few could have equalled in colour and dramatic context the triumph of the Apollonian English game over the Dyonisiac dance of Brazil.' From the earliest days to long after his formal retirement, the largest crowd of players and managers at the annual Football Writers' Dinner was always afterwards round the table of the man searching for the rainbow's end. Bill

Nicholson, from famous Tottenham, remembers Geoffrey's tattered brief-case, the bottom held together with safety-pins which still did not prevent his cigarettes from falling out. Why, enquired Bill, did the man from *The Times* not have a case more worthy of him? 'Sentimental reasons, old boy' replied Green, enigmatically.

After the publication of his obituary, I received a letter from a reader who had once met Geoffrey on a train, going to watch Manchester United, the favourite for both. 'He seemed,' the reader recalled, 'a bit of a Ralph Richardson of sports journalism: a rather eccentric air about him, a gleam in his eye, and lots of charm. If I remember rightly,' the reader added, 'he had a liking for whisky in his coffee: perhaps understandable on British Rail.' The charm was spontaneous. Prostrate in hospital, listening to the fussiness of other patients ordering their evening hot drink – two sugars, none, weak, strong – Geoffrey said to the nurse: 'I'll have Horlicks, and you can mix it *any* way you want.' Surgeons, leaving him stranded alone on the operating slab while they rushed to attend to an emergency in intensive care in the late afternoon, were told on return: 'Why don't you chaps go home and have a good night's sleep, and we'll come back *fresh* in the morning.' Asked by the Queen, upon presentation of his OBE, which teams he hoped to see in his last FA Cup Final for *The Times*, he replied: 'Ma'am as long as it's between fun and laughter, I don't mind.' In his final years he endured cancer, a heart attack and an artificial knee all with cheerful equanimity. If anyone greeted him 'It's good to see you,' the response was always, 'It's good to be *able* to see you.'

One of the last of that between-the-wars generation of sportsmen who personified the Corinthian ethic – and in fact himself an attacking Corinthian centre-half, as good, said Charlie Buchan, as any in the land, professional or amateur – Geoffrey was also special because men and women everywhere gathered round him like moths to the flame: whether he was at home in Twickenham, in Moscow or Mexico City. The late Christina Wood, correspondent of the *Daily Telegraph*, once said: 'I've loved him all my life, but thank Heaven I never fell in love with him.' Following Geoffrey's light, whether in sport, or in festive celebration, or in love, could indeed be a demanding exercise, for he had excessive stamina, and wilfulness, and an immunity to a need for sleep. He delighted many of us for so long. His absence leaves a gap in journalism, in sport, and in many lives, which no-one I know can ever so engagingly fill. His was a golden age: and for almost 80 years he represented it with his own distinct and beguiling style.

* Memorial address at St Bride's Church, Fleet Street.

WHEN PEGASUS SOARED ACROSS THE SKY

The amateur meteors who drew 100,000 to Wembley

9 April 1991

This is a nostalgic week, reminding me how long ago was my youth, how fortunate I was to be marginally involved in one of this century's passing, now long-forgotten sporting phenomena. In Oxford this week, Pegasus football club will be celebrating the fortieth anniversary of winning the Amateur Cup for the first time, against Bishop Auckland in front of 100,000 spectators at Wembley – an historic relic of the last era before money and sportsmanship spiralled in opposite directions.

For those too young to have any recollection, Pegasus was the combined club of Oxford and Cambridge Universities, an amalgamation of their respective 2nd XI names of Centaur and Falcon, inspirationally founded by Harold Thompson, the eminent Oxford chemist and later chairman of the FA.

For a mere 15 seasons, between 1948 and 1963, this echo of the turn-of-the-century Corinthian era soared like a meteor across the sky of English amateur football, illuminating the game with its style, borrowed from Tottenham Hotspur, and traditional ethics, setting a standard for schoolboys and universities, until the momentum of its own ideological aims prematurely withered and died in the expanding tide of individual expediency.

I feel entitled to make such claims, though involved, because the most illustrious days of Pegasus were occurring while I was still at school, open-mouthed in admiration as they rose from creation to double triumphs, winning the cup a second time in 1953 with a record six goals against Harwich and Parkeston.

I was subsequently to have the rare experience of pulling on the same shirt with players who were my boyhood heroes, an experience that has been a cornerstone of my years in sporting journalism.

The success was fashioned by some of the game's finest professional thinkers. Vic Buckingham, a disciple of Arthur Rowe's classic push-and-run style which had established Tottenham's early post-war fame, pulled together the threads which earned headlines after the first Wembley victory such as, 'Pegasus add to the blue-print'. George Ainsley, almost too eloquent to have come from the Leeds stable of that time, master-minded the second victory.

Joe Mercer and Rowe himself tried to maintain the momentum in the late Fifties, after the decline, through age, of the immediate post-war generation of undergraduates who had the physical and mental maturity of war-time service; men like Ken Shearwood, of the Royal Navy, who brought to the art of centre half a combination of Tommy Cooper and Freddie Mills.

Tactical pre-match discussion, punctuated by the perennially pes-simistic Thompson and the legal sarcasm and priceless irreverence of Jerry Weinstein, the assistant treasurer, were occasionally closer to the Goon show than to Schwarzkopf's Desert Storm; though in the years when I was travelling reserve for Tony Pawson on the wing, the exhilar-ating spirit within the club was something beyond compare. I trembled in anticipation of every cup-tie, and I was not even playing.

That collective spirit communicated itself to the public to an extent that persuaded followers in humble occupations to drive the length of England for away matches, drawn to the club's melody as to the organ grinder's tune, even on muddy inglorious afternoons far from Wembley; by inter-national stars such as Denis Saunders, captain and left half, and Johnny Dutchman, at inside forward, players wholly without self-acclaim. The story had begun in 1948 when I was 13. Thompson had contrived to gain exemption for his brainchild until the fourth qualifying round of the cup, shortly after the university match in December. The initial intention was that an arbitrary eligibility should be for current students and those one year out of residence – later to be controversially rescinded.

In the inaugural cup-tie, against Enfield, Pegasus were a goal down and it would have been two, but for one of many remarkable saves by Ben Brown, from Mexborough in Yorkshire, that were regularly to illuminate Pegasus's climb to the top. A shot by Rawlings, the Enfield inside forward, seemed bound for the net, only for Brown to dive full length and not only parry the shot, but hold it.

It was the first critical turning-point in the club's brief life; defeat would have forfeited exemption the following year, and a fragmented club, without league fixtures and with many of its players committed to a university programme, could not hope to successfully put together a scratch side in early autumn. Now, two goals by John Tanner, a goalscorer with, at times, the finishing skill of a Greaves and who played for Huddersfield in the first division, and a penalty by Doug Insole brought victory.

Pegasus had taken wing, and as success mushroomed, they drew unprecedented crowds to their 'home' ground at Iffley Road in Oxford. Five-figure attendances became common, surpassing the lauded amateur rugby team.

The 1948–9 run ended in the quarter-final against Bromley, the eventual winners. Players such as Tanner, Pawson (who represented Charlton in the first division) and Saunders, with the calm authority and touch of Ray Barlow, of West Bromwich, were becoming, if not national celebrities, a focal point of newspaper attention.

In 1951, Pegasus earned a semi-final replay against the formidable Hendon, thanks to Brown's stupendous save, among many others, from Dexter Adams's late penalty, in front of a 27,000 Highbury crowd. In the replay, 2–1 down with 20 minutes to go, Pegasus were swept to the final by Dutchman's two late goals. When goals by Jimmy Potts and Tanner brought victory over Bishop Auckland, there were those who said – Raymond Glendenning, of the BBC, among them – that Pegasus had done more for the prestige of the game than the contemporary professional giants, Blackpool, Spurs and Newcastle.

Everybody not only wanted to watch Pegasus but to play against them. Requests for fixtures poured in from all over the world. The fame was substantiated when, including a new wave of players such as Gordon McKinna and Jerry Alexander, the West Indies cricketer, at full back, and Jack Laybourne and Bob Lunn in attack, Pegasus defeated the powerful Hayes, Corinthian Casuals and Southall – in two semi-finals which left me numb on the terraces – and then overwhelmed Harwich in the final. Sport will probably not see their like again.

A STEADY HAND THROUGH ADVERSITY

Woosnam denies Olazábal to win thrilling Masters

15 April 1991 Augusta

For nearly four-and-a-half hours yesterday, Ian Woosnam lived with the thunder of American chauvinism pounding in his ears as he played the course with Tom Watson, the last pair on the last day of the Masters at Augusta National. Seldom has one of two men been more the favourite, and it is to Woosnam's enduring credit that he held his nerve to become the third consecutive British holder of this coveted title.

How often might his nerve have gone: never more so than when

Watson, himself playing with a wonderfully steady hand, eagled both the long inward holes, the 13th and 15th, to send the huge crowd into a frenzy of expectation as he drew level with three to play at 11 under. Ahead of them, in a three-way tie and playing the 16th, was Olazábal.

A steady par at the short 16th and the far away 17th, a huge gallery hushed among the towering pines, kept Woosnam in the hunt. Watson, with no less ambition, even though he has won before, was the gentleman throughout, the perfect playing partner as they duelled in sunshine which, in the early afternoon, pushed the temperature beyond 80°.

The chauvinism at times by the Georgia crowd was as wretched as when the crowd at Muirfield five years ago applauded Azinger's second shot into sand at the 18th. When Woosnam had birdied the 9th to return to 12 under – as he had been at the fifth – there was almost silence from the steep banks of spectators around the hole. And when he went into the woods on the left at the long 13th, dropping into the burn and having to take a penalty drop, there was a great roar of approval from the masses swelling behind the final pair.

But the little Welshman was to have the final say, never mind that it was preceded by near-disaster.

Hooking his drive at the 18th, he was 40 yards behind the crowd in no-man's land towards the 8th fairway, and marshalls had to carve a passage like Moses to give Woosnam a view of the final green for his bizarre second shot.

Meanwhile, Watson was into sand at the face of the green on his second: two men in trouble. Woosnam put his ball through the crowd onto the fringe of the green, Watson blasted out of sand 25 feet beyond the pin.

The edge now lay with Woosnam. Watson's down-hill putt went four-and-a-half feet past: Woosnam was putting from six feet for his first major title. In the stillness of the evening not a sound was to be heard until Woosnam's own cry of delight greeted the dropping ball that made him successor to Faldo.

Poor Watson three putted for double bogey, but his embrace of the champion was warm and generous.

Woosnam's presence of mind had throughout been exemplary, though his poor wife, following along the ropes beside the fairway in the public hurly-burly, was reduced to a tremble, especially by the proximity of so much overt hostility to her husband. 'Double bogey', they would cry as Woosnam addressed the ball on the green. The continuation of British dominance of America's most prized event is really becoming disagreeable for some American followers of the game.

16 April 1991

Having had the extraordinary good fortune of watching the first three British golfers to win the Masters, I think Ian Woosnam's victory brought the most pleasure. There are a number of reasons why.

With Sandy Lyle, Nick Faldo and then Woosnam – I missed Faldo's first victory – I followed, as much by luck as judgment, the whole of their final rounds. In Woosnam's case there was also the charm of Tom Watson. There are few finer sights in golf than Watson's short iron play when things are going well.

Not only that, but the Masters champion of 1977 and 1981 is one of sport's gentlemen and his manner towards Woosnam throughout 4½ hours of intense rivalry was everything anyone could wish: encouragement almost to the point of paternalism, by a rival who as dearly wished to win as the Shropshire lad.

Watson's graciousness was the more important to Woosnam, given the extreme partisanship exhibited by the huge following that progressively swelled, hole by hole, behind the last pair.

The British cannot be self-righteous; we saw the same at Muirfield in the British Open in 1987, when Faldo beat Paul Azinger, and in the Ryder Cup at The Belfry when Great Britain and Europe first won in 1985.

The characteristic, raucous enthusiasm for Watson was to be expected; especially when, having fallen from ten under par at the 10th, where he birdied with a 12-foot putt, to seven under by the 12th, when he was in the water, he eagled the 13th and 15th to share the lead with Woosnam and José-María Olazábal, playing one hole ahead, on 11 under.

The antipathy towards Woosnam, however, was wretched; on the other hand, it served to make him even more determined. 'The more aggressive I am,' he said afterwards, 'the better I play.'

At the par-four dog-leg 5th – similar to the Road Hole at St Andrews, according to Dr Alister Mackenzie, the designer – Woosnam had gone 12 under for the second time with a ten-foot first putt and Watson's miss from three feet set him back to nine under.

At the short 6th, a spectator was calling 'double bogey' as Woosnam, the back of his navy shirt dark with sweat under the fierce sun, addressed his first putt from 40 feet above the pin. He bogeyed; and, in front, Olazábal birdied the 7th to join him on 11 under.

Woosnam hit possibly the longest drive of the week, over 280 yards, down the 9th fairway, then pitched 140 yards to within 11 feet and holed, to return to 12 under . . . and there was barely a ripple of applause from the packed gallery.

For 20 years, Woosnam had said beforehand, he had watched the back nine as a bystander. Now he went into it with a lead that he would hold, during two final days, for a total of 27 holes. And he was impatient. 'I wanted to know the result,' he said. 'It felt like I was out there for ten hours.'

It was not impatience that cost him a shot at the 10th, where he chipped from off the green to 4½ feet and missed – Watson birdied from 12 feet – but it may have been at the 13th.

With two pairs stacked in front of them, he and Watson had more than 20 minutes to sit on the tee and think – Watson about the loss of three shots on the previous two holes. Woosnam wanted to get it all over; Watson was reckoning, he himself said, that eagles at the long 13th and 15th would put him back in the hunt.

Indeed they did. Woosnam, conversely, greedy on his own admission for another huge drive such as he had hit at the 13th on the second day, pulled his drive low in to the trees and the brook. The crowd disgracefully cheered and he was lucky to get away with a six at the hole where Azinger had a ten last year.

On the 14th tee, someone shouted disparagingly at Woosnam that Augusta 'isn't a links course'. The fatherly Watson quietly advised him to 'just think what's happening in front of the tee, not behind it'. On the only hole without bunkers, they each had par.

Approaching the 15th, where Olazábal had just returned to 11 under, Watson hit the best short iron of the week to within five feet from 180 yards.

It was here that Gene Sarazen hit a double eagle from 220 yards in 1935. Woosnam counteracted Watson's eagle with a birdie and there were three on 11 under.

With the skies overcast, the air heavily humid, the last pair held par on the 16th and 17th, every shot of Watson's received with clamorous applause. Beside the fairways and around the greens, it was like rush hour on the Underground and difficult to move.

The gentle Mrs Woosnam was standing midway between the 17th tee and green in a daze of anxiety, distressed by the hostility from the spectators.

While Watson was driving into trees at the 18th and Woosnam somewhere into no man's land between the 8th and 9th fairways, over and beyond the crowd – calculatedly, he would say, to clear the 18th fairway bunkers – Olazábal, going from one bunker to another, was taking a bogey. Now there were two in the lead with one green to play.

Watson's second went into sand; Woosnam's, via a gully carved by security men through the dense crowd, reached the lip of the green. Watson splashed 25 feet past the pin; Woosnam putted to within seven feet.

When Watson's downhill putt rolled past, those seven feet separated Woosnam from his place in history, nine years after he almost gave up tournament play in dismay. He put his head down, stroked the ball and, three feet from the hole, 'I knew it was in'.

'Perhaps,' he reflected afterwards, 'they'll now be able to say my name right. Maybe even spell it correctly.'

Regrettably, there are plenty of Americans who do not want to say it at all.

AN INTELLIGENCE UNCOMMON IN HIS FIELD

Lendl's torment extended by another year

2 July 1991

Even the tea-girls were sorry. 'He'll never do it now,' they murmured, amid the rattle of saucers. For Ivan Lendl, whose popularity swells with the passing years, his fourteenth appearance in the Wimbledon championships ended, prematurely for him, in the third round yesterday: defeated 6–3, 3–6, 7–6, 6–3 by David Wheaton, a fresh-faced 22-year-old from Lake Minnetonka, Minneapolis.

If an admittedly freelance crowd had tried, on Sunday, to turn the centre court into a South American football stadium, things returned to normal yesterday. Tennis, in my opinion, benefits from the theatrical hush of the opera house, and now they had drama enough.

Behind that almost gaunt, hollow-cheeked central European face of Lendl's lies a wide-ranging intelligence that is uncommon in his chosen field. Yet Wimbledon continues to taunt him. Next time he will be 32; fractionally less tangible for him each time, a scientist for whom the perfect formula, achieved eight times in other grand slams, slips by. He had no cause to complain yesterday. Nor did he. Lendl is the most honest of sportsmen.

There was no point in being angry, he replied to a questioner. 'I was beaten fair and square.' It had been, he said, a miserable European season for him, after a hand operation early in May to cure tissue damage in his palm near the thumb.

He did not attempt to hide behind this; it had been no trouble, he said.

Yesterday there was no argument. Wheaton, a quarter-finalist last year in the Australian and the US Opens whose prize-money earnings of $500,000 are barely a fortieth of Lendl's, overpowered the No. 3 seed. Lendl's second service, regularly necessary, took severe punishment from Wheaton's two-fisted backhand, and Lendl repeatedly misjudged ground shots that in his prime he would have put away with barely a glance. This was not the Lendl we know, losing finalist of 1986 and 1987.

He draws sympathy because he is so patently trying at Wimbledon to master a game that does not come easily to him. The instinctive hard-court game that became second nature as a child, under the guidance in Ostrava of his tennis-playing parents, has little scope at Wimbledon.

Here he is, at 6ft 2in, trying to play serve-and-volley, concertina-ing those legs to reach the low volleys: a trumpeter trying to handle the trombone.

He receives 'tons of mail' here in London, he said almost apologetically afterwards, 'but you try not to get caught up, you have to do it yourself . . . if you keep coming close, maybe one day it will happen'.

Not this time. Wheaton, an angular 6ft 4in yet with oddly delicate hands, set the pattern in only the second game, breaking Lendl's service with a flashing two-handed backhand and a lob. That was enough to take the first set, Wheaton's own service being particularly sharp to Lendl's backhand in the left court. If Lendl discovered that Wheaton's single-handed backhand volley was suspect, he could never build the dominance to exploit this.

There was a marvellously tense fourth game in the second set, which went to six deuces. On his third game point, Lendl broke for 3–1 with a backhand return down the line, sufficient to give him set-all.

Yet, the match continued to edge away from him. Wheaton broke for 3–1 in the third set, and though Lendl broke back to be 5–5, he surrendered the tie-break 8–6, his service faltering on critical points.

Wheaton broke him twice in the fourth set, surviving his own nerves in the eighth game when he served full toss into the spectators on one point and fell on another. It was a forlorn Lendl who wiped the sweat from his brow at match point, and Wheaton hit a stinging cross-court forehand at the first attempt.

NEW MODEL DOES THE TRICK

Becker sub-standard against rising Stich

8 July 1991

Michael Stich, the newest German serve-and-volleyer, played like a champion. Boris Becker did not, even though widely forecast to add a fourth Wimbledon title to his collection; this was very much sub-Becker.

That assessment should not diminish the performance of Stich, who has appeared almost magically as champion before an unknowing British public, like the rabbit out of the conjuror's hat. Any preconceived suspicion that this would be a boring shoot-out was banished by the splendid variety in Stich's game; familiar to those close to him but yet to become known worldwide. It soon will.

Here was one of those occasions when it was hard to tell how far the victor's dominance conditioned a seeming frailty within the vanquished. So distressed was Becker's form that his temperament, normally so predictable, so unshakeable, declined in parallel. 'I'm not enjoying this,' he bellowed in German at one stage, as though in some Monty Python sketch.

Yet here was no sketch. Here was the destruction of a player who has been a great champion, who had lost only twice in a Wimbledon final (to Edberg), who had been beaten only ten times in 83 on grass. Stich reduced this grass-court machine to a coughing, spluttering out-of-date model.

While Stich – who, like Becker, gave up football for tennis, though at a later point in his youth – was not as irresistible as the Becker who hurtled, meteor-like, past Curren and Lendl in the finals of 1985 and 1986, he has become, in the space of four days, a figure to be regarded in awe, successively dismissing three grand slam champions.

Yet a thought nags: were we watching the latest instance of premature burn-out? Have the fires of mental ambition and physical assertion that made Becker the world's No. 1 already started to wane at 23?

There was, beneath the surface as well as in the gripping fluctuation of the points, a special sporting drama in the third set as fascinating as anything we have seen at Wimbledon in years. As the set, and with it the match, was slowly, slowly prised from Becker, his reluctance to release his grip was at times sadly inept, at times heroic.

But to go back, momentarily, to the beginning. Spectators' fears of tedium instantly disappeared with a flurry of points against the server, Stich breaking Becker and saving a break point on his serve for 2–0. Becker broke back with the help of a glorious backhand pass for 3–3, only immediately to lose his service to love. It was already apparent that Stich's backhand was in destructive form and Becker's volleying worryingly shallow.

As the second set began to go the way of the first, Becker's nerves, extraordinarily, disintegrated. As he cursed, shouted and shook his fists at the heavens, the front row of Royal ladies smiled tolerantly like school parents watching someone misbehave on junior sports day. Becker was warned for time abuse; it was his reputation that was more threatened.

Midway through the second-set tie-break, with Becker trailing 1–3 on Stich's stunning backhand pass on service return, an ambulance wailed its siren outside. Becker might not yet be a stretcher case, but the brain was limping as much as the body.

Now came, for him, the agony of the third set. Eight times in his first four service games he was break point down as this disrespectful compatriot, slim, lithe, equally tall and ferocious, drilled the balls back at him like grape-shot. All the qualities that once typified Becker were now vested in his opponent: unflinching steadiness, power, accuracy, simplicity.

There might be nowhere for Becker to hide, but stoically he refused to lie down. At 4–3 and 40–30 to Stich on Becker's serve, Becker for once hit a marvellous deep volley to the corner of the baseline to save the game. The executioner at the other end was unrelenting; and served to love for 5–4.

As they changed ends, you could sense that Becker's intolerance of his decline had forfeited the crowd's sympathy. In that harsh way of the sporting public, they were ready for symbolic death.

At 0–30, having hit a pathetic volley, Becker still hung on: an ace, a diving backhand return in attempting to avert match point. But Stich closed in with a remorseless forehand return.

As the two young men embraced, you could sense the crowd's sudden forgiveness for the fallen champion's frenzy. He looked about 30. This modern game strips you bare. How long can Stich last in the goldfish bowl?

FIDEL STILL CASTS SPELL OVER ISLAND OF DECAY

Pan-American Games a credit to Cuba's people, not its system

7 August 1991 Havana

In Cuba's steamy humidity, everything – not least the economy – moves slowly. The opening ceremony of the Pan-American Games here overran by an hour, partly because the young women dressed in flamenco style who led each of the 39 teams into the stadium, walked as though down the aisle on their wedding day.

Economic isolationism – roundly denied by Fidel Castro – has not brought the nation to its knees, but these are hard times for this huge, unpolluted island of rare beauty without natural resources excluding its sugar cane, rum and tobacco leaf. Food queues are everywhere; paper is so scarce newspapers are slim or even suspended, while result-sheets at the Games are scarce enough to be collectors' items.

The Games flame at the main stadium burns smokily from paraffin. To alleviate the fuel crisis, Castro imported hundreds of thousands of bicycles from China. Fatal accidents abound, mostly among the young and fit: with transplant surgery advanced in Cuba, cyclists are cynically nicknamed 'donors'.

Lobsters come as large as rabbits from the warm waters, but press too hard with your fork when cutting one, even at a formal function at the Palacio de Convenciones, and the cheap implement will fold in two. Realisation of the export potential of its abundant, unexploited seafood to capitalist markets is just one of Castro's dilemmas.

At the recent Ibero-American summit of 21 Latin countries at Guadalajara, Mexico, Castro stated: 'Europe has united, why shouldn't we (the Latins) unite, since we all speak this marvellous language?' Diplomatic relations have been reopened with Colombia and Chile, and observers believe Castro's lifeline to economic survival and eventual harmony with the US will be achieved without loss of face via improved Central American relations.

A delegation of 20 technicians recently visited Toronto: there are plans to build 1,000 hotels, and Cuba needs more sophisticated bathroom, kitchen and front-desk equipment for the discerning tourist. Few of the shining Italian coffee machines installed at the Games refreshment bars yet work properly.

Tourist transport is not a problem. Cuba is littered with unused military airfields available for charter flights, one of them already serving the golden sands of the Varadero holiday resort on Bahia de Cárdenas peninsula.

Needless to say, the Germans have already discovered the Varadero haven, where prices for the moment are unreal: I rented a 20ft catamaran for under £10 an hour. There is the space here to build 200 golf courses without anyone even noticing them.

Havana is a revelation to the newcomer, a sad contradiction. Here is one of the world's truly magnificent cities, its wide tree-lined boulevards eloquent of a sumptuous colonial past. The sweeping six-mile waterfront makes San Juan look second-rate or Copacabana merely *nouveau*. Yet the city is crumbling like an old, abandoned wedding cake. The impressive pillared, stuccoed Spanish architecture decays, 30 years without paint, many houses without doors or window panes but still inhabited by the impoverished.

A feeling of unease runs through the city, of stirring, denied ambition. The young, exhorted by propaganda posters not to emigrate (illegally), know that there is another world. They can see it here and there: at Floridita's, Hemingway's old haunt and birthplace of the Daiquiri, a restaurant-bar established in 1818, then as The Silver Pineapple, and included by *Esquire* magazine in the 1930s among the world's seven best bars, together with Raffles in Singapore. Without money, youngsters gather at night in clusters along the sea wall, fishing, swimming, talking, courting, many still there at dawn.

Though Cubans have that languid, agreeable Caribbean nature and a friendship that is instinctive, service to the tourists tends to be half-hearted. The open-air Tropicana nightclub has a floor show that is wooden, much less erotic than the evening street scene, when regular brief thunderstorms bathe the city and the scanty dresses of young women without umbrellas become almost transparent.

Castro blindly dismisses market changes in Eastern Europe as 'crazy misfortunes'. Yet is is easy to see how this revolutionary, who in 30 years has transformed a country from 95 per cent illiteracy and relative rural slavery into a modern society, is revered. There is true affection in the public chanting of 'Fidel'. He is literally close to the people. His personal magnetism is undeniable, even if resident foreigners say he has become a self-parody.

He can be mocking. At a private function at the weekend for sporting VIPs, he said: 'We have 20,000 sports professors in this country . . . they are available to help anyone who needs them . . . there were so many at one time that I had to ask who was cultivating the fields.' Clearly, Castro has to take a new direction. Everyone waits to see how soon and where.

8 August 1991

Two days ago, my hotel, the most comfortable in Havana, ran out of everything but fruit for breakfast by nine o'clock. The day before the opening ceremony of the Pan-American Games, with several large teams arriving simultaneously, the village restaurant ran short of food for dinner. Cuba is in economic crisis.

With four days to go, the public face of the Games has been largely unblemished and a substantial international success. Some of the facts behind the scenes have been less happy. The Games have succeeded because of the people and failed because of the system.

It is said that, after 38 visiting nations have departed next week, and the almost unfailingly courteous officials, interpreters and volunteers have gone back to their normal jobs or studies – for many are students – the buzz of traffic along the spectacular sea front will halt. Havana will effectively have run out of gas. So much of what was even beforehand so little has been sacrificed to ensure the Games succeeded.

For the first three days, there was no soap provided in my bathroom, never mind a bath plug. Thirty years of travelling in Eastern Europe, however, conditions you to travel with some essential supplies, while a plug can always be fashioned out of a wad of toilet paper wrapped in a piece of duty free bag. Obliging you to shower, of course, saves hot water.

It has been, until now, the dream of Fidel Castro and his regime that Cuba, attempting the same totalitarian sporting platform as former fellow travellers in the Soviet Union and East Germany, might one day host the Olympic Games. That dream is dead, at least until the regime opens its doors to conventional incentive marketing.

The Games have splendidly shown the Cubans what they can, or could, achieve and, at the same time, what at present they cannot. They have concentrated, predictably, on serving the competitors, and to a degree have done it well. Press communication facilities, on the other hand, have ranged from poor to disastrous, even though every stadium has a range of working, relaxing and refreshment facilities not always to be found at other leading events.

Actually transmitting the news has been problematic. No collect calls, no fax, poor computer links, in some instances no credit-card slips on which to take a card payment imprint for overseas calls; delays on incoming foreign calls of an hour or so because of congestion, a malfunctioning local telephone system, disorganised seating, etc.

Watching Castro at close quarters, as I have had the opportunity to do at several private functions and in public at event venues, there has been the evident pleasure of every showman with a large audience: in Castro's case, with the not infrequent experience of embracing, literally, many members of the capitalist world.

If the message of the Games – the need for ideological osmosis – has not reached El Comandante, it has certainly penetrated many of his subordinates; not to mention the man in the street, who has to queue an hour and a half at one of the many pizza bars for a soggy slice of questionable quality.

Havana, indeed the whole country, is a waiting stage crying out for regeneration and development, denied only by its political soul. In revolutionising Cuba, Castro gave the country international self-respect, education, pride and a future. Now, he is preventing the furtherance of that future.

It has been apparent that Castro, and his former armed-forces lieutenant, José Remón Fernández, the Games chairman, fully appreciate the role played by Mario Vazques Rana, the president of the Pan-American Sports Association.

Vazques Rana has been in Cuba almost monthly for the past year and a half to ensure that the deadlines were met in a completion crisis proportionally just as critical as that of the Montreal Olympics in 1976.

If the credit for the fulfilment of the Seoul Games was Samaranch's, Vazques Rana's is the credit here, together with the efforts and sacrifices of the ordinary people. Whatever the objections, and I'm not familiar with them, Vazques Rana was a controversial addition in June to the IOC, some members afraid of his power. His altruistic contribution to Latin American dignity here – he surely has no need of personal prestige – has been substantial.

There will be many memories to take away. Recollection of a three-hour wait on arrival for my luggage, eventually discovering it unattended in another part of the airport, will fade, and the friendliness will remain; the enthusiasm of guides introducing visitors to details of the new venues. The good humour of house maids switching off the vacuum cleaner in the corridor when trying to phone on a bad line in the hotel bedroom; the willingness of interpreters to work long hours.

In Communist Russia, I used to find people helped you because it was a duty. In Cuba, they were doing so because it was a pleasure.

SPRINTING TO IMMORTAL STATUS

Lewis takes his place alongside Owens

28 August 1991 Tokyo

It was not records that Carl Lewis broke here last night, it was the boundaries of credibility. If there was any doubt about his place among the legends of not just athletics but of all sport, this was removed by a victory that was astonishing by every estimation.

As the gasping, wordless Japanese television commentator exclaimed, as Lewis soared like an antelope from being a yard down at half-way to take Leroy Burrell on the line: 'Aaaarrghh. Oooohhh.' It was a race that consigned the banished Ben Johnson to history's footnotes, defied the law of nature which determines that sprinters are young men surging on the flood of natural hormones in fluid muscles,* and overthrew the notion that Burrell, the boy, the record-holder, would bury him.

What Lewis achieved is not measured in seconds, but in the awe with which his name will be discussed in years to come. He had taken his place alongside the immortal Jesse Owens when he won his four gold medals in Los Angeles seven years ago. To have broken the world record here in the world championships at 30, following his moral triumphs in the Rome championships and Seoul Olympics, makes him a phenomenon to compare with the likes of Nurmi, Bobby Jones, Ali and Pele.

Such names are not spoken of, after their time, in terms of what they won, but of representing something beyond normal reach, of being on a plateau somewhere between us and the gods. Lewis now stands with them.

In the athletic arena – and he still has the long jump to come and Beamon's record to aim at – he obliterated the earlier fastest men of the century through the decades: Charlie Paddock, Mel Patton, Bob Hayes (of whom the rolling Burrell is so reminiscent), Jim Hines and Valeriy Borzov. Arguably, Lewis is superior even to Owens.

On that wondrous May day in 1935, when Owens broke six world records within one hour, it seemed there could never again be such a man. Owens was an early emancipation symbol for the black man, and confirmed an eminence that rose beyond sport in the Berlin Olympics. He might well have won further Olympic fame in the 1940 Games. Lewis, the athlete of the Eighties alongside Coe, remains awesome in the Nineties. 'It will be the highlight of the championships,' Burrell, exceedingly generous, said. Burrell is wrong; it will be the international highlight of 1991, never mind George Foreman, Ian Woosnam or the outcome of the rugby union World Cup.

It could be too easy at such exceptional moments to open the tap of exaggeration, but when Linford Christie, breaking the European record in what was the world record a few months ago, said 'he's the greatest of all time', that may be the simple truth. Burrell, who has almost schoolboyish innocence in the way he punctuates his conversation with 'gosh!', said that 95 per cent of the outcome was determined beforehand in the mind, and that Lewis had proved himself beyond all examination. Lewis reflected: 'My entire career had something to do with tonight.'

As significant as the race was the fact, as Burrell said, that 'this was real', a condition we must all fondly hope is so. Primo Nebiolo said at dinner the night before a little sombrely: 'We must hope this is no repeat of Seoul.'

There is a passion about both Burrell and Lewis, colleagues with the Santa Monica club, that conveys an honesty. Sport, Burrell said, has cleansed itself. 'It's about strong will,' he suggested; the inference being that those who use drugs lack the will. Another simple and obvious truth.

In mid-afternoon, the two spent an hour together, relaxing. Behind both lay the motivation of a father. Lewis's is no longer with us. But watching, his son said: Burrell's is recovering from open heart surgery. Their fathers' spirit went with them to the starting line. The thought moved Lewis to tears afterwards; Burrell said that once he had spoken to his father in hospital, hearing his voice following the operation, it liberated his mind to concentrate on the race. In vain.

'I broke the world record,' he mused, 'but he broke it a bit more than I did.'

* Lewis's muscle definition has remained constant since he was a teenager. I like to believe he is naturally exceptional and free of drugs.

AZINGER REAPS REWARD
IN TENSE DUEL

America's triumph benefits Ryder Cup

30 September 1991 Kiawah Island, South Carolina

It was good for the Ryder Cup, not just for the Americans, that the United States team won it. Emotionally crushing though it was for poor Bernhard Langer, missing from six feet on the final green of the final round, I would not have shared the European self-satisfaction that would have followed another triumph-by-tie.

When Couples and then Wadkins won their respective singles, matches 25 and 26, against Torrance and James – at the climax of the most dramatic three days I have had the fortune to see – the best that could be expected for Europe was another 14–14 finish by Langer beating Irwin. Over three days, the US had predominantly set the pace, even when losing Saturday's four-balls by 3½ to ½.

The Ryder Cup became important, as did the America's Cup, only when America lost it. The toil of getting it back has taught them something about themselves, about golf, and perhaps a little about life. It takes something out of the ordinary to reduce to tears hard men such as Calcavecchia and Wadkins.

The European team went into the match with the stronger individual reputations, and in defeat one or two of their players, such as Faldo and Woosnam, have cause now to reflect on their approach to the event, on why they contributed, relatively, so little in substance and spirit.

Langer, putter *par excellence*, should not feel humiliated by his one errant shot, historic though it will now become. The greatest of his contemporaries, Ballesteros included, would not have wished the moment for themselves. What it did was to encapsulate, yet again, the magic and, at times, the impossibility of this game. There is no equivalent in sport to the expectation placed upon Langer on the 18th green, just as there is no parallel to the concept of 28-matches-within-a-match. A Davis Cup tie for instance, has a mere five matches.

Dave Stockton, the US captain, spoke truthfully when, drained of all adrenalin, he reflected: 'I couldn't say it was an overwhelming success.' Anyone who had witnessed the passage of Stockton from pre-match optimism through caution into disappointment and finally transparent anxiety will sympathise. When Langer and Irwin went level to the 18th tee, strong Americans in the press tent departed in search of a beer to steady their nerves.

When I had passed Stockton between 17th tee and green during the Azinger-Olazábal match, his pinched demeanour, even with Olazábal off the green in the crowd, was that of Rod Steiger when playing sheriff and being seven down with eight to play against the Mafia. Under a burning sun and sea wind, Stockton was temporarily ashen. This event *shreds* people.

So does Pete Dye's Ocean Course. If I were to find the $120 green fee, I would need at the same time a boat, a sack of balls, and probably a spade rather than a sand wedge for digging out those balls I did find. Dye's design, scenically and in golf terms, is awesomely beautiful. It is the only course in the world, for a start, with about five miles of unbroken bunkers. The 18 holes are strung out between sea, sand, and alligator-infested dykes and marshland, some of it artificially recreated by Dye.

After three days and some 60 holes as a spectator, I am numb. The mental and physical concentration demanded of those who played in all five sessions – Azinger, Wadkins, Couples, Ballesteros and Olazábal – must have exceeded in endurance almost anything in sport. Azinger's drive on Sunday to the 17th – a prospect which, every time, is like making your first parachute jump – was one of many shots of the tournament: Woosnam's wedge from sand rough to three feet at the 17th in Saturday's four-ball, Olazábal's incredible five-iron uphill into the wind to within 25 feet at the 16th on Sunday.

The behaviour of the home crowd was nothing but good humoured. When Langer entered the patrons' tent at dusk nursing his wound, he was greeted by an affectionate American rendering of 'There's only one Bernhard Langer'.

The lager louts among the British trippers were a minority but worrying: vestiges of Empire Loyalists in search of a new empire. They regrettably raised the level of chauvinism and will be worse in two years' time at The Belfry.

Will Ballesteros be there? What a figure this Spaniard has been in fashioning the history of the game. The cornerstone of three cup victories, with Olazábal he was again the bulwark of the European team, a truly inspirational figure: that wonderfully expressive, anguished and determined face thrust forward in front of hunched shoulders, grabbing at his clubs from the bag like an impatient archer, Seve and Ollie have been the soul of the European team, young Olazábal this time the stronger of the two.

Because a Ryder Cup tournament teaches you so much, even the luckless Gilford should now be a better player, together with Broadhurst, Feherty, Montgomerie and Richardson.

In 1993, they will have the motivation from defeat that this time fired the Americans. As Woosnam might say in his football parlance, in a memorable match they done great.

1 October 1991

When José-María Olazábal stretched out his hand to concede the 18th hole to Paul Azinger, the American roar that drowned the sound of the surf signalled that this unforgettable Ryder Cup had tipped decisively towards the United States. In a fine competition, there had been no finer individual match.

Azinger has had his problems with Ballesteros, but yesterday with Olazábal, in what was perhaps the critical singles of the day, he shared a round of unequivocal sportsmanship, even including the moment when his opponent wished to consult the referee about his lie beneath a tree at the eighth. Tension was as taut as a bow string, yet both men conceded putts to each other with a generosity that epitomised the reputation of the competition.

For two days, Olazábal, together with Ballesteros, his Spanish compatriot, had held the European team together: two victories over Azinger and Beck on Friday, then Floyd and Couples on Saturday morning and a half against Stewart and Couples in the afternoon.

The demands of this treacherous Ocean Course, physically and mentally, are perhaps without parallel in golf. Azinger, defeated three times over the two previous days with one halved, must have been equally drained, yet now the two men fought a duel of unrelenting quality.

Azinger, from Florida, is 31, Olazábal a mere 25, the man who made that memorable putt to edge Europe towards victory at Muirfield Village four years ago. At Kiawah Island, Olazábal has played like a man with twice his years' experience, and now he needed every resource to match the supposed leading singles player of the US team. The balance of holes between them changed 12 times as the sun beat down and the wind sometimes rose to force six.

One down at the 1st, Olazábal immediately drew level, led at the 3rd, was pulled back, went one down at the 6th, was level again at the 7th. Three times between the 9th and 14th, Azinger would go one up only to be cut back instantly. It remained level to the 17th tee, where Olazábal hooked into the crowd and sand to the left of this frightening water hole.

Azinger went to the 18th tee one up again, with his match and the Ryder Cup itself hovering in uncertainty. Olazábal put his iron approach in sand to the right and Azinger's 70 foot putt from a hollow on the left of the green ran to within six feet. Olazábal's first putt failed for a bogey and, in the spirit of their rivalry throughout, he conceded for a two-hole victory and a critical point towards America recovering the trophy.

A tide of spectators had gathered behind the tall, lissom Azinger, runner-up to Faldo in the Open four years ago, from the moment he birdied the first hole. There is a distinctive way that American spectators at sporting events have of addressing competitors with a life-long familiarity, and now Azinger was the brother of 25,000 people thronging the course.

Yet repeatedly they were compelled to admire the Spaniard, as when he hit his iron approach into a crosswind at the 3rd to within seven feet and holed to go one up. A double bogey cost him the 4th. A marvellous four-iron second shot to the 6th seemed to give him an edge there, but Azinger immediately put his ball even closer, holed from five and a half feet and was one up again. Azinger bogeyed the par-five 7th to go level, and if Olazábal's putting had not deserted him he would have been one up instead of one down at the turn.

His touch returned, dropping the ball from nine feet at the 10th, only to miss from 11 feet at the 11th to go behind again. Putting his ball dead from 22 feet, he was level at the 12th as Azinger missed from seven feet, only for Azinger to hole from 12 feet at the 13th. The see-saw of fortunes was unbearable from the ropes, never mind having the club in your hands.

Both missed from six feet at the 15th. At the long 16th, Olazábal hit an iron approach out of sand, and it soared and veered in the wind like a gull and dropped 25 feet from the pin.

He putted to within two inches, Azinger holed spectacularly from 12 feet for the half, perhaps for him the final turning point of the round. And so to the 17th green. It was a match neither deserved to lose, and it truly was the stuff of sport.

HUMANITARIAN ALTRUISM RESOLVES AN ANCIENT EVIL

South African sport in the hands of three wise

men

6 December 1991 Lausanne

The other evening I had dinner with an Indian, an African and an Afrikaner. You wouldn't believe what good friends they are . . . considering they are all South Africans. The social-political equation in South Africa, so volatile, is solvable with such men as these.

Sam Ramsamy, president of the new South African Olympic Committee (Nocsa), Mluleki George, the vice-president, and Johan du Plessis, the general secretary, epitomised the three non-extreme ethnic faces of their country.

They are drawn together not just by sporting involvement but by the wish to ensure South Africa's future works. They make those who resist collaboration in British sports administration look incompetently foolish.

George is a former Xhosa political activist who spent five years on Robben Island penitentiary, where the form of physical activity operated by the police compatriots of Du Plessis's race left George with a permanently bent neck. You could say the strongest card in his hand in helping lead South Africa back to the Olympic games next years is forgiveness.

Du Plessis, a jovial, laughing man, comes from wrestling. He is chairman of the white former Olympic Committee, Sanoc, one of the five arms comprising the new committee. Regarded as a turncoat by some whites, Du Plessis's strongest card is that non-whites implicitly trust him.

Ramsamy, a former Natal teacher and former radical chairman of the international anti-apartheid body, Sanroc, has the job of trying to bind divisive racial forces into a cohesive Olympic team. He is the only one in South African sport with active knowledge of the international sports framework during 30 years of isolation but is short on administrative experience, which is provided by Du Plessis.

George provides credibility for the black majority as leader of the National Sports Congress and gives a direct line to Mandela.

Among many difficulties, Nocsa has found itself in trouble with the national government over rejection of the revered Springbok symbol, anthem and flag for use in Barcelona next year. That is why the International Olympic Committee (IOC) is sending a second delegation to Johannesburg in January.

'We had little choice,' Du Plessis said. 'Whatever we had decided, to use or not to use the symbol, there would have been criticism. The bottom line at the moment is participation, to be there. We can get the protocol right in due course.'

In their report to the IOC executive board, the delegation reported that they now have 23 affiliated non-racial Olympic sports – 20 summer, three winter – and eight affiliated non-Olympic sports.

The objections by the government on protocol detail is the more regrettable since De Klerk's administration has not yet put a single rand towards the preparation of the Olympic team, never mind his fulsome lip service to the value of South Africa's return at the time of the IOC's formal visit last June. Financial support is coming independently through ISL, the IOC marketing agents.

The IOC's second delegation to Johannesburg, again to be led by Keba M'baye, of Senegal, aims both to fortify and clarify the new integration, which was unanimously approved by the Commonwealth heads of government meeting at Harare in October.

Some remarkable events have taken place, such as the first dressage equestrian competition in Soweto. 'We have more black riders in South Africa than there are in the United States,' Ramsamy said.

Equally remarkable is that in tennis, table tennis and swimming, the amalgamation of white and black governing bodies – ignoring the dissident coloured bodies loyal to the South African Council On Sport (Sacos) – has led to coloured competitors deserting their organisation to join the unified body. Colin Clarke, the former general secretary of Sacos, has withdrawn his support of that political organisation.

Ramsamy, George and Du Plessis are setting an example: myopia will eventually be overcome, though it may yet be a bloody path.

CRUEL LUCK PRODUCES HISTORIC MONACO FINISH

Mansell thwarted by wheel failure and brilliance of Senna

1 June 1992 Monaco

Fate intervened. Just when it seemed that Nigel Mansell had a record sixth consecutive grand prix victory in his grasp, he was dealt the most wretched of cards. With seven laps to go, a wheel failure, not Ayrton Senna, overtook him to create one of the most remarkable finishes in the history of motor racing.

Now a contest that had seemed pedestrian, an unchallenged saunter towards Mansell's ambition and the first English world champion's title since James Hunt's in 1976 is suddenly alive and kicking.

By a mere two-tenths of a second Senna took his fourth consecutive Monaco victory, but what mental anguish there was for both men. It had seemed that Mansell had survived, mentally as much as mechanically, until he felt that wretched wheel-wobble coming through the tunnel and knew that misfortune was at hand.

Would the 28 seconds by which he led Senna be enough to survive a pitstop?

As he sat afterwards looking as hang-dog as a wet spaniel and physically devastated, Mansell tried to come to terms, sportingly, with the twist of fortune in favour of the man sitting beside him. It was, he reflected, the most important second place of his driving career.

When he felt the problem developing, he was halfway from the pits, riding on three wheels, and he lost 10 seconds or more in limping towards rescue. 'As I came out again I saw Ayrton go by,' Mansell said wryly.

For seven-eighths of the race he had had the race masterfully under control; then came misfortune. 'That's Monte Carlo,' he said, acknowledging that the bumpy track with loose dirt is a lurking hazard for any leader.

Now came a duel lasting some nine minutes that demanded the ultimate in driving skills from the two men and gave Monte Carlo and the watching millions on television a finish they will never forget.

The two drivers had been on nerve ends beforehand. This is a track, Mansell had said, with which the driver has a love-hate relationship, a track which you cannot attack, on which you have to hold back, a track where he had never won.

In the morning before the race, one or two of those who spoke to him had said he was as nervous as a witch, wondering whether fortune would hold good or whether, as they say, something was going to fall off. And it did.

Yet here he is driving as well as he has ever done, giving his bid for the title more attention, more concentration than ever before. The man who was the heaviest grand prix driver on the circuit was so busy losing weight over Christmas that he was almost anti-social, but the effort had been worth it, he said. He was breathing more easily, sweating less, was more mentally alert, more patient.

'My dedication this year is unsurpassed,' he said.

And that is how it looked as he raced round the houses beneath the cliffs of Monte Carlo for 71 laps, while the tens of thousands sat perched on balconies, rooftops and on the cliff face to the west of the harbour, just like the hordes at some *col des alps* during the Tour de France. Senna followed doggedly.

'You have a range in which we operate,' Senna said, haggard beyond his years. 'At the upper end you're vulnerable, to errors where there's no room to recover. Last year we were all at the upper limit. This year Nigel has a mechanical advantage that's so big he doesn't need to operate at that upper level. He knows it, so he doesn't expose himself to risks. That's the right way.

'But believe me, I'm still trying. Trying to maintain my motivation, which is not easy with so much frustration, knowing that I'm driving as well as ever, but that I'm only good enough to be a couple of seconds slower than the fastest car.'

Maintaining his own performance had become an end in itself, and this is what he was doing all yesterday afternoon, trying to keep the gap as small as possible, waiting for the moment when Mansell might strike unlucky. And it came. For seven laps, in a car with tyres that now had no grip, he fought every way he knew to hold off the challenge of the man sitting on his tail. With new tyres. This way and that they twisted, but as Mansell acknowledged, Senna was entitled to his tactics.

'He was fantastic,' said the runner-up, 'his car was just too wide!'

ENGLAND CONFUSED, LINEKER INSULTED

Taylor's muddled tactics fail

18 June 1992 Stockholm

It has to be asked, following the confusion of selection and tactics surrounding England's exit from the European football championship last night, whether Graham Taylor is the right man to continue leading England into the next World Cup.

Not only is there the obvious muddle of ideas between the manager and his players, but, in his own reaction to the defeat last night, Taylor appeared to be contradicting himself. He claimed that Sweden beat England playing English football. If that was so, then why not remain faithful to that principle? Yet it is Taylor who has been attempting to convince his squad of the need to use the continental style of spare man, or sweeper, in defence; even if he has twice used and twice abandoned this policy in the space of four matches.

It is, of course, a fundamental of the international manager's responsibilty that he should determine what is the best tactical way of playing internationally, and if Taylor has not made up his mind in the space of two years, then that personal confusion would seem to disqualify him from continuing in the job, no matter how likeable he is.*

To make seven changes in personnel, five of them positional, last night, to introduce, yet again, alterations in tactics and formation and to expect to win, required an enormous dose of luck. For 51 minutes, it looked as if Taylor once more might get lucky, but it did not last.

To embark on a European championship with the fluctuating policy that Taylor has utilised, against all traditions and experience within the game from previous successful managers, is to suggest that he is either a genius or foolhardy. Evidence of the former is in short supply.

To add to the confusion among his players, his final gamble, if that it can be called, was to remove his captain, his most experienced player and the man who has scored more goals for his country than anyone but Bobby Charlton, with half an hour still to go.

Whatever the merits of Alan Smith, who replaced Gary Lineker, I thought this was an insult to a great player in his last international match. While England were still in the match, Lineker had showed enough fire and positional sense always to suggest that he still had something to give to his side on this vital night.

Now they are gone . . . and although no one can celebrate an England sporting demise, at least the result brings the benefit of removing the violent elements of English spectators that threatened to ruin the tournament even more than the negative football.

Taylor's latest formation, abandoning the sweeper system for the second time in the tournament to play a flat back four behind a midfield quartet, always looked suspect.

The middle line would be positive going forward with Daley and Sinton on the flanks and, of course, it was agreeable to have Webb, a fluid passer, appearing for the first time alongside Palmer (a former sweeper). Yet England's middle line was likely to be under pressure if repeatedly attacked, and this indeed eventually happened. In the last quarter of an hour, Sweden not only won the match with the finest of goals but might have had two or three more.

For a long time, the Swedish team that had outplayed France and beaten Denmark was in relative shreds against an England side playing with conviction at the back and moving the ball forward quickly, both down the flanks and through the middle to Platt and Lineker: yet another fresh attacking partnership.

Though Platt mishit his shot for the goal, it followed a clean move between Webb, Batty and Lineker and, for the next 20 minutes, there were visions of England reaching their second consecutive championship semi-final. Now, however, Sweden began to find their feet, though it was Eriksson who had levelled the score early in the second half. Immediately, the tone of the match altered and there was a flood of yellow and blue towards the English goal.

For half an hour, England held out, but they were increasingly at full stretch to hold the flying Ekström. It was he who set in motion the lovely move that brought Brolin's winning goal. For the second time in their football history, Sweden had risen to the occasion as the host nation.

* Taylor continued, and failed to achieve qualification for the 1994 World Cup.

GRUNTING AND GROANING IS GETTING TEDIOUS

Navratilova, and tennis, have cause for complaint against Seles

3 July 1992

Most sports – football, rugby, cricket, boxing – get into a mess if they do not uphold their own rules. If the regulations of tennis had been applied yesterday, Monica Seles would probably not have beaten Martina Navratilova. The world's No. 1 is currently making the game sound like feeding time at the zoo.

The position is quite clear. The hindrance rule, under regulation 4/3/3 of the Women's Tennis Association rule book, states that 'any . . . continuous disruption of regular play such as grunting shall subject a player to a warning, and a penalty point thereafter'. Seles does not merely grunt on almost every stroke: she has a two-tone double-grunt which develops, when about to lose a critical point, into a squeal of complaint.

Seles was warned by the umpire twice, justifiably encouraged by Navratilova: at 2–2 in the second set and after Seles had served for 5–2 in the final set and been broken. Navratilova's complaint, she later explained, was less the distraction of a noise like strangled bagpipes than the fact that the sound of the opponent's racket on the ball, a key guide to velocity, was being drowned.

The critical game for Navratilova in a long and exciting match was the fifth in the final set. She had three break-points to lead 3–2 with her own service to follow: she won none. However, the one point of the match she would most like to have again, she said, was that at 15–30 when, at the end of a rally, she left a drive by Seles thinking it would be long. It had been struck less hard than she thought and was good.

Seles's vocal accompaniment is less offensive than all the nonsense which for years the sport needlessly endured from Nastase, Connors and McEnroe, but is incontestably an interference with the opponent's play. In the old amateur game, it would have been called bad manners. The rules, as always, provide an answer if officialdom only has the will to impose it.

Navratilova saliently made the point that Seles does not grunt when practising, which contradicts Seles's contention that she cannot help it. Seles further contends that McEnroe and Agassi are unrestrained grunters, that she is being penalised specifically because she is a woman and the No. 1.

Seles would be more believable had her tactics not included a nasty piece of gamesmanship when leading 4–3 in the final set: with Navratilova serving break point down at 30–40, Seles, waiting to receive, was leaping a yard back and forth from left to right. Navratilova refused to serve, began her rhythm again and there was huge applause when she saved the point in a baseline rally.

Seles says that she will spend the winter 'practising' the elimination of her melodic exhalation. She needs to, because it was clear where the neutral crowd's sympathy lay, as she may rediscover tomorrow against Graf. The crowd, predominantly, decided Seles was expedient rather than girlishly amusing, though you could see the funny side: there were moments when Seles seemed like some Disney character desperately baling out a sinking ship.

Navratilova, initially out-played, levelled at set-all, winning the tiebreak 7–3 with a succession of clenched, forearm gestures reminiscent of body-builders when photographed wearing little more than a clenched jaw smile. We knew that somewhere Virginia Wade would be telling listeners that 'Martina is getting pumped up'; and although the view of Navratilova pumped up is one which, aesthetically, many people seriously wish to avoid, there could be no doubting the sympathy now flowing her way.

She spoiled it a bit with her itsy-bitsy Marceau mime impersonations, but some sensational stop-volleys were leaving Seles stranded, physically and temperamentally.

Ultimately, however, that two-fisted backhand, which comes at you like a Foreman left jab, proved even more damaging to the former champion than any grunt.

A PARTNERSHIP FORGED ON SUPREME ABILITY

Redgrave and Pinsent toy with the opposition

3 August 1992 Banyoles

As a pair, they are as different as Ridgeway from Blyth and yet, in their way, as remarkable. Two unique men alone in a boat: in this instance, at Banyoles, the Olympic gold medal-winning coxless pair.

Steve Redgrave, the builder's son who left comprehensive school at the age of 16, and Matthew Pinsent, the rector's son from Eton and Oxford, are a social echo of that transatlantic coxless pair; NCO and officer. What they achieved here is said by the specialists to be the most exceptional partnership in world rowing today. They toyed with the opposition in the final, then crushed it.

The scene was inimitable: the apple-green viscous lake surrounded by the tree-shrouded hills, with reeds, willows and sandy paths fringing the water's edge. They came towards us out of the haze, from two kilometres away with a relentless mechanical-efficiency and graft, two massive tractor frames in perfect harmony, driving their slim, blue and white Aylings shell through the water as though on ballbearings.

When, with the race already won by the 1,750-metre mark, with Germany and Slovenia battling for no more than silver, Pinsent and Redgrave almost lifted their boat clear of the water in their final surge, it was one of the most impressive, muscular sights of the Games so far. And never mind the critics and sceptics; the rowing regatta, among many competitions, has epitomised everything that is irreplaceable in Olympic rivalry and mutual respect.

Respect which prompted Redgrave to say of his partner's record: 'He has achieved almost everything at the first attempt and has a great future.' Of Redgrave, Pinsent countered with: 'He is very aggressive, competitive and a great racer.' Renowned for their inter-boat chat, Pinsent added: 'He makes great calls. I have learnt a lot from him.'

Redgrave's Olympic string of three golds, thus joining five others in achieving the feat, makes his competitive reputation as formidable as his bio-physical reputation. His capacity for training work is legendary; yet for Pinsent to have stepped into the shoes of Andy Holmes, Redgrave's bow-man in Seoul, and become an equal figure alongside the great oarsman, is just as remarkable, especially to have done so at the age of 20, when they won their first world championship medal.

The acceptance by Redgrave of the adroit tactical switch by Jürgen Grobler, the former East German coach, promoting Pinsent to stroke, was a temperamental hurdle that many might not have cleared. The mental qualities within the boat have been anything but exclusively the Oxford man's. Yet the catalyst of their achievements has, perhaps, been the younger man's humour and his tolerance over the older man's severity. The matching has proved perfect.

As they crossed the line, Pinsent turned to his 30-year-old bow and said mockingly: 'Not bad for a has-been and a never-will-be.' The jest gives no indication of the anxiety ten weeks ago, just before the diagnosis of Redgrave's debilitating colitis, when Pinsent had been told by his girlfriend, who works in a hospital, that she has watched people die from colitis. Privately, Pinsent, at that moment, could not comprehend the future for either of them. Their recovery as a competitive unit is the most astonishing aspect of the medal they won so easily. For all the euphoria afterwards, for all the belief beneath the doubts that afflict every competitor, Pinsent could not express the winning sensation.

'It defies words,' Pinsent said, standing under the beating sun, no longer caring if he became dehydrated. 'I've loved the pressure, the nerves, looking back on it now, though I wouldn't have said so beforehand.' There was more pleasure than winning the Boat Race – twice – he reflected, because you were beating better people, training for four years, beating men who lived for rowing, yet competed without animosity.

'Now it's over, we can shake hands, have a beer, talk the race through and compare our feelings,' Pinsent said. A few yards away, Redgrave, characteristically, was the more serious, the more analytical, wondering about his future, about Atlanta. Two men united by supreme ability who had shared something that comes to few people. As Grobler said: 'They work so well together.' The novices among spectators had been able to observe that. As they had drifted back to the pontoon in the shadow of the trees, a crowd of hundreds waving Union Jacks had shouted their appreciation of a memorable morning.

ALGERIAN ADDS CRY OF DEFIANCE TO MOMENT OF JOY

Boulmerka strives for the liberation of the Muslim women of Africa

10 August 1992 Barcelona

There are many expressions to be seen in the face of an Olympic champion. Joy, relief, pride, awe, satisfaction. The look in the eyes of Hassiba Boulmerka, from Algeria, was one of unrelenting defiance.

Reviled by the Muslim fundamentalists in her country as a woman for stripping her arms, legs and her face bare in order to run, her victory in the 1,500 metres made her less a heroine than a martyr for the free expression of Algerian women.

As she crossed the line in triumph, despite that strange, ungainly gait, her instantaneous mood, like Sebastian Coe's at Los Angeles in 1984, was one of unveiled aggression: not, as with him, towards the press and television which had assailed him with doubt, but towards all those who questioned her right to be there, to express herself as a woman, never mind to be champion of the world, which she already was from last year.

Her gesture, with arms and legs spread wide and taut, as though still lunging for victory, said: 'Here I am, look at me, acknowledge me and accept me.' She tore at her bib-number, trying to reveal her country's name on her vest as the cameras closed in to convey her image to every corner of the globe. But the Olympic stage can carry a multitude of different messages.

Just under a year ago, Boulmerka, whose first recorded time at the age of 16 eight years ago was almost five minutes, had won the world championship in 4min 2.21sec, by a brief margin becoming Algeria's first athletic champion ahead of Noureddine Morceli in the men's event.

In Tokyo, Boulmerka had beaten the world's best to become also the first female African world champion in athletics (although Nawal el Moutawakel, of Morocco, won the Olympic 400 metres hurdles in 1984) and at home the insults and intimidation became intense. For religious fanatics, her fame was infamy.

Could she repeat the feat, against the same array of illustrious opposition: Dorovskikh, from Ukraine, and Rogachova, from Russia, the respective silver and bronze medal winners last year; the improving Li Liu and Yunxia Qu, of China; the veterans, Podkopayeva, 40, of Russia; and Melinte, 35, of Romania?

For three laps, Rogachova made the running, compact and confident, but the Algerian green shadow was dogging her footsteps, in turn trailed by the other Unified Team and Chinese rivals. On the final bend, Boulmerka let rip, a picture of power and willpower. Her splayed right foot has a plant more twisted than Cram's, but there was now nothing to stop her as she surged clear.

Her time of 3min 55.30sec was the fifth fastest all-time, and the race was the first with four runners under four minutes. Rogachova took the silver, the 20-year-old Qu the bronze with the 30-year-old Dorovskikh fourth. 'Algérie!' Boulmerka shouted at the cameras. 'Algérie!'

Her national pride was to be shared only with Hocine Soltani, a bronze medal winner in the 57kg category in boxing. Within half an hour of her victory, Morceli, after a season of injuries, would finish no better than seventh in a race surprisingly won by Fermín Cacho, a comparatively unknown Spaniard.

He gave his country one of the great prizes of the Games, a blue riband event. And who cared a jot that it was the slowest time, 3min 40.12sec, since Ron Delany won in Melbourne 36 years ago?

So astonished was Cacho to find himself leading, having made his effort down the last back straight to outpace the three Kenyans, Chesire, Birir and Kibet, Herold, of Germany, and Spivey, of America, that down the home straight he looked behind him five times.

Where were the others? Nowhere. In the last 50 metres, the silver and bronze were claimed by El-Basir, of Morocco, and Sulaiman, of Qatar. Morceli, badly boxed in from 800 metres to 1,200 metres, was never in the hunt. A bizarre race with a memorable finish.

ALONE YET UTTERLY SURE

Lewis, a British heavyweight challenger with genuine credentials

2 November 1992

The man who may be about to become the best British-born heavy-weight of all time entered the ring at Earls Court early yesterday morning more with the composure of an opera star than a prize fighter. It was as though Lennox Lewis knew, down to the movement of every muscle, exactly what he was going to do, rehearsed a thousand times. Within 226 seconds, he had done it.

There was an extraordinary look in his eye as he came into the ring, a look of being utterly alone yet utterly sure. You see it in a handful of competitors from time to time: in Ayrton Senna, Sebastian Coe, Rod Laver, Nick Faldo.

It is not the stare-him-down intimidatory gaze of some boxers before the bell, the macho bravado of a Tyson. It is the expression of someone who goes into the ring equipped with much more than a range of extravagant physical resources.

There are several ways in which the spectacular defeat of Donovan 'Razor' Ruddock was remarkable. Here is a British challenger for the heavyweight title with genuine, rather than contrived, credentials; a boxer-fighter to restore some dignity to a bruised international sport; a man with hands as fast as a middleweight throwing punches with the power of Samson; a serious contender rather than just another tree for a box office felling, as during Tyson's prime.

Yet there is more to it than that. If there can be intellect in the ring, as Tunney, Robinson, Ali and Leonard have shown there can, then Lewis, born within the sound of Bow Bells, seemingly has that quality.

Amid the euphoria of sending his opponent crashing to the canvas with a right hand some 11 seconds before the end of the first round, there was not a flicker of arrogance, no premature celebrations. Lewis was busy watching the feet and the eyes of Ruddock as he rose unsteadily on the count of six, the bell ending the round two seconds later.

'As he got up, his feet were wobbling and his eyes had widened, so I knew he was still feeling the pain,' Lewis said. 'But I knew I must stay cool and not waste the situation.'

It would have been easy to be over-confident, if only from relief. This was the opponent that others had avoided, in the musical chairs of the promoters' game, the man who had gone 19 rounds with Tyson. Half the battle of gaining a lucrative title bout, these days, is getting there without having to fight. Maybe Lewis could have gained a shot at Holyfield, or Bowe, a little later. Instead he chose to grasp the nettle. Or the Razor. Others said he didn't need to take the bout. It is the measure of him that he felt he did and that he could.

Violet, his adoring momma, has the ample form of Pearl Bailey, and you could see afterwards from whom the son gets his repose. 'I was very focused,' he said. Focused? As Ruddock leapt and danced and waved during the preliminaries, with the self-confidence that could not but seem feigned, Lewis stood quietly shifting his weight from foot to foot and gazing across the ring at the other man as though studying the questions of a tripos examination paper.

The response of a packed audience to the introductions beforehand had been informative. Frank Bruno, whose credentials now seem even more papier mâché than before, received a mixed reception of cheers and catcalls. Fight fans tend to be short on sentiment and long on reality. Betting shop reality. Henry Cooper, the only man to have made a real fist of a title fight since Farr against Louis in 1937, was given the bigger cheer.

There was a sudden transformation in the physical appearance of the boxers from the moment the bout began. As with weighing up horses in the parade ring, you would have said Ruddock looked more the part, imposing and mean, and you worried about what that left hand might do to the slimmer Lewis.

Yet the moment they moved in earnest, that slimness became a virtue. In an instant, Lewis was seen as the fitter of the two, Ruddock carrying spare weight around the shoulders and lower ribs. And Lewis, if not quite floating like a butterfly, was distinctly the faster with hands and feet.

For a minute and a half they fenced. Lewis threw a couple of tentative lefts that missed; Ruddock bored in on the ropes with his head like a rhino. It was no different to many a first round, the excitement existing almost wholly outside the ring, where a lot of money was going to change hands.

Then, suddenly, almost too quick for the eye. Lewis had delivered a fearsome right hand, above and down past Ruddock's left arm, exploiting his 6ft 6in in a manner never available to the shorter Tyson. Ruddock sprawled on the floor and, as he shuffled back to his corner, temporarily saved by the bell from a worse onslaught, his bemused expression was in sharp contrast to that of only a few minutes earlier.

Whatever Floyd Patterson in his corner might have told him, he was, all of a sudden, in no condition to absorb it.

Lewis almost strolled out for the second round, no hint of venom apparent, yet inside 15 seconds had put Ruddock on the floor again, this time with a stinging left that Ruddock never saw. We were witnessing a moment of boxing history in the making, I suspect. Ruddock rose like a man who senses that he has not only missed the bus but is left surrounded by seriously dangerous company.

He stared across at Lewis from the neutral corner after the count of eight with little but a longing for the refuge of his stool, and as Earls Court vibrated to the lust of the crowd, Lewis put him away with another right.

'His eyes looked blank,' Joe Cortez, the Puerto Rican referee gratuitously said to the press afterwards, leaning over the ropes several minutes later while various frenzied bystanders were being restrained from continuing the violence inside the ring. Not just his eyes, Mr Cortez, I thought.

In three minutes 46 seconds, Lewis had transformed the scene of British boxing. Dan Duva, whose Main Events consortium handles Holyfield, the world champion who defends the title against Bowe on November 13, stood leaning on the ropes during the post-knockout mayhem nodding to nobody but himself. He had just experienced, along with the rest of us, a revolution, and was weighing what it might all mean for Holyfield. Duva, of course, is one of those in the fight game who is comfortable whichever way the coin falls.

BOTHA TOASTS HIS FAREWELL WITH A SPECIAL DROP

Re-integrated South Africa returns to Twickenham

16 November 1992

It was a day for simultaneous celebration and worry. South Africa's return to Twickenham carried overtones of all the glories of the past and undertones of all the anxieties for the future. A beautiful sport still has enough bad vibrations, so that I found myself both happy and sad.

Happy to have seen the last international match of Naas Botha, one of the most remarkable and elegant kickers of the oval ball the game has seen, sad that South Africa's rugby rehabilitation remains clouded by ill-will and insularity on the part of some of their whites; an attitude so in contrast to their compatriots who are vigorously achieving change in cricket and other sports.

Anyone who had missed seeing Botha 12 years ago, as I had, should be grateful for a last glimpse of a special performer. The difficulty of handling and kicking a rugby ball is part of the game's fascination, something that hardly one percent of all those who play ever truly master. Imagine trying to hit a tennis or cricket ball that was triangular. Botha, marvellously proportioned physically and with that elusive secret of timing, makes his skills appear utterly natural to a degree that can unhinge the opposition in split seconds. He can swerve the ball off the outside of the foot and do things with it few can aspire to.

His kicking on Saturday, even in greasy conditions, was a marvel, rifling the ball 50 and 60 yards to stem English attacks and send them lumbering backwards. Andrew is an accomplished kicker, too, though his technique has a studied, mathematical calculation. Botha's art is altogether more spontaneous, and the nonchalance with which he spun away from on-rushing forwards to send a dropped goal attempt soaring between the posts after 25 minutes was a wonderful demonstration of his technique.

Two minutes before, Tony Underwood had accelerated through a groping South African tackle to score superbly in the corner and put England ahead 8–3; but with Botha's masterpiece and then Strauss going over the line to put South Africa ahead 16–8, the isolated *laager* of Afrikaanerdom was poised for the triumph for which it so longed. Whatever the tactical deficiencies caused by a decade's absence, South Africa's play had contained an electric quality that is unmistakable.

The mood when travelling to the ground had been typical of any international day. Knots of green-and-yellow decked South Africans were heckled good-humouredly by strident followers of the twice-grand slam champions, who think little beyond healthy sporting rivalry and a few beers, or more, afterwards. Theirs is not the world of racial division, of which they know and, frankly, care little. The fact that two Afro and two Asian-English were included in their XV was something they take for granted without any ideological consideration.

All that mattered on the 1.30 special from Waterloo was that the South African lot should be, in the nicest possible way, emphatically buried. The demonstration, just outside Twickenham's gates, by a throng of disenfranchised Asian South Africans, loudly supported by English sympathisers and solemnly patrolled by a few unblinking men in blue, was a coincidental distraction barely noticed amid the euphoria of expectation.

Nor was the crowd much bothered with the unfortunate, craven formal welcome given to President de Klerk by Sir Peter Yarranton, the immediate past president of the Rugby Footbal Union. This public indiscretion by a well-intentioned former second-row international implied the sentiment that South Africa should never have been away. It should seriously concern those involved with the projected UK Sports Commission, of which Yarranton is the proposed chairman. The traditional insularity of the Rugby Football Union is bad enough, but the UK Commission is in need of more statesmanlike intelligence than this.

De Klerk is to be commended for dismantling many fences amid controversy. He is caught in the domestic crossfire between his country's far right and the developing demands of the ANC and its National and Olympic Sports Congress. If South African rugby is to maintain its new-found international participation – and even host the next rugby union World Cup – de Klerk cannot be seen to be a party to continuing discrimination, still rampant in rugby. When he said, during an interview, that the world would miss out 'if rugby allows politicians to mix with it', and that 'rugby should be left to rugby administrators', contradiction was running at a gallop.

It was, therefore, perhaps a service to rugby in general, and South Africa in particular, that England reversed the tide in the second half, prompted by an early chipped kick ahead by Andrew that saw Guscott sail through a flat defence to score close to the posts.

From then on, England's recovery in the lineout, together with the inspirational tackling of Winterbottom and the opportunism of their backs, left South Africa floundering. Botha was now playing so deep that his three-quarters had no chance and not even his phenomenal kicking could rescue the situation.

The most points conceded in their history should send South Africa home to contemplate not only how they must reorganise the game tactically, but whether they might not be improved by giving 85 per cent of their fellow countrymen rather more of an opportunity to be involved.

It was symptomatic that, at the post-match press conference, Jack Abrahams, assistant manager of the touring team and a former official of the coloured South Africa Rugby Union, was not involved. He has apparently been barely visible throughout a tour directed by the old Broederbond brigade. If South African rugby is genuinely going to change, it has to change from the top. And it has been warned.

The sauciest of tries stolen by Morris from a South African put-in on the line sealed England's victory, and another by Carling salted the visitors' wounds. Botha came to the press conference and acknowledged the errors on the field. They would go home wiser, he said. His retirement leaves a void in their ranks, though his critics say that his captaincy has been devoid of genuine kinship. What a shame it is that lack of social enlightenment has not permitted his astonishing skills to illuminate the game these past 12 years.

Tactical wisdom has advanced almost every sport in recent times – not always for the benefit of spectators – and rugby is no exception. Geoff Cooke, the England manager, said with an undisguised hint of satisfaction that there was a considerable difference in judging what was happening in the game from what you saw on television compared with actually being out on the pitch.

Considering that South Africa are said to have doubled in efficiency during the course of their tour, it is apparent from that by how much they had fallen behind. This will leave them, for the moment, deeply unhappy, for rugby is ingrained in their soul yet there is more to one's soul than jumping, kicking and running with the ball and that is something they will have to carefully reconsider.

A PEERLESS DRIVER DISILLUSIONED

Senna appeals for F1 regulations to be changed

13 February 1993 Sao Paulo

They were saying a few years ago in motor racing, either affectionately, in awe or disparagingly, that he was just a little mad. Now it is Ayrton Senna, regarded almost unanimously as the finest driver since Jim Clark, who is waiting for Formula One to come to its senses.

Senna is not committed to drive for McLaren this season. Senna is not looking for another team. Senna is not worried about finishing second to Nigel Mansell or anyone else. Senna is not moody, greedy or sulking.

He is, simply, a peerless driver disillusioned at the path down which his sport is heading. Away from the driving skills that for 70 years have distinguished Campbell, Fangio, Ascari, Moss, Clark, Stewart, Lauda and Prost. Away from drivers' character and intelligence, and into the lap of computers beyond the reach of all but a minority of Formula One teams.

Senna is renowned for being detached, aloof, exclusive. A perfectionist. Now, at 32, the Brazilian finds that his perfection is redundant. Machines, he asserts, have taken his sport away from him, away from the public who clamour in their hundreds of thousands to watch him and Mansell and Alain Prost duelling at near impossible speeds.

'I want to be challenged,' he said. 'By my own limits together with someone else's limits, by someone who is made of the same skin and bone, and where the difference is between brain and experience and adaptation to the course; not challenged by someone else's computer. I don't want a car from Ron Dennis to let me win, but a car to let me compete.'

That was no longer so last season, Senna said, and the situation is becoming progressively worse. It is the drivers who make the show, and the show has been taken away and sport is being killed. 'The regulations *must* be changed,' he said, speaking with the authority of a three-times world champion with 36 grands prix victories. 'The machines have taken away the character, and it is the character that sponsors and public are looking for.'

Sitting behind his desk at the top of a new office tower block in São Paulo, where he can land his helicopter on the roof, Senna is resigned to the possibility that McLaren's new car – belatedly due for testing this weekend – may be inadequate. Maybe he will sit out this season, and spend his time developing the farm at Angra dos Reis a couple of hours' drive from Rio de Janeiro, the hobby he shares with his father Milton, the components manufacturer who set him on his way 20 years ago as a kart racer.

Senna is the technical genius who came closer to the limits than any driver before: so close that he generated resentment. At the peak of his rivalry in 1989 with Prost, then his McLaren colleague, Prost stated: 'Ayrton thinks he cannot kill himself because he believes in God, and I think that's dangerous for other drivers.' Senna would argue that he was not so much close to God as to perfect harmony with his car, to the discomfort of others.

'If I give a hundred per cent to my driving, which is my hobby as well as my profession, I can compete with anyone, but not with computers,' he said. 'I've got to have that feeling. Now, it does not exist. In 1988–9, we still had to figure out the problems [as drivers]. Now the difference between the [computerised] cars is huge.'

Only Williams, McLaren and Ferrari have a chance, he said, and last season even the gap between Williams and McLaren was unbridgeable. Mansell simply ran away with the world championship.

Never were Williams-Renault overtaken between the starting grid and the first bend last season. The driver now puts his foot flat on the acclerator, thuds in the clutch at the green light, and the computer takes charge. As the engines scream at 14,000rpm, the skill of the driver in finding the balance between either the wheels spinning in a cloud of burning rubber with the car stationary or maximising the acceleration into the first bend is now superseded by computer. Computerised gear changing means that the car comes out of the bend and moves through the gears from second to sixth with never a missed change, with never any damage to the box.

Even more significant, Senna reflects, is the electronically-controlled suspension, regulating in conjunction with the aerodynamics the height of the chassis and the inclination of the car at every curve.

'The computer knows where you are on the course and actually *designs* the lap,' Senna said. 'It is no longer the driver who determines the difference between first and second place, or second and sixth. Last year, we [McLaren] had a similar system [to Williams], but were adjusting and developing all season. You could not judge Mansell against the rest of the field, only against his fellow driver with Williams. Nobody seems to see the hole we're going into. Formula One is not a matter of just six cars, it has to be a proper race, with many having a chance.'

This is why other teams are showing hostility to Williams, and Senna argues that it is imperative for Fisa, the sport's governing body, not only to change the regulations – to ban computer systems, the development of which at absurd expense has no bearing on conventional motoring – but also to alter the Concorde agreement from ten years ago.

This required that any agreement to change must be unanimous among the teams. 'Unanimity is impossible,' Senna said. 'There has to be a majority decision, so that we have what is best for Formula One. On the Indy circuit, all the cars are comparable, they don't have computer electronics. The current problem is that there is no leader among the drivers. At the top, you have a few characters of conflicting personality while the rest, without good results, don't have any credibility. So Williams, McLaren and Ferrari go their own way for what they can get.

'Yet everything has a limit, and we must change the rules to find a way in which we can all work. To reduce the costs, so that we return to an era where the emphasis is on people, on building, developing and maintaining a team, dependent on the ability of those people and not on computer.'

Senna has abandoned any interest in the Indy circuit for this season. One or two of the richer rivals of the top three have approached him, but he is for the moment more concerned with the future of the sport than with his own. He is prepared to mark time until sanity returns.

The inclusion of his name on McLaren's list of potential drivers is a precautionary cover for both of them. He can be added at any stage up to three days before the opening grand prix in South Africa upon payment of a $10,000 penalty. 'If we come to an agreement.'

Both he and Dennis, McLaren's owner, accept that there was no value in McLaren's assurance that they would have a more competitive car this year. Only testing would prove that. 'It's worth waiting,' Senna said, enigmatically. Perfection is not something that can be snatched at. Senna has already been there. He thinks he has many years left in him, but as his opponents well know, he is not a man to compromise.

DANCING TO A FADING BEAT

Parreira optimistic for revival of Brazilian fantasy

22 February 1993 Rio de Janeiro

Poetry in motion. This may be a cliché, but it is reality in summer-time on Copacabana Beach. Nowhere else do you find boys playing frisbee and catching the still-spinning disc with their foot or knee, or 'passing' it in mid-flight with a flick of the forehead. Spontaneous exhibitionism is a way of Brazilian life.

So it is on the football field. Relative failure in the World Cup brings anguish, shootings and suicides. Nowhere else does football so express the soul of the people.

Last week, against the tactically superior Argentina in Buenos Aires, Brazilians were attempting skills I had not seen in nine World Cup tournaments. Bebeto was taking passes on the turn, simultaneously dragging and chipping the ball a foot high, so that it would pass above the instantaneous tackle from behind. If Bebeto's legs could ride the tackle, then the ball was free.

He and Raí, Careca and Valdo were constantly dribbling at opponents and *through* the oncoming tackle, gathering the deflected ball with quicksilver reflexes, the way Pelé used to do. The sight of Celio Silva dribbling round three opponents in his own penalty area before clearing would have brought a nostalgic gleam to the eye of Sir Matt Busby, who used to cause heart failure in the Manchester City directors' box when doing likewise in the Thirties.

There is truly no team like Brazil. To have drawn in Buenos Aires against a formidable Argentina side welded by Alfio Basile – with a commendable degree, especially for Argentina, of fair play – was an exceptional performance.

The Brazilian press raged afterwards in disappointment. Carlos Parreira, the manager, was happy nonetheless. 'Against what is probably at present the best team in the world, in our first game of the season, I think the result was OK,' Parreira said, 'especially when our midfield did not have a good day. The midfield is the lungs of a team, but if they don't coordinate, the team doesn't move well. We're not worried. We'll get in real shape when we have the time. What mattered was the strength of personality to come back from one down.'

The most colourful football nation is tormented by not having won the World Cup in five tournaments over 20 years: fourth, third, then eliminated in the second round, twice, and quarter-finals in the last three tournaments in which they could and should have reached the final. Defeat by a late, single goal against Argentina in Turin two years ago was less galling because Brazil had dominated the first 80 minutes than because they had betrayed their heritage by using, of all things, a sweeper. Back home, they burned effigies of Sebastião Lazaroni, the manager.

Fifteen months later, after the brief reign of Falcão, Parreira, the former physical training coach of the 1970 winning team, was appointed. He had subsequently spent seven years with Kuwait, leading them to the 1982 finals. He then managed Brazil for one year, won the national league with Fluminense in 1984, and spent the next six years back in the Middle East.

He feels it is his destiny to revive the old glories in the finals in the United States next year.

'We believe we'll only be successful again if we go back to our roots,' he said. 'There have been many changes in the game in 20 years; every continent has its own school. Ours has to be retained: our unique skills, our natural rhythm, our zonal marking, our possession game. In the last few years we became confused, using power instead of technique. We must return to creativity, to fantasy, to players' freedom.'

He leans back in his chair at the CBF (national federation) offices and fondly relives the second goal against France in Paris last year, by Luiz Henrique: 16 passes without the French getting a sniff of the ball.

That was something from the past. So, he considers, was the 1–1 draw at Wembley, when Brazil flowed. Parreira's record in 18 months is 14–10–2–2 (the defeats home and away to Argentina without his European players).

Parreira believes that a sweeper and man-for-man marking limits a team; that it conditions them to the other team's tactics. With an old-fashioned flat back four, used in the 12 years of victory, quick defenders have more chance for interception instead of tackling, more chance to play one-touch passes for the rapid development of attack.

I went to watch Vasco de Gama against Bangu in the Rio league at Maracana. Both sides appeared at times to be playing a sweeper, yet my eyes deceived me. 'Not really,' Carlos Alberto, captain of the 1970 side, said. 'One of the centre backs is always covering the flank where the ball is, making it seem like a sweeper, while the other centre back is marking. It requires rapid thought and movement.'

In order to generate the mood of 1970, the CBF has reassembled the administrative team: Mario Zagalo, then manager and now coordinator; Dr Lidio, the physician; Chirol, the physical trainer; and Parreira, then trainer, now manager.

Parreira's first target is this summer's qualifying tournament against Bolivia, Venezuela, Ecuador and Uruguay between July and September, with two to qualify. 'We had no time to adjust to the *libero* system in '90 [under Lazaroni], and I know that I don't have time,' he said. 'That is a huge philosophical change, so we will play the way we know. With what we know, you can succeed.'

In spite of the financial collapse of the Brazilian league, Brazil continues to produce outstanding players. But for how long? 'In the final analysis, you need more than spirit to win the World Cup, you need quality,' Parreira said. 'We are now, I am convinced, at the right moment.

'We have a squad of players around 28 or 29, with maturity and the experience. Several have played in two World Cup tournaments. We need to rely on those like Mozer, Branco, from Genoa, and Luiz Henrique, from Monaco. If we don't make it this time, it may take another 12 or even 20 years. Eight of our squad were in Italy, and that is always the key factor of successful teams.'

Whatever the critics may say, Parreira will continue with the experienced men until the qualifying tournament. Between then and the finals, he may consider one or two of the remarkable younger players: Cafu, the São Paulo right back, star of the world club championship final against Barcelona, or Celio Silva, a centre back who tackles like a tank yet dribbles like Rivelino.

Brazil's gift to football is immeasurable. It is in all our interest that they should triumph next year.

'THEY NEVER GAVE US A CHANCE'

Ruthless Cambridge complete ultimate Boat Race humiliation

23 March 1993

Seldom in the history of any two-horse event have the bookmakers been worse informed. The Boat Race odds of 1–4 on Oxford belonged to the realm of Canute. Cambridge, in a different league from the first stroke, buried Oxford within the first two minutes.

Cambridge used to perfection the big cleaver blades, scorned on the day by Oxford. There is no team so emotionally bankrupt as a beaten Boat Race crew and distressed Oxford finished as though with a hatchet in their backs. Beefeater, the sponsor, which has put £1 million into the race over three years, will have been delighted at such a contradiction of predictions.

The reputation of this now globally transmitted event, never mind the reputation of Cambridge, was revived by a victory that was crushingly conclusive, terminating what had become an Oxford closed shop for 16 of the past 17 years. So synchronised and so overwhelming was Cambridge's superiority that they exceeded even their own expectations: that they would match Oxford for about a mile, establish a marginal lead then burn them off.

'We knew we could do it after about 25 strokes,' Malcolm Baker, Cambridge's amiable American postgraduate, said. Others, such as James Behrens, the restrained president, gave conventional, more modest, reflections: like being sure at Barnes Bridge.

Baker, part of the engine room at No. 6, grinned in a tidal wave of pleasure. He said: 'The intention was to wait until Martin Haycock, our cox, was about to level with their No. 2 [over half-a-length lead] and then to open it up so they had no hope of coming back. We never expected it so early.'

Early! Cambridge began as sweetly as a swallow diving off the willow's bough and had taken the centre of the stream before the mile post. It was a march of triumph thereafter.

If you were looking for illumination on the prospects beforehand, during that long anxiety-ridden countdown on the stake-boats that has no equivalent in sport except perhaps the Formula One grid, it was to be found in the eyes of young Will Mason, the Cambridge stroke.

An imponderable of the race, the experts had said, was the inexperience of the respective strokes and coxes. Yet as the pencil-slim craft interminably slewed off line, and the starter waited, Mason's gaze was clear and focused.

The agony of the burden of his and the hopes of thousands was there in the face of Mason's rival, Gardiner. And when, an hour or so later, showered and blazered and trying to hide his sorrow at the boat house, Gardiner passed a jubilant Mason, still in singlet and chatting to interviewers, the Oxford stroke had to look away.

Mason reflected: 'I could have thought about many things, waiting for the start. But I thought of nothing but simply the first stroke, how important it was.' What a lesson in sports psychology from this near-adolescent.

All sport, in the ultimate moment of realisation, can be cruel. Richard Phelps, a veteran of 27, of the Olympics, world championships and Henley, knew enough of losing to Oxford to savour the satisfaction of victory. 'The idea was not to beat them but to shatter them, to leave them humiliated,' he said, without apparent aggression.

'When we were a length up, we felt we'd win. But for the rest of the race, we were mentally stamping on them. The relief is more than anything I can imagine.'

The joy, Phelps admitted, was making Oxford feel bad, the way Cambridge have felt bad for so long. The mental approach is one of destruction: winning a place in the boat, then winning the race. This is a competitive arena. The Cambridge motto stretches back more than a century: 'G. D. B. O.'. God damn bloody Oxford.

The intensity of the event is hard to describe. Jon Bernstein, Harvard land economist, attempted to do so. 'You wake up on the day three hours before you want to, with a sinking dread and a tingling in your fingers. The whole day is a cross between these two emotions. You do nothing but watch the second hand of the clock, hoping that when the moment arrives you can focus all that desire.'

How extravagantly Cambridge did just that. There was disbelief among two generations of Cambridge coaches in the pursuing launches and on the banks as hope become reality; as all the years of oppression rolled away behind the swinging rhythm of clean, crisp, almost mechanical, unity as Cambridge left Oxford grovelling.

'We were *flying*,' Bernstein recalled. From his faraway gaze, you could sense how it must have felt at the time. As the generous Mathew Pinsent, the Oxford president, said: 'They never gave us a chance.'

ON COURSE WITH STANDARDS SET BY THE MASTER

Bobby Jones: 'You play the ball as it lies'

12 April 1993 Augusta

'The Masters has long been the genesis for every serious player's season . . . a tournament where the true feeling of the game is not tampered with in any shape or fashion.'

Those words were written by Ben Crenshaw and addressed to Augusta National's chairman, Hord Hardin, shortly after his victory in

1984. Crenshaw added: 'I shall always attempt to carry this victory with the conviction that The Game is the thing, not anything else, along with a happy and life-giving memory.'

The legacy from Bobby Jones, winner of US and British both Open and Amateur championships in 1930, is indeed the most perfect of any sporting week, of any year. So, when Dan Forsman's challenge to Bernhard Langer slipped on the third day, and Nick Faldo equalled his worst previous Masters round with a 79, they did no more than bite their lip.

Crenshaw recalls visiting Bobby Jones to commiserate during the great man's last years of serious illness, and Jones reproving him: 'You play the ball as it lies.'

Those who knew Jones say that he revealed more resolution in his times of tribulation than he did in his many triumphs on the golf course.

As a young player, he had had to overcome an instinctive temper. He once withdrew from the Open championship, at St Andrews, in mid-tournament because he was so angry with his poor form. Thirty years later, they would give him the freedom of the borough.

Charlie Yates, 60 of whose 80 years have been entwined with the Masters, since its launch in 1934, knew Jones from boyhood, living across the road from East Lake country club, in Atlanta, where *the* master played much of his golf. Yates would follow behind him, an awestruck 11-year old.

'Occasionally, he would play with us around a short, par-three course beside the club,' Yates recalls. 'Unbelievable'.

Yates went on to become twice Georgia state champion, aged 17 and 18; national inter-collegiate champion in 1934; British amateur champion at Troon in 1938, beating Cecil Ewing, of Ireland, 3 and 2 in the final; twice a Walker Cup player and then captain in 1953; three times the lowest amateur in the Masters, with a best round of 70; and recipient in 1980 of the Bobby Jones award, the US Golf Association's most prestigious recognition.

He became, other than Jones's father, who was affectionately nick-named The Colonel, the most regular playing partner of the legendary amateur.

Yates reflected: 'I have occasionally written about his swing, which was exceptional. He played with unhesitating dispatch. His putting was wristy by comparison with today's method, and when he came back in 1934 four years after retirement, for the first Masters, or National Invitational, as it was known at first, he had not the same touch.

'He was one of the most intelligent people I've known, with an engineering degree from Georgia Tech, an arts degree at Harvard and a three-year law degree taken in two years. He was most helpful to me when I first started work in banking.'

Yates's serious playing ended with the war. When he returned home, the fluency had gone, though it did not stop him singing songs in the shower with the extrovert Colonel.

Stories of Jones's father abound. Before rules had been formalised, the Colonel would occasionally be enlisted at Augusta as a rules official. Sent to oversee Amen Corner, he was confronted by a player with a plugged ball on the bank above Rae's Creek; what Yates calls the most perfect hole in golf, where the players on the tee for the 155-yard hole are oblivious to the wind blowing down the 13th fairway and swirling around the precipitous green.

The player asked if he was entitled to relief. 'How do you stand against par?' enquired the Colonel. 'Seven over today, 19 over on the tournament, sir.'

'Then put the son-of-a-bitch on the green.'

When Yates once partnered a preacher against Jones and father, Jones shooting 64, the Colonel bunkered himself at the 16th, took two to get out and three-putted for an eight, every stroke accompanied by a vehement oath, the errant clubs beaten upon the turf.

'We should have known better' murmured the preacher in an audible pulpit-whisper, 'than to have tried competing against a combination of proficiency and profanity.'

Yates attributes much of Augusta's success to Clifford Roberts, Jones's friend, financial adviser and the first club chairman. Particularly important was the decision to invite golf clubs within 200 miles of Augusta to apply for series passes, thus ensuring a sell-out beforehand. One effect of this, Yates believes, was to eliminate the bad behaviour evident among day-pass purchasers at the gate, who brought with them the hollering and booing common to other professional spectator sports and the kicking of balls hit off the fairway into better, or worse, positions, depending on their mood.

Roberts also insisted on photographers and writers remaining outside the ropes, so as not to obstruct the spectators' view. 'Yet Augusta was the first to create the interview and press facilities that are now common to major tournaments,' Yates said.

What finally cemented Augusta's glory was the post-war appearance of Eisenhower, a golf fanatic, and then the simultaneous arrival of television and Arnold Palmer. Whence Arnie's Army.

It was Jones, however, who more than any perceived the importance of the media. In 1953, he wrote: 'To gain any sort of fame, it isn't enough to do the job. There must be someone to spread the news.'

Try telling that to some infantile contemporary professional footballers. Or even Linford Christie.

AMERICA PROVES A SOFT TOUCH

US golfers strangely untroubled by Langer's Masters victory

13 April 1993 Augusta

It had to come. When Bernhard Langer put his three-iron to the par-five 13th no more than a limousine-length above the flag, he had already narrowly skirted the possibility of a sensational round. He was due something.

His demeanour had throughout been mesmerising. The pursuing pack was not given a glimmer of light. Blond, dapper in primrose shirt and lime slacks, inscrutable and relaxed, he was a model of German efficiency. A Porsche on cruise-control. Impassable.

Six times in 11 consecutive holes played to par, after bogeying the first, he had been within four inches or less of a single putt and a birdie. When he had faced, unwaveringly, the daunting 12th, he might have been 15 under par instead of nine.

Shrugging off the demon that, only moments before, had devoured the luckless Dan Forsman – quadruple bogey for a seven when twice in the water – Langer now stood on the 13th green with Chip Beck, his only remaining challenger two shots astern, with the chance of an eagle three for each of them.

If the 12th at Amen Corner is the meanest hole in major championships – ask Nick Faldo – then the 13th is one of the most elegant. The golfer is asked to perform on what could be a canvas by Manet or Sisley. There is as much aesthetic pleasure to be had from an afternoon spent sitting there as at a concert or opera.

Now, Beck had to putt first from some 24 feet, a club length beyond Langer. Beck grazed the cup, and it served to give Langer the correct line and pace down the slope of the green. His ball was swallowed.

Though Beck birdied, Langer was now three shots clear with five holes to play. As his arms were raised aloft in fulfilment, everyone on the course, watching the red figures blink on the scoreboards, knew the Masters was over for another year.

There remained one more chance for Beck, only the second man ever to have hit a 59 on the American tour. The two men stood on the fairway beside their tee shots, at the top of the gradient that falls away to the water in front of the par-five 15th. Beck had the choice: to lay up safe and short of the water, or to hit a three-wood into the wind for the distant green. Go for eagle. Go for broke.

Langer had done just that at the dog-leg 13th, conscious that it was the moment to apply the pressure. Now the decision confronted Beck. 'The only choice was to go for it, he had to,' Langer reflected later. Beck laid up instead.

Worse still, he then struck his pitch over the water, through the green and off the back. Langer pitched to eight feet, birdied, and went four strokes up. When Beck then three-putted the short 16th, Langer was five up with two to play. The American challenge had disintegrated.

That was, is, and will continue to be the American talking point. What has happened to their golf? All afternoon, the leader board never showed serious threat to the imperturbable German. Forsman's charge collapsed, Beck never found the steel that was needed, Wadkins had a brief flutter that blew out, Daly's power proved irrelevant and Lehman's promise deceived.

The home of ruthless stroke play, of Hogan, Snead, Palmer, Nicklaus and Watson, was as empty as the words of Greg Norman had proved to be. Europe had taken the green jacket for the eighth time in 14 years. Is the welfare state's soft life the farewell state of American golf, never mind the Ryder Cup victory and Langer's agonised missed putt at Kiawah Island two years ago?

The picture of Langer and Beck together on the course provided a contradiction, a sporting conundrum. As they strode down the seventh fairway, the cheers out in front indicating that Forsman had closed to within a shot of Langer and one ahead of Beck, the two rivals were engaged in conversation, all smiles.

What a perfect picture of sportsmanship, one might say. How splendid that two rivals playing for the ultimate prize in golf should be able to do so in such a mood of friendship.

Beck was asked later whether he was happy, under the pressure of the event, to have such informality with his rival. Beck caused laughter by replying: 'This is not Herzegovina. This is the kind of tournament I want. We had a good time. I don't want his game to fall apart. I was hoping he'd have a good day . . . and that I'd play better.'

Admirable sentiments. Yet, if Beck had had a good time, he had lost. I do not think we would ever have heard those words from, say, Palmer, had he spent six holes only two shots behind the winner.

I remember following Palmer at the World Match Play at Wentworth. Palmer was long past his prime. As he played an iron approach, I was standing inside the ropes a full 220 degrees round from his stance and backswing, out of even peripheral vision. He missed the green.

As he turned to hand the club to his caddie he saw me and said crisply:

'Please try not to stand in my line of sight.' With Palmer, any missed shot hurt, never mind the stakes or his age.

You sensed on Sunday that Beck was not hurt by defeat. American golfers have to rediscover, perhaps, that sensation.

HOW COULD TAYLOR GET IT SO WRONG?

England's unnecessary elimination from World Cup

3 June 1993 Oslo

The moment I heard England's selection an hour or so beforehand, my heart sank. Their many limitations were to be compounded by sending out a radically changed team that would struggle to find each other on the field. So it proved. A scientific result cannot be achieved with a lottery selection.

England's World Cup prospects plummeted with this deserved defeat by moderate Norway in a performance substantially more embarrassing than the defeat here 12 years ago under Ron Greenwood. Any lingering sympathy for Graham Taylor, gamely doing his best to build bricks without straw, has evaporated. His plans never had a genuine prospect of success.

The faultiness of the strategy – three marker centre backs behind a four-man midfield, with Gascoigne floating behind Sheringham and Ferdinand – is beside the point. Taylor was voluntarily dropping his side into the same pit as Don Revie did: believing that impromptu tactical team changes can work among players who meet less than a dozen times a year. And this was not even a particularly sensible plan.

It is hard enough to build one formation at international level. To toy with two or more always courts disaster. England reaped almost inevitable punishment in a defeat that will, I fear, come to be seen as a watershed in their history and decline.

A team with alterations in each area is going to spend the first half, or more, establishing its own positional contact, let alone mastering the opposition; the more so when only one of the players, Gascoigne, is a fluent passer of the ball. From the first minute, England were little more than a smothering, blocking, fudging, clearing bunch of optimists, with little hope beyond hope itself.

Again and again, England were passing the ball into spaces of the field where there was not a single white shirt. Embarrassment was acute. It was as though England, not Norway, were the international apprentices. What ignominy when an England side is persistently whistled for its incompetence.

The back three, Adams, Walker and Pallister, were constantly unsure of their relationship and adjustment against Fjortoft and Flo, and their use of the ball expressed little but anxiety. In midfield, Sharpe, replacing the anonymous Barnes, was wholly at a loss, Platt and Palmer could seldom settle into a creative mould and Gascoigne was as ponderous as he has recently been. Sheringham and Ferdinand were as desolate up front as rural pensioners awaiting the village Sunday bus that never came.

It was not as though the folly of changed teams in the midst of a phase of critical matches had not previously been demonstrated. Revie believed he could do with England, unsettled and insecure in 1976, what he had done week by week with Leeds. He made six changes against Italy in Rome and lost 2–0. How could Taylor look for a second team, so to speak, when he had barely found a first?

Taylor had talked at length beforehand about how the Norwegians would be glad for a draw, on how they had respect for England. I had always doubted this, sensing that Oslo would prove a much sterner arena than Katowice. I have seen Norway beat Holland here, seen them at Wembley. They were much more of a unit than Poland, who played above themselves last Saturday.

I always thought Egil Olsen would play to win, and Norway did so with a passion and verve that was stirring to watch, even if England did collaborate in their own demise.

How could the England manager get it so wrong? I take no satisfaction in previous convictions being confirmed. We all want the England manager to succeed, to be a fount of knowledge from whom those in the game can learn. Taylor, however, has I fear moved from the gloom of last summer to an even more severe reversal.

This defeat was more fundamental than anything England have experienced since that by the United States in the 1950 World Cup. The team then was poorly organised, but at least there was still a stream of talented players at home. Now the cupboard is almost bare of alternative players. And that is why continuity of selection, as achieved by the smaller countries out of necessity, is the only course.

CHER HENRI SO CLOSE YET SO FAR

Leconte's genius eclipsed by power of Becker

29 June 1993

Henri Leconte's kneecaps may be all wrong for a great athlete, but the racket in his left hand can be a magical instrument. In vain, the crowds again came to the centre court in fond expectation and hope, *cher Henri* once more being close yet so far, an ephemeral genius.

Boris Becker advanced upon him like a wall of lava. Sooner or later, we knew, the German would engulf the Frenchman, the way he has eight times in ten meetings, including the quarter-finals and semi-finals here in 1985 and 1986 respectively, when the young German was champion. Yet how charming and beguiling the doubt was while it lasted.

Becker's victory gives him now a quarter-final against his compatriot, Michael Stich, who defeated him in the final two years ago. 'Friends we are not,' Becker admitted later, in the wake of controversy that goes back to Olympic participation last year, and was refuelled by Becker's non-appearance in this year's Davis Cup. 'But we're not enemies,' he added, 'and this is not a critical meeting, because I expect to play him another ten times in the next few years.'

A score of 6–4, 6–4, 3–6, 6–3 against Leconte yesterday may not suggest an epic battle, yet it lasted the better part of three hours, and now and then the cannon thundered. At the merest hint of a revival by Leconte – even an assault? – the crowd would throb with encouragement on his behalf. There were, indeed, hints about every half-dozen strokes, but Leconte could never join them together consecutively in what might have become a real counter-attack.

There at one end stood Becker; his hair cropped as close as Burt Lancaster's in his meanest role, shining like burnished copper beneath an unbroken sun. There is a toughness in the demeanour of a more mature Becker which is quite different from the irresistible athleticism of his earlier years.

The 30-year-old Leconte glided this way and that at the other end, reaching out for those occasional shots which are invisible until he has struck them, the ball itself sometimes too fast for the eye of opponent or spectator. That left wrist can conceal the direction, until impact, of the wickedest strokes in the game.

Leconte had break points to recover for 4–4 in the first set, and to lead 2–0 in the second, yet failed to exploit them. Becker's solidity in serve and volley continually stopped him in his tracks. How the crowd tried to will the match the other way, but it was not to be.

It is not just the beauty and speed of Leconte's best shots which enchant, nor the soulful glances and grimaces of those Gallic eyes. Never mind that the game-score may not be going well, he will produce a sequence of follow-throughs that are even more dramatic than the strokes which have fallen out or in the net. His most triumphant points are concluded with gestures to the gallery as histrionic as Leonard Bernstein at the climax of Mahler's Fourth.

As for his opponents' unplayable winners, Leconte has a delightful way of utterly ignoring them, as though he were not actually involved in this particular match, and indeed is overdue for an appointment elsewhere. It is no surprise that young and old alike take to him uncritically, for he brings to the court a charm similar to that of Jean Borotra, the champion of 1924 and 1926 and now in his nineties, who was here watching his *enfant* yesterday.

Becker, whose game is rediscovering the edge he will need to defeat Stich – his conqueror at Queen's – was generous to yesterday's opponent afterwards; as indeed he could afford to be. No, he was not put out by the partisan nature of the crowd. 'All spectators enjoy Henri Leconte. He's one of the most exciting shot-makers in the game, and I'm a fan. I like to watch him,' Becker said.

There was not too much of Leconte to watch early on. Becker broke him in the first game, and although the cheers rang out intermittently as the Frenchman's forehand would find some impossible angle, Becker proceeded machine-like towards his objective.

When he fell, trying to half-volley at 4–3 to give Leconte 40–30 against serve, he saved the situation with a drive that clipped the baseline and two games later served out for the set with barely a blink.

In the second game of the second set, two glorious backhands by Leconte gave him break points, only for Becker to respond with a telling lob and a kicking second service, and in the third game, Becker broke for 2–1 with a drive to the line which brought a pained questioning look from Leconte towards the linesman.

Excitement mounted when Leconte saved four set points at 5–4, but Becker served an ace for the fifth, and was seemingly out of reach at two sets to love. Not so. A wonderful backhand cross-court pass and a forehand down the line gave Leconte a break for 2–0, and with services being held thereafter, emotion was on fire when he held his second set point for 6–3.

For a few games, Becker had seemed wooden, but at 3–2 in the fourth set, he played perhaps the best shot of the match, an acute cross-court backhand from the baseline which left Leconte open-mouthed.

With a double fault and netted stop volley by Leconte, and a teasing lob by Becker, the match had drifted beyond Leconte's reach at 4–2. The cheers, however, were not spent, and at 5–2, he saved two match points. Then his sun went down as Becker served out with an ace.

A MAN REMEMBERED
FOR DIGNITY AND GRACE

A letter to Arthur Ashe's daughter Camera, aged six

28 June 1993

Dear Camera, you do not know me but I am one of thousands of people who regarded your father as one of the best people we ever met. Like a great many of them, I am white but, as you will come to discover, for your father that was not something to separate us but a starting point for closer communication and friendship.

What he attempted to encourage among millions by his own example were the fundamentals for humanity, such as tolerance, understanding, generosity and, above all, fair-mindedness.

If you should read this letter again as a teenager, you might wonder why an ordinary writer on sport should presume to try to tell you something about your own father. There are three reasons.

First, although he wrote with characteristic self-discipline, during his last days, a book in which almost every page bears evidence of his special love for you and your mother, his description of his efforts to close the gap between black and white people can never fully convey the degree to which other people of all races admired him. You can only discover that from them.

I am one of the least of his acquaintances but, for me, he was not only one of the most intelligent, gracious, humorous and dignified people I ever met in sport but, through his intelligence, he strove to make sport a vehicle for wider communication. While keeping sport and his own fame in perspective, he tried to utilise the common language of sport to break barriers in the way it had broken them for him. When he first revealed his marvellous backhand in England, at Beckenham, all he wanted to talk of was the impression upon him of that country and its people.

Second, your father was a sportsman who had the truest philosophy about sport – an Olympian concept about attitudes to competition, and especially the difficulty for women, to winning and losing and how we should conduct ourselves, how we should examine our attitudes and those of others, especially when we do not like them, in case in our judgment we may have misunderstood them.

As he said: 'The lessons of sport cannot be duplicated easily.'

Your father was in thought and deed the definition of a good man to such a degree that others more experienced or cynical sometimes questioned his sincerity and motives. For those who knew him, those qualities withstood any examination.

As my retired colleague, Rex Bellamy, remembers: 'He opened windows with an ever questioning mind.' Your father was among the people whom it has been a pleasure to know because they have always left you feeling better for having been with them.

Third, perhaps most important, your father was passionate about you, about his family. I hope it will fortify you all your life. Not enough parents nowadays sufficiently cherish the lives of the children they create. Our obligations to you must always be greater than yours to us, and your father profoundly regretted that he might not be able to fulfil some of those obligations.

You should be grateful for the possibility to have been Arthur Ashe's daughter, for it might never have happened. In 1975, at a tournament in Lagos, Nigeria, which was interrupted by a military coup, his match was broken up by troops and, amid gunfire, he was pinned to the wall with a machine gun in his neck.

One of the things you should do and probably will is come to Wimbledon and witness the moment that was your father's supreme sporting achievement, the winning of the men's singles.

Anyone who is there will tell you that it was perhaps the finest application of intelligent tactics against supposedly superior ability in the history of tennis.

Jimmy Connors was the defending champion, an overpowering left-hander who reached the final without losing a set. He was 22 and your father was 32. They had met three times previously, Connors winning every time, notably in the 1973 final of the South African championships. From that occasion, the older man had learnt more.

So confident was Connors now that his warm-up with Ilie Nastase was conducted in almost comic fashion. Yet your father had reached the final by eliminating, both times in five sets, the formidable Tony Roche and then Bjorn Borg. Beforehand, your father reflected: 'My best shots go to his weaknesses . . . I'll refuse to give him the angles he likes, I'll be restrained.'

Your father, with typical application, had carefully studied the semi-final of Connors against Roscoe Tanner and this, together with his own performance against the left-handed Roche in the quarter-finals, convinced him that this was about to be his moment.

Before Connors could adjust to such astute analysis, he had astonishingly surrendered the first two sets 6–1, 6–1, tormented by being given no pace that he could return with interest; nothing but slice and lob and services to his weaker backhand and the best volleying your father ever produced.

Though Connors took the third set, your father became Wimbledon's first black men's champion with a glorious smash to win 6–4 in the fourth. It was a moment in history and one of the only times in 34 men's finals that I have been on my feet in exhilaration. Yet so self-analytical was your father that, in later years, he came to question his tennis fame, whether instead he should have been among those sacrificing themselves in the human rights campaign of the Sixties and Seventies. His passion for justice for African-Americans might have been almost as strong as his love for you. I hope that, with the pride you will bear from his many deeds, you will never feel the life-long sadness of living in the shadow of being black that he admitted to. It was something that involuntarily conditioned his almost every thought and action, never mind his defiant and dignified allegiance to his race.

For your father, as he has written, being black was more of a burden than suffering the illness of Aids, which he bore with an extraordinary fortitude. Having unluckily been infected by a blood transfusion at the time of by-pass surgery, he would no more say 'Why me?' than he would ask the same question when winning Wimbledon. He took life as it came.

Yet he resented the racial conditioning in his reactions to other people that he believed should be free of any racial context. So many things made him feel guilty, not least the wanton attack by blacks on a white truck driver during the Los Angeles riots, and what he regarded as the damage to black intellectualism by the Black Power movement of Stokely Carmichael, which he considered abandoned morality. Some of the attitudes of Malcolm X he found preposterous.

The racial geography of the 21st century, Asian-Pacific orientated rather than European-Atlantic – how fortunate America is with its access to both oceans – will continue to provide you, and all races, with the challenge that your father fought hard to resolve. Whatever you may do, you have a special inheritance being his daughter.

'YOU EITHER WIN. OR LOSE'

Martínez withers under Graf's onslaught

2 July 1993

Conchita Martínez, the youthful Italian Open champion who strikes the ball down both flanks as well as any woman at Wimbledon, could do with the advice that Helen Wills once gave Lili de Alvarez, likewise from Spain. It might have helped Martínez to stretch Steffi Graf that much further in her grand slam semi-final debut yesterday.

The flamboyant, emotional de Alvarez, who lost three consecutive Wimbledon semi-finals from 1926 to Kitty Godfree and Helen Wills, twice, was another who demonstrated that, at the top, winners need more than wonderful timing. The videotape of yesterday's 7–6 (7–0), 6–3 defeat will remind Martínez, if she needs reminding, that following the marvellous eleventh game, which she won after six deuces, she took only one of the next 15 points.

Wills, who won eight Wimbledon singles titles, was listening on one occasion to de Alvarez relating, at length, how she had *nearly* defeated the redoubtable Elizabeth Ryan in a particular match. Wills silently drummed her fingers on the table, and at last interrupted. 'Lili, dear,' she said, in that crushing way no man can emulate, 'you either win. Or lose.'

Martínez is not a loser by any means. She was the first Spanish woman to win in Rome this year since de Alvarez in 1930. Last year, she reached five tour finals and took a set off Graf in Florida; this year, she has won three titles. Yesterday, however, her game collapsed at the very moment she was captivating the centre court with the flow of her flat drives.

As Graf suddenly began to run rings round her, like a labrador toying in the park with a poodle. Martínez cast imploring glances at the sky, at the linesman, at her impassive parents in the stand. Her shoulders sank, her feet trailed between points, and Graf, changing up a gear, accelerated away into her sixth Wimbledon final in seven years.

It had all looked so promising for Martínez early on. Forcing the ball on to Graf's sliced, less penetrating backhand side, she was forcing her famed opponent around the back of the court, preventing her getting to the net. Winning two rallies in the fourth game, against service, as Graf was manoeuvred into backhand and then forehand errors, Martínez led 3–1. She served for 4–1, and was 30–0 on Graf's next service.

Her temporary domination ended in the seventh game. Graf, never seeming flustered and having the comfort of a 7–0 record against Martínez, broke back for 3–4 and then three big serves gave her 4–4. Then came the best game of the match, the eleventh. Three times Martínez found herself game point behind but each time rallied. Three times she had game point herself but could not clinch it, finally doing so at the fourth attempt with a big smash. Would Graf falter, serving to save the set?

Anything but. She served a love-game and then took seven points in a row to claim the tie-break. The girl at the other end was suddenly unrecognisable, and so it continued into the first game of the second set.

When Graf broke for 3–1, with a drive to the line on Martínez backhand side which the Spaniard thought was wide, you could see the last shred of resistance vanish.

'When I lost my serve going for 5–2, that was a little bit bad,' Martínez lamented afterwards. 'Then, I don't know . . . she played really good and I couldn't do a lot . . . The tie-break? What can I say? I mean, she was serving really good and it was difficult for me to return . . . Now I know that I can come back and play OK on grass, that it's not difficult.' This was her second Wimbledon.

Maybe Martínez will decide that her future lies primarily on clay, such as Rome, but she did enough in that first set yesterday to show that an attacking player, even in the class of Graf, can be kept away from the net by those superb passing shots. What she needs is the confidence to believe that winning is not beyond her.

Graf looked unplayable in those moments when her serve was deep and her forehand was booming, but there was an element of inconsistency that Novotna might well exploit in the final. Herself a volleyer, Novotna could well work on Graf's backhand, and if she returned service the better, then Graf might not be assured of her fifth victory.

'It took me a little while to start,' Graf reflected. 'After I got the feeling of what she was doing, I simply tried to rush the net a little bit more than usual, and it paid off very well. Novotna? I've been saying it all along. She's got the talent, she's got the game and we had a lot of close matches last year. I'll have to have a very solid serve and work on my return, which hasn't been particularly good today.'

HEADING BOLDLY FOR THE BEARS' CAVE

Atherton exudes leadership

15 September 1993

There is an unusual feeling when interviewing Michael Atherton. This boyish young man, who leads England's cricket team to the West Indies, is only 25, modest and unassuming in manner. Yet beneath the mop of shortish blond hair, the clear blue eyes gaze at you unwaveringly, giving an unmistakable sense that it is you who are being interviewed.

The Australians this summer experienced, occasionally uncomfortably, that penetrating, unflinching stare when he was at the wicket.

There is the clear impression that England's new captain, taking charge at one of the lowest moments in the country's cricketing history, is a sharp observer, preferring to listen rather than talk. During an hour or so, he never once laid claim to what he intended, or expected, to achieve. Yet he exudes leadership.

There is not much of that quality about, whether you look at politics, industry, the church or sport. West Indies have not lost at home for 25 years, and Atherton is heading for the bears' cave, but is anything but intimidated, while remaining realistic.

'This is a break-point' he said calmly. 'The younger players are keen to do something. Improvement depends on the base of players you have around you. You don't get many good captains of poor sides. I am not for a moment saying we're bad, but they've [W.I.] not been beaten for so long. We're trying to set a plan for two or three years, long term. Previously, England have been playing tour by tour, using older players. They've not been doing it.'

The inference is that, if the captain has had anything to do with it – and he left small doubt that he had – then today's party will represent a quiet revolution: a new England, uncomplicated by former rebel tourists or ailing, ageing reputations. Atherton is his own man, and hopes to generate a fresh spirit of collective comradeship. His nature rides that uneasy line between being gregarious and selective, something critical for any captain.

'You need to feel you're playing with mates,' Atherton said in his measured way, the phrase carrying an equal ring of the Lancashire of Cardus and the Fenner's of May. 'Obviously the first point [of the tour] is selection. It was a reasonable side at the Oval, the attack for the first time this summer looked decent. I'm hoping to progress from there.'

It is easier, he reflects, to generate spirit on tour; and important, when you go as underdogs to a hostile environment. That spirit manifested itself at the Oval against Australia. Today's will be a younger party, reflecting that victory.

The making of Atherton took place steadily if unspectacularly. Captain of most teams at Manchester Grammar School – 'something I've always found comfortable' – the same experience with Cambridge, outclassed by the counties, might have been intimidating. Instead, he learned to cope. Handling players who were overwhelmed, he learnt not to blow a fuse every five minutes. He developed further with the Combined Universities XI, uniquely reaching the quarter-final of the Benson and Hedges; and, significantly, established a close friendship with Nasser Hussain, a player whose abilities he values.

Along the way, he was acquiring, too, a retentive memory: important, he observes wryly, if you stay around long enough to play against teams or individuals twice. At the same time, he was gaining a 2:1 degree in history at Downing College, another vain, coincidental poke in the eye for college entrance tutors actively prejudiced against games players.

Aged 21, he was a candidate for the West Indies tour of 1989–90, and was keenly disappointed when omitted, instead being selected for the A tour of Zimbabwe. 'In retrospect, that did me good,' he said. 'Keith Fletcher was the manager and I developed my batting to the extent that I was good enough [for England] the following year, where I hadn't really been the previous summer.'

He pays tribute to the master technician, Geoff Boycott, who was coaching the squad prior to Zimbabwe; showing how Atherton's feet were commendably quick but wrongly placed, causing him to play across the pad, a common fault. He worked diligently at technique during that tour.

Atherton's concept of captaincy is less one of helping to advise fellow batsmen, or his bowlers, on technique than making sure that the side's emotional chemistry is right.

This is something that has long been missing: a sense of service. Gooch was dedicated and loyal, but less than inspiring. Gatting's instability and indiscretions are well documented and Gower's captaincy by osmosis, an impression that the game developed around him rather than through him, equally apparent. Botham's buccaneer attitude, notably on the Jackman-interrupted West Indies tour, when it included daily roistering along the Barbados coast in the *Jolly Roger*, was undistinguished. The last truly perceptive captain was Brearley (1977–81), the only long-term post-war captain to have won more matches than he drew or lost: 18–9–4.

'In the modern game, the captain's technical influence is less, because most teams have a manager and/or coach,' Atherton said. 'My role is the match situation – though I'm not exactly totally experienced! – which is wholly mental over five days. Everybody can *play*. You do look at technique, but the most important quality is character, tenacity, people with a bit of ticker. It was these players we chose towards the end of the summer.'

Atherton is not conventionally, outwardly tough, as measured in millimetres of chin stubble. It is more a mental, intellectual resilience. You suspect he may be immune to media harassment. 'If things start going wrong, there'll be criticism, as always' he said. 'But I think I'm tough enough inwardly to handle that, strong enough still to make my own judgments and stand or fall by them. The last thing you should do is whinge about injuries, illness or the wicket. You have to be honest.' He is not dismissive of the press, however, recalling that newspaper-power probably first pushed him into the side at 21.

He questions the extent to which the Oxbridge factor is in any way a complication. There is the old story of someone in the Lancashire team initialling Atherton's kit-bag F.E.C.; ostensibly 'Future England Captain', but open to another, more mocking interpretation.

An article in the *Sunday Telegraph* contrasted the difference in backgrounds between Atherton and Stewart, the two potential successors to Gooch. Both men were big enough to ride it. 'I think the Oxbridge consciousness is still there' Atherton said. 'Look at the comparisons made between Hurd and Major at the time of Thatcher's replacement. But the difference between Alec [Stewart] and me is not as wide as made out. He mentioned the *Telegraph* article to me, it annoyed him, but he joked about it and has been excellent since I was appointed. I hope I would have been the same, and I didn't have his expectations.'

Atherton did not consider that he would be selected: that Gooch's recommendation was probably for Stewart, the vice-captain, but he thinks the Oxbridge factor was never relevant. 'Much was made of the Gooch/Micky Stewart regime being anti-university' Atherton reflects, 'but I don't go by that. They stuck by me, except in India last winter, when I felt harshly treated. Besides, I want to be thought of as a Lancashire cricketer.'

A measure of Atherton's maturity is that he feels the captaincy will help rather than hinder his batting. He was happy with his performances in the last two Australian Tests, given the added burden of leadership.

'If I have a bad time [with the bat] in the West Indies, it won't be because of the captaincy' he said. 'I can still go to the wicket *isolated*, totally concentrated, not taking with me the responsibility for other players, only the responsibility of being captain, which is positive. If I'm not getting runs, maybe that will change, I admit.' You sense, however, that here is a player with a degree of control over his and others' destiny. It should be a fascinating winter.

MOTIVATED BY A LOVE OF THE GAME

Busby's immense qualities as a manager

21 January 1994

With the passing of Sir Matt Busby at the age of 84 yesterday, British football has lost not only the most notable of all managers of the modern generation, but also a man who personified, both as player and manager, almost everything that was best in the game.

With those he played with, and those he inspired to play for Manchester United as manager, his objectives were motivated by a love of the game, by a love of chance, a desire to take risks, a thirst for skill, the will to entertain.

What distinguished him was not simply the quality of the teams he built and the players who filled them, but the way in which the majority of those who came to Old Trafford would pay tribute to his influence upon their game if not upon their life.

It is said that he made three famous teams but, in fact, there were four. First came the cup-winning side of 1948, with victory over Blackpool and Matthews, including some of the best of United's post-war players in Carey, Morris, Rowley and Mitten.

Nine years later, after regularly dominating if not winning the championship, there came the immortal team of 'Busby Babes' that was denied a supposed certain victory over Aston Villa at Wembley by the injury to their goalkeeper, Wood. Those who failed that day included Byrne, Colman, Edwards and Taylor, all killed in the air crash at Munich the following February, and survivors Foulkes and Charlton.

Temporarily, with Busby lying for months in hospital recovering from fearful injuries, United languished but they were back at Wembley in 1963, with Crerand and Law, defeating Leicester. The fourth side was that which gained Busby's ultimate triumph, defeating Benfica in the European Cup final at Wembley in 1968. If the youthful Best was a hero of that performance, so too were young Kidd and Aston.

Busby's immense qualities as man and manager were formed by his upbringing. Born in 1909 in the Lanarkshire mining village of Orbiston in a row of 32 two-room cottages, where the bath when his father came home from the pit was a bucket on the kitchen floor, he learnt to appreciate life the hard way. His father was killed by a sniper at Arras, obliging his mother to take a job at the pithead.

Encouraged by his headmaster to remain at school until he was 18 because of his academic ability, the young Busby thought of emigrating to Canada, discovered the delay was too long and fulfilled his mother's worst fear by going down the mine.

But his ability on the football field with Orbiston Cannibals, so named for their treatment of the opposition, ultimately earned him a trial with Manchester City and a wage of £5 a week. Yet he felt lost in Manchester and wrote home to his fiancée, Jean: 'I feel I'm out of my sphere . . . I dread the approach of every season'.

The Manchester United scout, Luis Rocca, almost bought him for £150 but the deal fell through and by one of those strange strokes of luck, Busby's career turned a corner. Selected as a late substitute for a reserve match when someone was injured, he switched from inside forward to right half for the day, and never looked back.

The experience was to help formulate several of his attitudes when he became a manager, such as never to discard a player too quickly and to realise the value of transferring a player further back in the team to exploit his intelligence or skill. It was a principle he would put into practice with Carey, Aston, Byrne, Jackie Blanchflower, Colman, Brennan, Sadler and to some degree Charlton.

As a wing half, Busby was noted for his attacking play, and together with Syd Cann, a colleague at Maine Road and later manager of Southampton, Busby was one of the first to obtain an FA coaching certificate.

Although City lost the FA Cup final of 1933 against Everton, Busby was back again the following year to help City defeat Portsmouth. The *Daily Telegraph* reported that he was the best right half ever seen at Wembley and an appreciation in the *Manchester Guardian* that year said: 'At best he has no superior as an attacking half back. It is his shrewd footcraft which notably delights the crowd. His crouching style is not pretty but the control is perfect. His dribble is a thing of swerve, feint and deception.

'Few opponents are not hoodwinked by his phantom pass. He scorns the obvious. His passes not only look good, but sound good . . . He has a spirit of adventure and there are things which make the directors feel old before their time.

'But who would have him different? He laughs equally at his blunders and his triumphs, which is the privilege and proof of a great player'.

That characteristic was the foundation of a reputation that was unrivalled in Britain and far abroad. He brought to management not merely an intelligent use of tactics based on the underlying principle of attack but a sense of fairness as well as discipline with the players he handled. Busby was the first, controversially, to pay the then maximum wage to any player appearing in the first team, whatever his age, and he was to transform Manchester United's position by the combination of three factors: scouring the country, and especially Ireland, for the best young players; a willingness to invest the club's income for the benefit of the public by purchasing star players; and by his insistence on attacking play, a refusal to be negative. 'Go out and fizz it around' was about the limit of his usual tactical instruction.

It dismayed him that the game became increasingly physical through-out the Sixties, his own players being persistently fouled, so that he tended, disappointingly, to turn a blind eye to the indiscretions of some of his own hard men, such as Setters and Stiles.

It was sad, too, that by the time Best reached his prime, Busby was no longer in his and lacked the energy to impose the discipline on Best that might have helped keep the boy-hero on the rails.

Busby was a legend and created a legend around him, one that drew fanatics not just from every town in Britain but from all corners of the globe. He was one of those precious few who, although football gave him a fine life, put infinitely more into the game than he took out, genuinely a father of modern football.

RIDING ALADDIN'S CARPET

Total mastery of Torvill and Dean

21 January 1994 Copenhagen

If we allow that dance can be sport, an ambition to achieve the most exceptional comeback in the history of the Olympic Games still burns with the colour and intensity of magnesium.

Jayne Torvill and Christopher Dean moved into the lead in the ice dance section of the European figure skating championship, here in Copenhagen yesterday, with their flawless original dance programme, a rumba, that left even their admirers short of description. A class apart ten years ago, they remain so now; though they must prove their point again today in the free dance and then at the Winter Games in Lillehammer, Norway.

How do we say it, moderately, about them all over again? As a part-nership it is as remarkable, in mutual understanding, as Pinsent and Redgrave or Edwards and John. We watch them and we marvel: at the supernatural level of athletic synchronisation.

If the physical element, the product of months and years of training, is more about refinement than power, the aspect of interpretation – which arguably is where they depart from sport – lifts them beyond anything we have seen other than Rogers and Astaire or Fonteyn and Nureyev, with whom they have been not exaggeratedly compared.

Where they remain solidly within a sporting ambiance is in balance and discipline. Their performance yesterday was apart from everybody else because there was not one moment of visible muscular stress. This alone is exceptional in their mid-thirties. So fluid and frictionless is their motion that it is as though they are no longer in touch with the ice, and have become an animated Disney creation, riding Aladdin's carpet.

They transcended their rivals yesterday because they are not just impeccable technicians but have become, over ten years of professional entertainment, even more accomplished actors than in the old days of *Bolero*. 'We were in love for the two minutes we were dancing,' Torvill said afterwards in that friendly but matter-of-fact way she no doubt used to talk to customers when still a building society clerk.

Oksana Gritschuk and Evgeny Platov, the No 2 Russian couple with whom Torvill and Dean had shared second place following the compulsory programme, in my view skated more appealingly yesterday than their supposed superiors, Maya Usova and Alexandre Zhulin, the first-day leaders. Gritschuk and Platov, she in vivid magenta, were respectively pliant and lithe, she entwined around him like ivy; but they were less accomplished technically, being unsynchronised in their last sequence.

The marks for composition reflected this, with only three 5.8s, though they had three 5.9s for presentation. Arbitrary judging will always remain an imponderable, but it was hard now to understand the four 5.8s and one 5.9 for composition and the six 5.8s and three 5.9s for presentation by Usova and Zhulin, who were flamboyant only from the waist up.

Skating is about legs and feet more than head and arms. Yet Torvill and Dean were a picture of total mastery. Their three 5.9s for composition were reward for the seemingly computerised harmony; two skates, two legs, move and turn as though one, identical in lift, timing, angle.

As Torvill observed, years on stage have given them unrivalled experience and experiment, the scope to explore possibilities of related balance, so that several times yesterday the upright woman was sustaining a reclining man with no appearance of stress. 'The years [of professionalism] have made us versatile,' Torvill said. 'And it was a challenge to create something within the restrictions of competitive rules.' Or back to basics, as Dean reflected.

They brought a tingle to the skin, a buzz in the crowd – disappointingly small – that is common to the best sports performers and the best entertainers. They are both. They have transparently lost nothing in the interval, even though, while rivals do exercises off-stage beforehand, Dean says that his 35-year-old limbs now instead need a hot bath in preparation.

Some foreign critics thought Torvill and Dean's rumba lacked physical visible emotion. Dean's answer was that, for a dance of love, total mental intimacy was their intended interpretation. It was as though, just as in *Bolero* in Sarajevo in 1984, they were in a trance unconscious of all but each other. There is still some way to go to the fulfilment of their ambition. The Olympic arena is not the Lido, and thereby hangs much of the excitement. Can they do it?*

What they retain, uniquely, is that rare twofold capacity: physical and technical harmony, plus a quality of fantasy, the impression that they live for each other. Whatever the reality of their individual marriages and private lives, the indelible sense on the ice is that they still do, and that is why millions are again following their fortunes.

It is fortunate that an indiscretion by Betty Callaway, their coach, had not, at least yesterday, had a disadvantageous impact upon the judges. It was imprudent, to say the least, for Mrs Callaway to have launched into criticism of Usova and Zhulin, following the compulsories, for alleged technical errors.

In the opinion of Britain's wisest skating official, that is neither fair to the Russians nor helpful to the British cause, in mid-competition, especially in a sport that is notable for the subjectivity of its judging. We are all still wondering what the Austrian judge was up to with a mark of only 5.5 for Torvill and Dean's composition.

* At Lillehammer, they were awarded the bronze behind the two Russian pairs, the judges subsequently admitting an error in marking.

NORWAY SHARES ITS SECRETS WITH THE WORLD

Fairy-tale opening to Winter Olympics

14 February 1994 Oslo

Beneath the earth in Norway there exists a secret, mystic people, the *vetter*. They are gentle, shy and peaceful, in harmony with nature. They live in the fantasy and poetry of the Norwegians, and offer in part an explanation of the humanity of the Norwegians themselves.

In the most enchanting Olympic opening ceremony I can recall,

Norway shared its secret with the rest of the world. It was as though they were lying on the consultant psychiatrist's couch, and the television cameras had crept in the door. Norway bared its heart, and what we saw was not funny or embarrassing or silly, but one of the fundamental truths of mankind: that we share this earth with creatures and spirits of which we know not, of which Prospero spoke to us. They are there in the recesses of our imagination, which we discover in childhood and all too often dismiss as unrealistic.

The *vetter* are Norway's conscience as well as their secret culture, and to give their guests a glimpse of this was a brave step. As the rest of the globe tuned in on Saturday, Norway wished simply to say: 'This is the way we are, we want you to see and share our sensibilities, to understand us and accept us.'

Here was a masque, set amid fading misty-mountain light and gently-falling snow, that was itself a fairytale, its unblemished style devoid of pomp or brash presumption, and fashioned around two ideologies: the perfections of youthful sporting competition, and the fantasies of a peaceful mountain people. For such a day, both the Norwegian organisers and the much criticised International Olympic Committee (IOC) can take immense credit.

The afternoon began like some nineteenth century public holiday, with musicians arriving by pony and sled, wrapped in fur rugs. Dancers swept down the ski-jump slopes, the girls in ankle-length skirts to join the throng. It was all disarmingly unpretentious, including the arrival of the royal family, the king's presence being greeted like that of a benign uncle. As the curtain of darkness closed across the surrounding valley, the 66 teams strode into the stadium, the Bosnians with their symbolic white flag and simple emblem. The British were so formal in dark overcoats they looked as if they were on the way to the office.

There was heartfelt applause for Juan Antonio Samaranch, the IOC president, when he asked for a silent pause, among everybody watching worldwide, in sympathy for the dead and beleaguered of Sarajevo, a former Olympic city. And he pleaded: 'Stop fighting, stop killing and drop your arms.'

The Olympic flag was raised. Then Stein Gruben, astride the pinnacle of the towering slope above us, received the torch. Trembling, he launched himself down the jump, landed perfectly, and passed the flame to another. There was a huge cheer when Crown Prince Haakon, heir of two former Olympic competitors and himself an athlete, ignited the pedestal.

The floodlights dimmed. All was still. And slowly, from beneath the snow, there emerged, in ones and twos, the strange, crouching, tumbling, laughing figures; hesitant at first, in awe of the crowd surrounding them. By degrees, they grew in confidence. Then they were joined by more figures from the higher slopes, cascading joyously downwards, until a whole throng of hundreds was engaged in a shadowy, mystic ballet. The creation of the midnight sun: of new life and opportunities for our future, that must be in harmony with nature. It was simultaneously a hymn and a parable, and when it was over, we wound our way back down the hillside and into the little town twinkling among the snow-laden firs. Enchanted, and wiser.

HALF SMILING, HALF SWIMMING IN TEARS

Dan Jansen's world record in last-chance race

19 February 1994 Hamar

If proof were needed that the standing of the Olympic Games still ranks above all other competitions, it came with Dan Jansen's victory here in the men's 1,000 metres speed skating event. The man, the performance and the audience conspired to create one of the most memorable occasions it has been my pleasure to witness at 12 winter or summer Games.

Not only did Jansen, denied his just reward at three previous Winter Games, and then again in the 500 metres on Monday, finally triumph in what was certainly his last Olympic race. Not only did he do so with a world record at a distance that is not his speciality, with a will that refused to succumb to intolerable self-doubt over the past four days. Not only did he achieve a private tribute to the sister who died just before the Games in Calgary, in which he was to fall twice.

He won with such a mixture of tangible relief and overwhelming happiness that an entire stadium of 12,000 people, most Norwegians, responded as though he were one of their own. For Jansen, this one prize, as he would later state, counted for more than all the other records and championships and World Cup victories and it was something he could not, for the moment, measure.

As he crossed the line and saw the record time of 1min 12.43sec flash on the screen, he clasped his hands to his head and held them there as he coasted on round the track, momentarily alone. When he walked out for the medal presentation, he had less the look of a victor than of a hostage unexpectedly released. A hostage to bad luck.

His demeanour spoke of gratitude more than triumph. The last champion I can remember with such an expression was Mary Peters when she won the pentathlon at Munich in 1972 – a feeling that a rare kind of honour was being granted.

As Jansen stood upon the dais and received the gold medal from Anita DeFrantz, the United States member of the International Olympic Committee and former rowing medal-winner, he looked down at it and held it almost disbelievingly. You knew that in the intervening hours since the failure on Monday he had not dared to believe it would happen, not when the man now standing next to him as silver medal-winner, Igor Zhelezovsky, of Belorus, was the acknowledged master at this distance.

As the Stars and Stripes were raised, Jansen's eyes were half-smiling, half-swimming in tears. And then came the most touching finale. The lights of the Viking Stadium dimmed and the victor set off on a lap of honour hand-in-hand with Kristin and Haakon, the Games' mascots. Halfway down the finishing straight, his eight-month-old daughter, Jane, named after his sister, was passed into his arms and gracefully the four of them circled the rink in time to Strauss's *Skater's Waltz*. Another perfect touch by the host nation.

It was a genuinely sensational race. Zhelezovsky, in the first pair out, set an Olympic record of 1min 12.72sec. In the second race, Grunde Njos, of Norway, a potential medal-winner, crashed violently into the barriers on the second bend.

Then came Jansen and Junichi Inoue, of Japan, fourth pair out, with the crowd fiercely exhorting the American. His split-times, unusually fast, brought a fever-pitch of expectation for something way beyond the ordinary. Yet twice Jansen nearly slipped, although not as seriously as in the 500 metres. When the finishing time was seen, the crowd was still applauding when the next pair were halfway through their run.

Zhelezovsky said the victory was deserved for the way Jansen had been skating in the past two months. No polite gesture this, but the recognition of a rival's claim.

The past three days, Jansen admitted, had been difficult, mentally: 'I don't know why it worked out,' he said, still in a daze. 'It's a little bit ironic that I should beat Igor who's been dominant as long as I can remember at the 1,000.'

Yes, he reflected, the Olympics were different from everything else for their rarity. Ever since Monday, he and his coach had talked of one thing: the last 200 metres. 'I seemed to get to that point and have a mental block,' Jansen said, 'and I didn't feel good today when I got on the ice, my timing was off so I didn't push too hard. I was very surprised. I was so fast to the 600 mark.'

LIFE FINDS THE RIGHT SOLUTION

Bayul collapses in moment of triumph

26 February 1994 Hamar

The woman who, come what may, is destined to make millions, came second. The girl who, in a sense, has nothing, was triumphant. Life sometimes finds the right solution.

The women's Olympic figure skating gold medal last night came to Oksana Bayul, the 16-year-old Ukrainian, amid tears flooding in the belief that she had failed.

Seldom has an Olympic competition been so wrought with emotion. Nancy Kerrigan, 24, the American who had survived a clubbing assault, had come to the Winter Games amid intolerable controversy and pressure. Yet, armed with her open-faced equanimity that is so appealing, Kerrigan had skated, if not like an angel, then at least like a potential champion – with poise, charm, grace, and almost enough technical polish.

By the tiniest of margins it was not sufficient, for she led only as long as it took Bayul, skating immediately after her, to complete her routine. The largest American television audience, winter or summer, in history was going to be disappointed.

The doe-eyed girl, her legs so frail she appears incapable of those triple jumps, the shoulders so slim, it is a wonder how she can generate enough power, earned the favour of five of the nine judges, three of them – puzzlingly – on her technique rather than presentation.

Bayul's mother and grandmother are dead. She never knew her father. When she stood on the victory rostrum to receive her medal, her sad face, with hollow eyes, and cherry-red mouth seemed on the point of disintegration – from a mixture of joy and the tribulations of her young life which included a painful collision during training the previous day, for which she had a pain-killing injection. One prays that she will be able to handle her stardom, and that it can fortify her spirit rather than expose her to the pitfalls that await the unprotected.

Her coach had emigrated to Canada, and only the protective attention of her fellow Ukrainian, Viktor Petrenko, the 1992 men's Olympic champion, provided the necessary financial support, while Galina Zmievskaya, Petrenko's coach, gave her housing refuge.

From such bleak circumstances rose an Olympic champion, although she already had the reassurance of being last year's world champion in Prague.

Earlier Tonya Harding, the American champion perceived as the villain of the piece because of her alleged association with the attack on Kerrigan, had threatened to steal the headlines. Within forty seconds of starting her routine, Harding missed a jump and, in tears, skated to the judges' desk to reveal a fault in her boot. She was given permission to restart at the end of her group but her previous poor technical programme and a moderate performance now left her in eighth position overall.

As the evening progressed Yuka Sato, of Japan, and then Lu Chen, of China, had successively taken the lead. Sato, 20, elegant in royal blue, confident in her jumps from powerful, short legs and graceful with her tiny hands, gained no mark higher than 5.7, while the 17-year-old Chen had 5.8s on both technique and presentation.

Then came Kerrigan, smiling and assured in her coffee-coloured lamé, those warm dark eyes looking fixedly at the judges as she began. Her lines to a melody of Neil Diamond numbers was flowing and assured, the applause at the end was rapturous, and her presentation earned six 5.9s. Could Bayul do better?

The magic was instant. While Kerrigan was a skater, doing figures, Bayul was a theatrical whole, something of subtle complexion and uncertainty as to what she would do next.

The applause for Bayul was not as prolonged as for Kerrigan but none the less appreciative. Yet when the technical marks flashed on the board, including a 5.5 from Canada and a 5.6 from Britain, the waif collapsed in dismay on the shoulder of a friend, unable to comprehend what must have seemed to her like a physical assault. She left the rink grief-stricken, seemingly unaware of the fractional superiority she had gained from the five judges.

The only question remaining, really, was whether Surya Bonaly, of France, or the veteran, Katarina Witt, German Olympic champion of 1984 and 1988, could steal the bronze from Chen, Bonaly, with a fall, was inadequate on technique, while Witt, giving us the best of her old script, could do no better than finish seventh.

CLEAR MESSAGE FROM WINTER WONDERLAND

A letter to sports enthusiast John Major

1 March 1994 Lillehammer

Dear Prime Minister, a truly exceptional social and sporting event has just concluded here in Norway. Perhaps you have had the opportunity to observe some of it and, if so, you are sure to have noticed several characteristics of these seventeenth Winter Olympics.

Foremost of these have been the spontaneous joy of the Norwegian people at the opportunity to be hosts to the world, and the pride and satisfaction that has been generated throughout a country of only four and a half million people by the performance of its team. These are experiences which you believe could and should be attained for the British people, though it has to be admitted that Britain is unlikely to finish second in the medals table.

These Games have enabled Norway to present their face to the world and to enjoy a collective identity that brings a national sense of confidence and well-being. This is a feeling which we in Britain would like to have.

As someone with an active interest in sport, you have demonstrated your commitment to Britain's attempt to regain international status and recognition by your support last year of Manchester's bid to host the Olympic Games in 2000. The performance of an inspiring team is something different, though the roots of its creation are similarly founded.

The message from Lillehammer is that, although in a modest way the British team achieved better results than in any Winter Olympics since 1948, the administration of British sport is still regarded as lightweight and insignificant in the corridors of international influence. The platform for producing medal-winners remains narrow, underfunded and self-dependent to a degree that is not always motivating.

That is not going to change without powerful persuasion and direction from the top. Management determines the success of any enterprise. The British Olympic Association (BOA) does manage our team effectively within the means at its disposal, but the continuing fragmentation of British sports administration, the undermining element of divided authority, leaves us short-changed on the field and dismays our traditional friends, who look to Britain for leadership and find petty preoccupation with domestic rivalries and relative trivia.

In Olympic sport, Britain is seldom any longer great in any sense. When greatness does occur, as with Ovett and Coe, Christie and Gunnell, and, in their way, Torvill and Dean, it tends to be self-generated, despite the system.

This debility is to a degree self-perpetuating. The general attitude of the British press to the Manchester bid was dismissively unhelpful and reaction to the Winter Olympic team has been largely negative; this despite the fact that for the first time two bobsleigh teams in both events have been placed in the top ten, something also achieved only by Switzerland.

Your present minister for sport, Iain Sproat, would not be able to tell you too much about all this. His responsibilities are also fragmented. Far from directing the course of sport, he is still trying to learn about sport. It was a shame that in the 16 days of the Games he was unable to find the time for even one day here to learn about the mood, requirements and attitudes of those who are working energetically in Britain's name, on and off the piste.

The secretary of state for national heritage, Peter Brooke, who has sporting interests, did put in a long weekend, was politely interested without being able to be reassuring on further improvements in financing or department support. It was a shade too much a politician's rather than a sportsman's visit. British performance and credibility will only increase when there is a single identifiable national body, preferably an amalgamated organisation called the British Olympic and National Sports Federation, which deals with all elite sport, leaving a more stream-lined United Kingdom Sports Council to handle grass-roots developments.

Nobody suggests that 'money buys success'. This premise has in the past been disproved in other Western European countries, such as France, and is demonstrably less than successful in the United States. No national Olympic committee has more money at its disposal than the USOC – in excess of $10 million a year – and its 13 medals here are a poor, almost accidental, reward for its expenditure.

Yet it is worth reflecting on the achievements of Spain, in the last summer Games in Barcelona, and Norway and Russia here. Their respective tally of medals can be directly related to central government funding and support. Nobody wants British winners to be money-motivated rather than sports-motivated, yet that is no excuse for leaving them without adequate opportunities to compete in key preparatory events.

Brooke, during his visit, heard of the experience of our freestyle skiers who, by saving their daily allowance when accommodated free at one event, were able to pay for their participation in two subsequent World Cup competitions. Is this how we wish to run a national team?

Norway spent £6.6 million per annum between the 1992 Games in Albertville and Lillehammer preparing their summer and winter teams. Britain's government grant for elite sport is some £1.7 million per annum, plus private sector Sports Aid Foundation grants and BOA subsidies. On a population pro-rata basis, the government grant to the British team would be £100 million.

Winning a lot of Olympic medals does not make Norwegians superior. Such superiority as they do have lies in their dedication to the preservation of our natural habitat – evident in their Games organisation – and in their magnanimity towards all races. For the past two weeks they have shown nationalistic fervour, but never at the expense of spontaneous appreciation of every medal-winner of whatever nationality. The Games did not make Norway better: they gave its inhabitants the chance to show what a good people they are.

British people yearn to do the same. Success in the Olympic field is a doorway to self-esteem and foreign approval, and is not to be under-estimated.

SWEPT AWAY BY POWER OF TYPHOON

England help to make Ambrose look unplayable

30 March 1994 Port of Spain

It is tempting to say that England were destroyed by a force beyond resistance or even comprehension here yesterday. The devastation caused by Curtly Ambrose in a spell of 7.5 overs was from a tornado that left England as flattened and derelict as cardboard houses.

In barely an hour and a half England's tenuous visions of a victory that would restore some dignity was in utter ruin, and they will have left the ground to return to their hotel, awaiting the formality of today's finish, in a daze from which it is difficult to know how they can recover.

So absolute was their capitulation that it will remain impossible to define accurately the degree of Ambrose's astonishing performance. Here was sustained hostility with barely a single ball not directed like a bullet at the stumps rather than at the head. It could not now be said that this was a victory by physical intimidation other than the intimidation of exceptional legitimate bowling.

It will also be said that England's batsmen helped to make Ambrose look unplayable. The truth is that at many moments he was.

Atherton went, leg-before, to a stinging first ball of the innings which caught him unawares. Smith, third out, may have played fractionally late to a ball that hit his off stump and Hick and Thorpe may have marginally misjudged the line. Yet the ball that swept away Stewart's off stump to terminate the only straw of resistance that England had mustered was lethal.

At no time was it seemingly possible to play forward to the pitch of the ball from Ambrose, such was his pace. How the crowd loved it, laying low the old colonial masters.

I had not shared the same optimism as many regarding England's capacity to win a Test that, until four o'clock yesterday afternoon, had fluctuated so absorbingly throughout four days. This was not because of any lack of commitment on England's part up to that moment, for they had mostly been resolute, but because of the memory of the Test against South Africa at Barbados two years ago. Just when South Africa seemed set for victory on the final day, Ambrose and Walsh respectively took six for 34 and four for 31 and the result was turned on its head. That typhoon of fast bowling was less overwhelming than that which hit England now.

Certainly, there were contributions by the English to their own demise. Ramprakash will be embarrassed by the absurdity of his run-out in the first over within moments of his captain having already been sent, head hanging, back to the pavilion. Never was there such a moment for granite-like calm, yet here was Ramprakash calling Stewart for a second run on a glance to fine leg, sending him back when Stewart was too far committed and leaving Ramprakash himself stranded.

Earlier, there had been the miserable errors of Hick in the slips, dropping Chanderpaul when he was only four and then again when he was 29. The 50 that the 19-year-old Guyanan was allowed to make, leaving West Indies at the moment of his dismissal 191 in front, was itself enough to have lost a match that was winnable. Yet the significance of Hick's errors became swiftly lost in the maelstrom that was about to overtake England at the crease.

The West Indies have long been distinguished as the best in the world by their ability to recover from periods of lax concentration to accelerate and deliver knockout blows to opponents who have become unjustifiably confident. They did it again now with a vengeance.

LOSS OF A TRULY MAGIC DRIVER

Ayrton Senna dies at Imola

1 April 1994

Unnatural death for someone you know is always a numbing shock. Ayrton Senna's horrific fatal crash in the San Marino Grand Prix at Imola is appalling not just for those who follow motor sport, which he distinguished, but for all who even casually admired the courage and excellence of a man unique in physical achievement.

Behind those dark, soulful eyes burned an emotion that the public seldom saw. Senna may have been resilient, but he was one of the most calculating of experts within his pursuit of the past 40 years.

Senna, three times Formula One world champion, with 41 race victories and an unequalled 64 pole-position starts, crashed from as yet unidentified causes when leading in the seventh lap of yesterday's race. His Williams Renault left the track at 186mph at Tamburello corner, hitting a wall head on. With multiple head and internal injuries he died in hospital.

When I heard the initial news of his accident on the car radio, the commentators, reporting the re-started race, referred only to the accident in passing. A broken gear box, I supposed. Then came the black details. I did not want to believe it. Ayrton, I had always felt, was indestructible.

As Stirling Moss, himself long ago the victim of a serious crash, said last night, comparing Senna to Juan Manuel Fangio and Jim Clark as one of the greatest drivers: 'He was certainly the greatest of his day. A real racer, excellent whatever the conditions. He had amazing car control, a truly magic driver.'

Senna's death reminds us, though none should have needed reminding, how close to death racing drivers are every second of their glamorous, unrealistic existence. Everybody had recognised this with Roland Ratzenberger's death during practice on Saturday.

Senna himself had said: 'To survive in grand prix racing you need to be afraid. Fear is a very important feeling to have. It helps you race longer . . . and live longer.' Ironic words, even when safer tracks and carbon fibre cockpits, capable of absorbing the momentum of extreme impact, had brought 12 years free of death.

Senna, with that extraordinary detachment from the dangers with which he lived – and from which he made many millions of dollars – had had the aura that, by touching the hem of perfection as he regularly did, he was somehow immune. He had reached a level of mastery in his sport to which no other great contemporary professional I have watched, not Sampras, not Faldo, not Morceli, not Tyson, has come even close.

There were those who said, and his fellow champion, Alain Prost, of France, was one of them, that at times Senna would push his fellow drivers intolerably hard from behind. But as Moss observed: 'He may have pushed them hard, but he pushed himself even harder. He had seemed fireproof.'

If Senna claimed an association with God that those in the media world may have found exaggerated and even unacceptable, there was about him a strange, almost religious-like mood of conviction; that with the ability and experience he had assembled since he began kart racing in 1975, he could do almost anything he wished with a motor car travelling at 200 miles an hour.

And so he could, until yesterday, when those who knew him will wish to believe that it was some mechanical failure and not his own error that precipitated the end of a remarkable life.

The difference between Senna and the rest of the contemporary field was apparent to all, whether or not you liked him, which many did not. In the pits only an hour or so before a race he was simultaneously as calm as though going out to play a game of Sunday croquet, yet as concentrated as though going into a world championship chess match.

While on the one hand the intellectualism of the mechanical development of modern racing fascinated him, he also recognised that science, the computerisation of technology, was in danger of removing his skill. He wanted motor racing to remain a sport.

He was a rare man, obsessive without ever being disorientated, intent on touching the top of the mountain just so that he could know what it felt like to be there.

The deaths of sportsmen in their prime, whether boxers like Johnny Owen or Bradley Stone, or racing drivers such as Jochen Rindt, Jim Clark or Ronnie Petersen, always bring grief, bring an outcry from those who would like to control our lives that such activities should be banned. Yet the mastery of danger is an inherent part of human character, man or woman, and we should never attempt to tell the Sennas of this world how to live their lives.

NO PLACE FOR ANDREW IN QUEST FOR NEW ADVENTURE

My debate on the tactical limitations of a hero fly-half, acknowledged by his contemporaries, was hostage to fortune: that day, he kicked England to victory

4 June 1994

England's rugby union team, under Jack Rowell, the new manager, stands today at a crossroads. The future success of both is dependent on the calculated termination of one of the finest careers in this or any international sport. Rob Andrew has to go.

In today's first international against South Africa here in Pretoria, against a background of criticism for unimaginative play in the five nations' championship that continues to dog England on tour, Andrew extends his record as the world's most-capped stand-off half to 56. Against expectation, and seeming logic, England persist with the Geoff Cooke syndrome – containing, unattractive yet, in the wetter northern hemisphere, persistently successful ten-man rugby.

England may revive a so far disappointing tour with victory today against the odds to deny a confident South Africa side that will attempt to run the ball. The evidence of the tour has suggested, forcefully, that unless England change their style to fluent, running rugby, they have little or no chance of repeating here next year their 1991 achievement of reaching the World Cup final.

The bottom line for Rowell, therefore, is this: unless he discards Andrew, the fulcrum of the team that Cooke built – and does it soon – he cannot hope to break the mould of kicking, stifling rugby of which Andrew is the master. Andrew is an intelligent games player, but together with Cooke and morally supported by Will Carling, his captain, he has squeezed the maximum gain from the dominance of England's pack, in all three departments, over the past four years. It is not by accident that England have defeated France in Paris four times in a row.

Rowell, bravely and controversially, accepted the succession to Cooke with the conviction and the intention to take a different route – to let the ball run, to revive threequarter play, to take risks. Andrew's is the fail-safe mode: kick, pin the opposition down, let the pack grind the ball forward, free the ball only in the last third of the field. If that.

Why, therefore, has Rowell stayed loyal to the Cooke policy for the opening international, when there are so few matches – two on this tour, two autumn friendlies against Canada and Romania and the next five nations' championship – to fashion a team to his own design? The excitement generated by the more adventurous play of the second XV last Tuesday in a narrow defeat at Kimberley cried out for a gamble today.

Yet Rowell was in a cleft stick. He has admitted to feeling partially compromised by inheriting a squad relatively close to the World Cup. Additionally, he finds himself leading what is so far a losing streak. To change the pattern, to get wiped out by a South African team substantially more effective up front than when defeated at Twickenham, would be to put his head on the block. A loser either way.

The truth, however, is that, in a sense, the two matches with South Africa over eight days are unimportant, at least in comparison with developing a side that can adapt to firm-ground rugby in time for the World Cup. The options, however, within a squad that he did not select, were limited.

Stuart Barnes, his own man at Bath, is already effectively resigned to being the man with the international career that never happened: his path habitually blocked by Andrew, his flair passed by. He was at less than his best in Kimberley – though the ball did flow – and is bothered by a pelvic strain.

Paul Hull would be a possibility at stand-off half, but has stated a clear preference for full back, while Mike Catt is feeling sore and is perhaps not ready for the temperamental demands of such a confrontation.

None the less, time is perversely already running out for a manager who has only just begun. Apart from other considerations, a No 10 ready to release the ball would reveal whether or not Carling should retain his place for the World Cup, or whether a fit Jeremy Guscott and Phil de Glanville might be the better centre combination. The dilemmas facing Rowell are daunting and fascinating. Whatever today's result, it is unlikely to resolve them.

LOW STANDARD OF WOMEN'S TENNIS

Impending exit of Navratilova exposes the flaws

29 June 1994

Admiration for the Women's Tennis Association is the only possible reaction to yesterday's singles quarter-final between Martina Navratilova and Jana Novotna. Any organisation that can negotiate for a semi-finalist to receive £86,250 – equal pay with the men – following such an indifferent, error-prone match must be smart. Navratilova, with around £14 million career prize-money, was doubtless unconcerned about the cash, only in prolonging the legend.

For the moment, the legend lives on, but this was hardly the stuff of dreams. The debate on comparable values of men's and women's tennis is too old a bone to dig up again – even by one denounced a year or two ago as being a 'closet mysongynist', whatever that may be – yet by women's standards this was a drearily average second-division affair.

None will begrudge the former queen of grass her enduring Indian summer, in what is allegedly her retirement year, but where does this place the rest of the women's game? The performance of Novotna, one of only a handful of volleyers, was often abysmal whenever the door for her was opening.

Although she won the first set, you sensed thereafter that she could not have won a critical point – 30-all or game point – even if Navratilova had been sitting in a chair beside the umpire. Seventeen times Navratilova either reached or won game point on her opponent's error, often a crass volley at the net with an open court. In a disastrous second set, which she lost to love, Novotna hit only 43 per cent of first services in, and won only 24 per cent of her second services.

At last year's final, when Novotna crumbled from a 4-1 lead in the final set against Steffi Graf, the Duchess of Kent consoled her reassuringly by saying: 'You'll win it one day.' Not this way, she won't. Her temperament is transparently as fragile as eggshell.

Novotna had 11 break points against Navratilova's service, and won only two of them, both in the first set. So average was the play initially that the match was being conducted in near silence, broken only by some half-hearted exhortations for Navratilova, the affection being for her longevity rather than her present sparkle. It was not until the twelfth game – the second of the second set, when Navratilova broke service on her fourth game point – that there was any stirring of the pulse, any evidence that this was the last eighth stage of a grand slam tournament.

Consistency is a condition as yet unknown to the 25-year-old Novotna, never mind her appearance in the Wimbledon and Paris finals and her £2.5 million prize-money. Evidence of this had been apparent in her third-round match against Dominique Monami, of Belgium, winning the first and final sets 6-0 while managing to lose the second 6-4. Although Navratilova was afterwards gracious about her fellow Czech, the truth was that Novotna lost the day rather than Navratilova won it.

That, sadly, was not how Novotna saw it, and until she adds realism to her equipment, a recognition of what is her flaw and the need to correct it – if indeed that can be done at her age – she will continue to be an ultimate loser crying on somebody's shoulder, not always a duchess's, and wondering why her talent, which is undoubtedly considerable, does not reward her better.

At her press conference, Novotna hid behind compliments to her opponent: played well, returned well, and so on. Asked why she had played so poorly on the important points, she deflected the question. 'It happens,' was her stark answer.

The matter of Navratilova's service return really did not become a factor until the third set, by which time Novotna's state of mind was such that she would have had difficulty holding a dry bar of soap. There were two killer blows that ensured Navratilova's victory. She broke service for 2-0 with a forehand return, cross-court backhand volley and two backhand returns, and when Novotna had four points to break back for 2-3, that formidable left forearm saved every one of them with winning volleys.

Not, mind you, the volleys of the nine-times former champion. Novotna admitted she had never played her opponent at her peak. That, she ought to know, would have been a wipe-out, the Navratilova who beat Chris Lloyd in straight sets ten years ago.

Although Navratilova has become somewhat regal in her interview manner, she is also more modest than when she believed she was the axis upon which the tennis world revolved, as she once did. No, she hadn't expected anything (from Wimbledon), she said. She was surprised how easily she had won her last two matches, against Sukova and Novotna.

She has been a great champion, if never an endearing one. In her, relative, old age, you wish her well.

SPONTANEOUS GENIUS, MORE SINNED AGAINST THAN SINNING

Maradona, the boy from the back-streets of Buenos Aires

1 July 1994

When I first saw Diego Maradona as a teenager, in 1979, the impact was even more electric than the debut of Pelé in the World Cup 21 years earlier. Maradona was, in a word, unmarkable.

Cesar Menotti, the manager of Argentina, had been much criticised the previous year for excluding the boy genius from the team that was to win the World Cup in Buenos Aires, saying that premature exposure would damage this remarkable talent. Argentina went on to win, defeating Holland.

A year later, the two teams met again in a charity match in Switzerland. Now Maradona was included. It seemed a formidable foreign baptism, for he would be up against Neeskens, also skilful but additionally one of the hardest Dutchmen who ever played. Maradona destroyed him as if by magic.

For much of the 90 minutes, Neeskens was within a yard of the ball yet never touched it. He was humiliated; it was as if he was trying to catch a salmon with his bare hands as it glinted in the sunlight beneath the water. On that day, those who had not previously seen Maradona knew that here was one of the most sumptuous players in the game's history.

The final indignity this week in a chequered career is enough to make you weep.* Maradona has been destroyed as much by villainous treatment on the field over 15 years, and by media hounding, as by his own weaknesses. It is wretched how the public are too unforgiving and sanctimonious towards fallen sporting heroes, when we accept without challenge the idiosyncracies and psychological failures of the tortured genius in art, science, music or literature, such as Gaugin, Mendel, Elgar or Ibsen.

There has been a tiny handful of players who were different from all others, even from great players. A player such as Finney or Bozsik or Beckenbauer lifted skill to a pinnacle, to a refinement that was breathtaking, doing the same as others but at a sublime level.

Above and beyond them are those who do things which, until the moment they are done, you never thought possible. This is genius and we have seen it in Matthews, Di Stefano, Pelé, Best, Cruyff . . . and Maradona.

It is a combination of rare physical dexterity with a mental perception that may be calculated, as with Di Stefano or Cruyff, or was simply instinctive. Maradona's genius was wholly spontaneous and a thing of beauty.

Those who now leap to condemn him, especially from within the game, should pause to consider their degree of blame from a maze of problems which have enmeshed him over the years. Like Best before him, he was a boy from humble surroundings overwhelmed by money and fame, which he had not the education to handle, and was kicked a thousand times a season by cynical defenders under the eye of indifferent administrators and referees.

If Maradona is a victim of self-indulgence, he is also the victim of foul play, inefficient refereeing and disciplinary incompetence. Fifa, the sport's world governing body, which now expels him from the World Cup, has much to answer for.

By the time of the World Cup in Spain in 1982, he was already, metaphorically and literally, a marked man. Belgium, Italy – notably Gentile – and then Brazil endlessly tackled him from the waist down with their legs and feet and from the waist up with their arms. Ultimately he cracked, retaliated against Brazil, and was sent off.

He moved club to Barcelona and it was even worse, Spanish referees being among Europe's most inefficient, not least with their bias towards Real Madrid. Maradona was all but put out of the game by a deliberate late tackle from behind.

By degrees, predictably, he became as cynical and expedient as his tormentors. Here was a player who, like Best, was miraculous at remaining on his feet when illegally scythed from all sides. When countless fouls went unpenalised by referees, he took to diving; and nowadays, one could throw a brick at the television screen when ignorant commentators – not to mention English managers who live by condoning foul play – hypocritically question whether Maradona is exaggerating the force of the millionth tackle aimed at his knees.

Sure, he handled a goal against England in the 1986 World Cup quarter-final, but hundreds of English players handle the ball every season. Three points should be made concerning that incident: an alert Shilton should have jumped higher than tiny Maradona to punch clear; Bobby Robson had no complaint about Fenwick elbowing Argentinians in the face; and Maradona's second goal was the most glorious you ever saw.

Of course, Maradona has been weak, greedy, temperamental, manipulative and many other things common to most of us. As he departs, we should feel sorry for him and grateful for the fantasy which he has given to a game dragged low by the unlawful play of so many 'honest professionals'.

* Suspended from the World Cup for a positive drugs test.

A LION ON THE COURT, A LAMB OFF IT

No shot the incomparable Hoad could not play

9 July 1994

In a lifetime's association with sport, there has been only a handful of performers for whom my affection, from first-hand observation or through the old Pathé newsreels or television, amounted to hero-worship. As a boy, there were Jesse Owens, Lindsay Hassett, Joe Louis and Stanley Matthews. In later, equally impressionable youth, Bobby Charlton, Pelé . . . and Lew Hoad.

It has been my good fortune to have talked with all of them, with several at length. Hoad's death last Sunday was a particular personal wrench. Of all the famous sporting champions, he possessed not only unparalleled heroic, athletic quality but also, almost uniquely, a special debonair charm. He was my contemporary and definitive hero, defeating Tony Trabert memorably to win the Davis Cup against the United States in 1953 at an age when I was still doing chemistry A level.

Hoad at full throttle had a lion-like beauty. When I recall him at his regal prime, aged 22, defeating Ashley Cooper – the champion the following year – at Wimbledon in straight sets within 57 minutes, it makes me angry that myopic administrative bureaucracy drove him, and others such as Pancho González and Ken Rosewall, into the ostracised limbo-world of honest professionalism. For ten years, Hoad's withering, electric skills were lost to the 'official' game; until, for him, it was all too late.

For that final of 1957, I stood on the lamented free terrace, recently abolished, barely an arm's length from the baseline. With the temperature approaching 100°F his performance was awesome. The power of Hoad's wrist and forearm – shaking his hand was like gripping a shoulder of ham

– was such that he turned looping top-spin drives into attacking shots.

In *The Daily Telegraph*, the respected Lance Tingay wrote: 'It was a display of genius and it is to be doubted if such dynamic shot-making was ever sustained with such accuracy. He was super-human.' The following morning, Ted Tinling, a close friend, went to Hoad's hotel room with the Champions' Ball gown he had made for Lew's wife, Jenny – the former Australian Open finalist, Jennifer Staley – and with the morning papers. 'You have a fantastic press, the critics say your performance was the greatest ever,' Tinling said. Hoad casually deflected the acclaim. 'What's Peanuts doing today?' he inquired about his favourite comic strip.

This unaffected manner, his disarmingly quizzical raised eyebrows, made him uniformly popular among players. Jack Kramer, for whose professional circuit Hoad had already signed before retaining his Wimbledon title, recalls the attitude of González, that loveable raging bull who was then dominating the professional game: 'Lew was so damn popular with everyone that even when he was clobbering González, Gorgo [González] wanted his respect and friendship.'

Even before turning professional, Hoad was beginning to be bothered by chronic lumbar pains. Kramer considered him 'potentially the greatest tennis attraction of all times', while González, who beat Hoad 51–36 after trailing 18–9 on their initial head-to-head tour of 1958, reflected: 'When his game was at its peak, no one could touch him.'

Not for Hoad the expedient, no-risk percentage game of today's professionals. He went unhesitatingly for the winner, so that, when he was not in tune, he could be erratic. Yet he could be almost equally at home on a clay court as on grass. In 1956, besides the Wimbledon and Australian titles, he won the hard-court championships of Italy, France and Germany and was only denied the grand slam by Rosewall in the United States Open final. His physical strength was phenomenal. During 48 hours on a world tour, he played four matches in Nairobi, Karachi and Lahore with no sustenance other than tea or beer on two long flights, or drinks on court. 'His body could withstand almost anything,' Kramer wrote, 'but like a lot of strong kids, personally he was as gentle as a lamb.'

Although losing the United States professional finals of 1958 and 1959 to González, Hoad regularly overwhelmed him in every department: service, overheads, volleys and ground strokes. There was no shot he could not play. In 1957, we were astounded at Wimbledon by some of his acute, dipping cross-court shots at the net, hit with a flourish rather than desperation, on seeming winners from Cooper.

Some of the happiest evenings of my professional life were spent compiling, during several summers, Hoad's column for *The Sunday Telegraph*. Every other moment was a laugh. Generosity and wry humour coloured his critical comment. I never once found him bored or boring; such a contrast to the majority of today's introverted, over-rewarded players, whose character is limited to their head-bowed, interminable plucking of their racket strings.

His affectionate irony was evident in family life, which he and Jenny sustained even when, in the early professional days, they barely saw each other for 12 months on end. Glancing through the receipts from a shopping expedition to Harrods by Jenny with their three young children, he would gently, mockingly murmur: 'And which child had the leopard-skin coat?'

Jenny has been a strong, loyal and original partner. She and Jane, Peter and Sally will miss his magnetism even more than we.

BULGARIA HUMBLES THE HOLDERS

Germans' disbelief in World Cup capitulation

11 July 1994 New Jersey

In one of the most notable surprises of the World Cup since Germany themselves defeated Hungary in the 1954 final, the champions were ousted in the quarter-final here in the Giants' Stadium yesterday by Bulgaria, the rank outsiders. Until 14 minutes from the end, Germany had looked calm, clear victors.

Then, suddenly, they were toppled by two goals in three minutes, the winning header coming from Yordan Lechkov, who plays with Hamburger SV and whose 27th birthday had been the day before.

It is hard to describe the look of dismay, disbelief and, so unusual for them, capitulation on the faces of the German team in the instant that Lechkov soared above Helmer to meet a looping cross from Yankov. With barely six minutes remaining, the Germans knew that, barring some unlikely stroke of fortune, their dominance that has extended through three final matches since 1982 – twice runners-up – was, for the moment, at an end.

How the Bulgarians, who now play Italy in the semi-finals, relished their triumph, as did those of their supporters billowing their red-white-and-green flags here in this huge stadium. As the Germans dragged themselves dejectedly away from the scene and down the tunnel after the finish, the Bulgarians, the substitutes, the trainers and just about anyone present from Sofia who could get a foot on the pitch, staged a photo-session for the benefit of posterity that was worthy of Hollywood. You would think they had won the trophy.*

It is indeed a remarkable story for this former Soviet satellite, at present grinding its way through the throes of a new democracy and economic survival. Bulgaria are only here in the finals thanks to an injury-time goal in Paris; in five previous World Cup final tournaments, their record was no wins, four draws and six defeats. Yet what a scalp this was!

Dimitar Penev, the Bulgaria coach, said his side had played the perfect tactical match. 'I'm very happy, not just with the result but with the way we played,' he said. 'Tactically, we did everything we had to do and if we had taken our chances, we would never have had to come from behind.

'We will start thinking about playing Italy in the next few days. Our last three games have all been very difficult for us but we'll have the same players on duty and we will try to do the same thing to them.'

Germany's record over ten previous quarter-finals was nine wins and one defeat and, once they had survived a purple spell by Bulgaria during which Balakov hit the post in the first quarter of an hour, it had seemed that the familiar German machine was marching on relentlessly. They went ahead four minutes into the second half with a penalty by Matthäus, after Lechkov had chop-tackled Klinsmann inside the penalty area. Here was a referee's decision, by José Torres, an energetic Columbian, at which none could complain.

As the second half wore on, with the mid-day temperature now approaching 90°F, there was the appearance of the men against the boys. Germany were looking physically stronger, more assured, tactically compact, and the Bulgarians' flair, which in the first half had been so fluid and imaginative, seemed to have withered. From where could they find a reply?

When they did, it was too little, too infrequent. With just over 20 minutes remaining, Kostadinov, the striker with FC Porto, Bobby Robson's team, cut in from the left and let rip with a drive that Illgner fumbled on the line. But the ball rolled around the post for a corner. A header by Kostadinov a few minutes later flew wide of the top corner.

In between, Germany pressed forward, the blond, confident Klinsmann and Völler defying their years to create a threat almost every time they were in possession. So close were they to going beyond reach with a second goal moments before Bulgaria's astonishing revival. Buchwald, who had played a commanding role in central, deep midfield, thrust forward and found Hässler on the left.

He made ground along the touchline, feigned to cross and then pulled the ball back into the path of his midfield colleague, Möller. With one of the most powerful shots seen in three weeks, Möller battered the ball against the left-hand post from 14 yards. Germany felt they might score from the rebound only for Klinsmann to be given offside.

Now came the climax. What looked like a harmless free kick was given away by Germany a few yards outside their penalty area on the left; maybe 26 yards from Illgner's line. Stoichkov, who had suffered that barren European Cup final with Barcelona, stood waiting, content, while Germany lined up a five-man wall. With a little staccato run, Stoichkov moved forward, clipped the ball left-footed, and it curved over the wall and inside the left post with Illgner stranded.

Germany braced themselves for counter-attack, for extra time. How deluded they were. Back came Bulgaria almost immediately, Yankov floated the ball right to left and there was Lechkov's balding head to put his country in a semi-final for the first time. What a field day the photographers had. Mind you, everybody gets their picture taken here. Even the police team posed afterwards for theirs.

GERMANY (1–4–3–2): 1 B Illgner (Cologne); 10 L Matthäus (Bayern Munich); 14 T Berthold (VfB Stuttgart); 4 J Kohler (Juventus); 5 T Helmer (Bayern Munich); 17 M Wagner (Kaiserslautern; sub: 2 T Strunz, VfB Stuttgart, 59min), 6 G Buchwald (VfB Stuttgart); 7 A Möller (Juventus); 8 T Hässler (AS Roma; sub: 3 A Brehme, Kaiserslautern, 83min), 13 R Völler (Marseilles), 18 J Klinsmann (AS Monaco).

BULGARIA (4–1–3–2): 1 B Mikhailov (Mulhouse); 16 I Kiriakov (Lleida), 5 P Hubchev (Hamburger SV); 3 T Ivanov (Neuchâtel Xâmax), 4 T Tzvetanov (Levski); 6 Z Yankov (Levski); 9 Y Lechkov (Hamburger SV), 20 K Balakov (Sporting Lisbon); 10 N Sirakov (Levski); 7 E Kostadinov (FC Porto; sub: 14 B Guentchev, Ispwich Town, 90min), 8 H Stoichkov (Barcelona; sub: 13 I Yordanov, Sporting Lisbon, 85min).

Referee: J Torres (Columbia).

* Bulgaria lost to Italy in the semi-final.

JUSTICE IS DONE, UNSATISFACTORILY

Baggio misses penalty to give Brazil fourth Cup

18 July 1994 Los Angeles

Justice, of the most unsatisfactory kind, was finally done. Brazil, consistently the most attacking team of the fifteenth World Cup finals and of the ultimate match against Italy, became the first to win the trophy on a penalty shoot-out. They thus became the first four-time winners.

There is no more wretched conclusion to a great match than this, but the truth is that Brazil had been dominant throughout much of 120 minutes. Moreover, the luck that had patronised Italy for four weeks stayed with them when a shot by Mauro Silva in the 75th minute, fumbled by Pagliuca in goal, rebounded into play off the post.

In extra time, too, the initiative belonged to Brazil. In the third minute Bebeto missed from two yards after a cross by Cafu, while in the fourth minute of the second period of extra time Romario, latching on to another cross from Cafu, hooked a shot wide from no more than four yards.

The renowned defensive qualities of Italy enabled them to survive for two hours, their attack blunted by the evident injury to Roberto Baggio. It was ironic that the last kick of the match, Baggio's miss on Italy's fifth penalty kick, giving Brazil a 3–2 advantage, should have decided the destiny of the cup. It was the most ill-judged decision to allow Roberto Baggio to take a penalty; for with a hamstring injury it is not possible to pull the foot back properly for the striking blow.

After receiving the trophy, which is such wine for millions back home, the Brazilian players paraded a memorial banner for Ayrton Senna, as did many in the crowd.

It is said that this Brazilian team is not of the standard of their better, more famous teams of the past. Be that as it may, it was a revelation to see, in a first half in which more than two thirds of the play was conducted in Italian territory, the Italians being surpassed in technique time after time.

In a contest as fascinating as the chess match between England and Brazil in the first round in Guadalajara in 1970, Brazil played some lyrical football, exhibiting the full range of their wonderful skills.

When Cafu, a substitute after only 20 minutes for Jorginho at right back, made the kind of technical error which you see every 30 seconds in the Premiership, the 30,000 or so Brazilian supporters in the stadium sighed in dismay in unison.

From the kick-off, Italy's game plan was clear: to always keep more men goalside of the ball than the opposition. That was often nine or ten men. Never mind, the Brazilians came at them persistently like a cloud of yellow bees. Here were the Italians, whose own skills are of the highest order, being left flat-footed.

There was a moment that took the crowd's breath just on the half-hour when Romario, 30 yards from goal, pulled the ball backwards with his right foot on to his left and in one instant flipped the ball with his left over an oncoming Italian.

Yet half-time came without score and in any such situation the chance must always be that the team under the whip will score on the breakaway. Not that there had been many of these moments for Italy. The nearest they came to scoring was in the eighteenth minute when Aldair slipped making a tackle on Massaro, who ran through to drive a 14-yard shot straight at Taffarel when he might have put the ball either side of him. That was an escape for Brazil but, beyond that, Italy had little to cheer them.

The rest of the time, the crowd sat back, entranced by the weaving patterns of Brazil. After 12 minutes, a cross by Dunga was headed by Romario hard at Pagliuca and five minutes later Romario, dragging three men with him on a waltzing run, slipped the ball left to Bebeto whose shot from wide on the left was turned behind by Maldini.

In the 25th minute, Brazil's best chance of the first half came and went. Mussi fouled Zinho on Brazil's left. Branco's 30-yard drive was fumbled by Pagliuca and, although Mazinho reached the rebounding ball inside the goal area wide of the left-hand post, he fell as he attempted to turn it back to the waiting Romario and Bebeto.

Italy had replaced Mussi after 35 minutes with Apolloni and, within a few minutes of coming on to the field, he was booked for upending Romario as the two Brazilian forwards exchanged a flicker of passes. As Italian players in the defensive wall for Branco's free kick refused to retreat ten yards, Albertini was booked.

Italy opened out more in the second half, although it was still Brazil who were calling the tune. Their frustration showed when Zinho shot wildly and wide from at least 30 yards.

The evidence of Baggio's injury was apparent when he scooped the ball high over from 16 yards towards the end of normal time with a restricted right-leg action that he would repeat when missing his penalty kick.

Exciting breakaways by Cafu on the right again and again produced danger for Italy in normal and extra time, while the introduction of Viola for the second half of extra time produced a new nightmare for Italy. His powerful dribbling all but floored the wearying Italian defence. However, in the last ten minutes his colleagues, having run their lungs and legs empty for two hours, were on the point of collapse.

The teams were:

BRAZIL (4–4–2): 1 Taffarel (Reggiana); 2 Jorginho (Bayern Munich; sub: 14 Cafu, São Paulo, 20min), 15 Marcio Santos (Bordeaux), 13 Aldair (AS Roma), 6 Branco (Fluminese); 17 Mazinho (Palmeiras; sub: Viola, Corinthians, 106), 8 Dunga (VfB Stuttgart), 5 Mauro Silva (Deportívo La Coruña), 11 Romario (Barcelona).

ITALY (1–3–4–2): 1 G Pagliuca (Sampdoria); 6 F Baresi (AC Milan); 8 R Mussi (Torino); 2 L Apolloni, Parma, 34), 5 P Maldini (AC Milan), 3 A Benarrivo (Parma); 14 N Berti (Internazionale), 11 D Albertini (AC Milan), 13 D Baggio (Juventus; sub: A Evani, Sampdoria, 95), 16 R Donadoni (AC Milan); 10 R Baggio (Juventus), 19 D Massaro (AC Milan).

Referee: S Puhl (Hungary).

SPORTING REUNION OF WARTIME FOES

How Mikhail Bobrov helped to save St Petersburg

30 July 1994 St Petersburg

During the Rome Olympic Games in 1960, Mikhail Bobrov, then modern pentathlon coach to the Soviet team and now honorary chairman of volunteers at the Goodwill Games here in St Petersburg, noticed a man he recognised but could not place. He was one of many in the crowd of competitors at St Peter's Square listening to the Pope's address, and theirs was a reunion as extraordinary as any I have heard told.

The two men smiled, but did not speak. A few days later, at the football final at the Flaminio stadium, the same man was seated a few rows behind Bobrov. Mutual recognition fell in to place. They embraced, and wept. Arm in arm, they walked back to the Olympic village overwhelmed with emotion.

The threads of this story began 20 years earlier. Bobrov, then aged 17, had become an expert skier. He won the national under-18 skiing championship, and an athletic scholarship to the Caucasus mountains, 4,000 miles away, where he slalomed down the 17,000 feet of Mount Elbus. The same year, he graduated as a mountain climber and, now in the army, was middle-distance track champion.

During the Second World War, he became a frontline infiltrator of Germany's advancing forces, spying on their base camps and ammunitions movement. On his fifth return from behind the lines, an exploding artillery shell temporarily deadened his eardrums and vocal cords. While he was recovering, city leaders in St Petersburg – or Leningrad, as it then was – came to him in hospital with a nightmarish request. He and three others – Olga Firsova, Ella Prigogeva and Alois Zenbo – were required to darken the city's many golden-domed churches, from which the terrifying German artillery was gaining its bearings on other civilian targets, such as schools and hospitals, in the siege of the city that was to last 900 days.

'Nobody had been able to understand the Germans' accuracy,' Bobrov now recalls. 'Then some of our spies recovered photographs from

German gun positions, carrying exact bearings and distances from the 17 churches with golden roofs, that gave a reflection, even in moonlight. There had been many suggestions about how to disguise them, including covering them with wood, but the fire risk was too great. The proposal for camouflaging them with paint was alarming, even if you were fit and strong, because autumn weather had arrived and the winds were strong.'

On September 20, 1941, the four climbers, working at night, began their heroic task. Though rendered appallingly weak by their starvation rations, they abseiled down the precipitous roofs, blackening them out with grey warship paint. The first assignment, St Isaac's Cathedral took a week.

Working square metre by square metre, and using enough paint to cover two destroyers, they completed the task in six months. As Bobrov, the youngest, worked – necessarily – by day on the 120-foot needle spire of the 360-foot Saints Peter and Paul Cathedral on the banks of the Neva, German fighter planes attempted to shoot him down. The spire took him six weeks to complete.

'We were starving, like everybody else,' he recalls. 'All four of us were weak and ill.' Within another two months, Prigogeva and Zenbo had died of malnutrition. Bobrov remembers the dates as if it were yesterday. St Petersburg, with its incredible array of 400 historic buildings, survived.

Bobrov was then drafted into the Russian mountain regiment on the Caucasian eastern front. Not long afterwards, Bobrov's platoon ambushed a reconnoitring force of 15 German skiers. In a machine gun battle, all the Germans were shot.

While collecting the identification papers from the bodies, Bobrov discovered that two of them, though seriously wounded, were still alive. Strapping them to skis, the Russians made the descent and took the wounded to hospital. There, the Germans recovered . . . one of them, Lt Otto Bauer, later coach to the combined East/West German Olympic team of 1960, was the man whose eyes met Bobrov's in St Peter's Square.

For the Soviet Union's inaugural participation in the Olympic Games, Bobrov was a modern pentathlon competitor, but he fell from his horse while training, was trampled and badly injured, and never seriously competed again.

He became the coach, attending five Olympics, and was deacon of Leningrad's University of Physical Education, which generated a profusion of Soviet champions. In 1988, Bobrov was awarded Russia's Order of Friendship by President Gorbachev, for his heroism during the siege. In January this year, he became an honorary citizen of St Petersburg.

'THE PROBLEMS IN SPORT ARE NOT DIFFERENT FROM THE REST OF LIFE'

Tshwete calls for patience in South Africa's sporting race

23 August 1994 Victoria, British Columbia

Not long after the England rugby tour two months ago, Steve Tshwete, the new South African Minister of Sport, was out shopping in a Johannesburg supermarket. When he reached the checkout counter, the queue of other customers agitatedly surrounded him. 'Where were *our* people?' they demanded in unison.

The England squad had contained six black players, the home team only one, Chester Williams. What had happened to the shift in representation that was intended to follow, they supposed, the peaceful election of Nelson Mandela?

The embarrassment for Tshwete, a man of the same unswerving philosophical ideals as Mandela, with whom he spent years in prison, has intensified here in Victoria. Upon South Africa's Commonwealth readmission in June, a team scrambled, against the clock, for August take-off; a team of 105 whites and seven blacks, determined by selection on merit.

Despite the emotional pressures back home – where, inexplicably, television is screening nothing live in spite of morning events here suitable for evening viewing there – Tshwete is rigidly holding his ground.

'It's a problem for the ordinary black person in the street and even some parliamentarians,' he said. 'They ask why we are not pushing for a proper reflection of the demographic situation and argue that there is no way they can identify with this team as *their* team. The embarrassment became sharper after the England tour. It's still seen as the old "they" and "we". It's a crisis.'

Yet Tshwete fervently believes that the struggle to rebuild South Africa's social structure depends as fundamentally on the development of sport and the retention of competition's basic principle – best is best – as on the development of education, housing and health.

On Sunday, South Africa won its first Commonwealth medal for 36 years, Willem Engelbrecht's bronze in the cycling road race, following the disqualification of Lillywhite, of England. A cheer went up at an official reception being given by Tshwete when the decision was announced by Michael Fennell, of Jamaica, the Games federation's new chairman. It was significant to see many white members of the team having their photograph taken arm in arm with Tshwete.

'I cannot consider conceding to tokenism,' Tshwete said. 'It's bad for everyone. If we were to play 5–5–5 in the World Cup next year, blacks, coloureds and whites, we would be trounced, it would humiliate the players, the country, and increase polarisation. So we have to be patient.

'The problems in sport are not separate from the rest of life. None of it is going to be easy, it will require explanation every inch of the way. Development is not an event, it's a process. The heritage of apartheid is not going to be swept away overnight.'

Like any sports minister anywhere in the world, only ten times more so than most, Tshwete finds his budget impossibly stretched two ways: by the need to support elite international sport and produce national heroes – perhaps, this week, Makebula, the light flyweight, or Sepeng, the 800 metres runner – and also to supply the facilities absent in most townships.

Tshwete said: 'It is useless to talk of development if you don't have the instruments to make it viable. Yet sport can be the counteraction in the attempt to halt the crime wave that threatents to wreck our country. Sport is central to culture, it's aura of self-discipline is invaluable. You cannot provide houses in which people will breed the next generation of youth and not offer them opportunities to fill their lives instead of playing on the streets or drinking, robbing and hijacking.'

Tshwete points to the motto in use in New Zealand: A Child in Sport is a Child not in Court. Yet the most important race in South Africa is the race to generate racewinners. This week Tshwete has told Sam Ramsamy and Mluleki George, the national sports leaders, that they must accelerate their work to increase training opportunities for blacks in the key sports of boxing, athletics, cycling and tennis, as well as football.

'This is the last time I'm going to be put on the platform to defend our policies,' Tshwete said. 'We must accelerate development and I know that that means more money. We are going to finance it, but they must do the work. At the same time, we must try to persuade people to forget the colour of their skin.'

THE WORLD'S MOST DEBATED COACH

Can Ma produce male athletes as successful as his women?

15 October 1994 Hiroshima

Ma Junren, the revolutionary, impassioned coach who so controversially inspires the world's fastest middle and long-distance female runners, sets an odd example.

Sitting in the late afternoon sun yesterday at Hiroshima's £30 million new stadium, and reflecting on the first gold medal by one of his male runners at the Asian Games, Ma was chain-smoking so compulsively that at one point he had a cigarette between the fingers of each hand. Yet he acknowledges he is a sick man.

A few yards away, the women such as Wang Junxia – who would become millionaires if the China Athletics Federation was not limiting their commercial appearances – padded obediently round the warm-up track. Sun Ripeng, who had just set an Asian Games record in the steeplechase, eased away the lactic acid.

Having become, in one season, the world's most debated coach – after the achievement of his women runners in the world championships and the National Games in Peking last year – Ma's life is, at 50, in turmoil. He is so unwell, on the one hand, with serious stomach and blood pressure disorders, that he needs prolonged rest, yet is under pressure on three fronts: from a sceptical sport, which wants him to prove his worth by producing successful men; from obstruction by his own province and the national federation from gaining full exposure for his runners; and in his desperation to generate the finance that will sustain his private training school in the city of Dalian, in the northeastern province of Liaoning.

He says that at the moment he is smoking 'simply to stay awake'. Ma dismissively waves aside performances at these Asian Games by his runners. 'You haven't seen their real standard,' he said, 'because there's no challenge.' In the men's 800 metres, Mu Weiquo, improving his time by three seconds in six months under Ma's guidance, had set a national record of 1min 46.44sec when taking the silver medal behind Jin Il-lee, of South Korea.

Ma concedes tht the phenomenal achievements of his women runners last year, at all distances from 1,500 metres to 10,000 metres, failed to impress some coaches. 'They say that improving women is nothing special, you must improve men [to be properly recognised],' he said.

So, after the National Games, he took on board eight men. He admits women are more susceptible to discipline and hard work than men, and that he is at present short of facilities for men, but predicts that his men will be setting world records 'within six or seven years'. This is the period it took to reach that standard with women, under his regime of severe training and controversial herbal diet.

Sun yesterday ran to instructions: staying with the leaders for four laps, then increasing the pressure over the last three. He sprinted away from rivals from Qatar and Saudi Arabia in the final straight.

Yet Ma admits that the reason why his women's performances, though still impressive, are below those of last year is that they needed to reduce their training workload or risk incurring injuries. 'They need more resting time this year,' he said. There is also the question of the Chinese athletic calendar.

For Ma, achievement by his runners is paramount when representing Liaoning in the National Games. Before 1993, the National Games were last staged in 1987, in Canton. With an inevitable downbeat in 1988, they did poorly in the Olympic Games in Seoul. The national federation therefore rescheduled the National Games to follow the Olympics; so it is now the Asian Games, midway between Olympics, that suffer the downbeat.

Just before agreeing to an interview, Ma was in a huddle with a young Japanese. It was the first time he had directly received an invitation for his athletes to compete in one of the profusion of high prize-money marathons, in this instance Osaka's.

The regular experience for marathon organisers – such as London's – when making formal approaches to the Chinese national federation, is to receive little or no collaboration. In other words, the invitations never reach Ma. He admits that he has no influence on selection for any inter-national events, such as continental or world championships, or the Olympics, never mind marathons. Financial envy – with arguments in China about who keeps the money – is not confined to British administration.

This means that Ma's superiors – primarily Zhu Xhenling, the all pow-erful woman within the federation – will determine whether Ma's runners compete in the expanded, high prize-money grand prix series next year; though there is, of course, the corollary that absence will assist their per-formances in the world championships in Gothenburg next year and the Olympics in Atlanta.

To finance the 'Ma's Army' training school, he contracted the rights, in April, to market his patent herbal medicine – on sale in downtown Hiroshima supermarkets at £20 a small bottle – for £7 million with the Sheng Yang First Medical Company. He holds a 46 per cent interest, but says: 'The investment is such that the project is not yet making a profit.'

Because of conflict with the province, he needs to generate private money to sustain his athletes – 'We eat, sleep and train together' – whose allowance from the province is only £1 per head per day.

Are there problems of rivalry with the Ministry of Sport? 'I don't care,' he said grandly. 'We need to travel, to have special food, if we are to survive, so we need money. I'm following the [expansionist] policy of Deng [Xiaoping].'

The world should be warned that, if his health allows, Ma is far from finished. He has a 16-year-old girl, Wang Xiaoxia, who has run 8min 49sec for the 3,000 metres, who he believes can win in Atlanta. 'And I have some more, only 14 or 15-year-olds.'

Random drug testing results – four times by the international federation in the past year – suggest that Ma's ambition to continue conquering the world may be legitimately based, contrary to the cynical view.

EGOTISM TO THE POINT OF PARANOIA

Why the brilliant Clough would have been bad for England

4 November 1994

The debate on whether it would have been good for English football if the brilliant, eccentric Brian Clough had been appointed national team manager, in succession to either Sir Alf Ramsey or Don Revie, is never-ending. Clough has now supplied the answer. No.

Clough, whose bloated egotism sometimes approached the point of paranoia – and is exactly portrayed in a fascinating autobiography related to John Sadler – needless to say himself believes exactly the opposite: 'We would have had one of the most exciting, positive England sides of all time,' he characteristically asserts.

Yet he goes on to admit that the Football Association did not want someone who could publicly call the Italians 'cheating bastards', after Derby County's European Cup semi-final defeat by Juventus in 1973 and a subsequent inconclusive Uefa inquiry.

He further relates, almost with pride, how he gratuitously insulted Professor Frank O'Gorman – a friendly, altruistic surgeon – for intruding on an England youth team discussion at half-time *with the oranges*!

The Mad Professor – as Clough dismissively refers to the equally-controversial Sir Harold Thompson, internationally renowned chemist (not mathemetician, as Clough writes) and FA chairman, who had created the most famous of Amateur Cup winners, Pegasus – rightfully put Clough and Peter Taylor, his assistant, in charge of the youth team, under Ron Greenwood, to see how they would handle it. The FA committee included Sir Matt Busby. Clough and Taylor proved they did not have the patience.

That was a pity. Clough could have become more famous worldwide than Ramsey, could have given English football immense prestige, yet he lacked a fundamental quality, taught him at Sunderland by Alan Brown and one that he demanded in all his players – self-discipline.

That wild streak of genius laced with a resentful feeling of inferiority, from being internationally ignored and then cheated by injury as a player – after a career encapsulated by a phenomenal record of 267 goals in 296 league and cup matches – made him intolerably, splendidly bumptious, the darling of cynical television producers and his own worst enemy. To appear on *Parkinson*, understandable in the boy from the back streets, had become more important than personal dignity.

He admits the worst error of his life was needlessly resigning, with Taylor, at Derby. They had become consumed by their own sense of power, authority and their public acclaim.

'I knew I'd finish up with a team of league champions,' he states, upon leaving Hartlepool. His talent, on which he unashamedly gloats, for motivating players was so immense and Taylor's, for finding and blending them, so astute – Taylor, the former goalkeeper-friend, mentor, humorist, work-dodger, financial opportunist and ace scout – they could, you sense, have climbed any peak.

They were Butch and Sundance. Whenever Taylor had made one of his crass personal miscalculations with the board, he would confide in Clough: 'I think *we're* in trouble!' The tale of their inspired-yet-calculated, often reckless-yet-rational course, gambling on their exceptional, contrasted judgments, has produced one of the few worthy football books.

Clough's condemnation, as an aspiring young coach, of Charles Hughes, the FA director of coaching, is utterly damning – 'never worked with anyone who knew less about football' – but the contradictions that have confused his own career are starkly apparent.

He worshipped his mother, an angel of love and warmth in terraced, working-class Middlesborough, who would have been ashamed of the needless expletives with which he has allowed Sadler to mar the narrative. Only occasionally sliding into clichés, Sadler is otherwise tellingly faithful to the vernacular of the game.

Clough dumps Birtles off the team coach in the middle of the countryside for complaining of an early start – 'find your own way' – yet within the hour pulls his team off a plane bound for the Middle East, scared by an abortive take-off, saying: 'I couldn't care less what happens to the match guarantee.'

He derides the excessive money players now receive, exposing the greed of Stuart Pearce when attempting to double his salary with Nottingham Forest – 'He couldn't tackle . . . was murdered by real wingers' – yet himself took all he could, though he categorically denies the infamous, alleged 'bung' from Tottenham Hotspur for Sheringham. He eulogises Hoddle and what he might have done with him for England, yet significantly never attempted to buy him. The fascination of the story is his assembly, with Taylor, of often improbable, ultimately triumphant players and scintillating teams, uniquely, with two clubs: O'Hare, McGovern, Hinton, Mackay and Gemmill at Derby; then the derelict winger, Robertson – 'a slob . . . furtively smoking in the corner' – the underestimated striker, Withe, declining centre half, Lloyd, anonymous full back, Clark (now Forest's manager), allegedly uncontrollable central defender, Burns, and unknown centre forward, Birtles, with Nottingham Forest. A double miracle.

We tended to take it all for granted at the time, to have forgotten how the emergence of Forest from the bottom of the second division to win the European Cup in successive seasons was truly astonishing. The recreation of Robertson, as with Hinton, was the mark of managerial genius, as was the way Clough and Taylor produced successive teams devoid of fear, in which the sum of the whole exceeded the sum of the parts.

Taylor's instinct for blend is generously and affectionately told: how Taylor, without optimism, sent Clough off to 'get Mackay' from Tottenham, how they diverted him from imminent appointment as assistant manager with Heart of Midlothian and then, extraordinarily, persuaded this hell-fire attacker to become their sweeper.

'When Mackay, the truly great Dave Mackay, put his foot on the ball under the most intense pressure in the six yard area and calmly played us out of trouble at Huddersfield . . . I remember Taylor's reaction . . . "That's what we bought him for, we're on our way" . . . the Derby era was born.'

Yet this managerial genius so often failed to read the tealeaves: with Stuart Webb, a scheming Derby secretary; with Sam Longson, generous but envious chairman; with Matt Busby; most of all, at Leeds, with players he had criticised and still despised as cheats when he, briefly, took charge. They were out for revenge. And got it. How could he have so misjudged the situation?

Finally, after his anti-climatic decline and relegation with Forest, Clough admits to his drinking problem. 'I do drink too much . . . I have allowed [it] to take a hold . . . I will face it and bring it under control.'

The old, old story: tearaway, talented son of devoted mother. Like so many of us, Brian Clough has been the prisoner of his childhood. It would have taken an exceptional chairman to have replaced his mother, which was what he needed.

A NATURAL COACH

The rise and rise of Gerry Francis

26 November 1994

Not even the greatest players can play football without the ball. Someone, therefore, has to win it. A simple enough maxim, you might say, but it has been a central factor in the career of Gerry Francis as both a player and a manager.

Francis was on the verge of becoming the most complete England midfield player of the modern era until struck down by a back injury when with Queens Park Rangers, falling on the base of his spine on a frozen pitch. As dynamic, with or without the ball, as Neeskens then was for Holland – or as Mackay had been when Tottenham last won the League in 1961 – Francis was appointed England captain by Don Revie in 1975, when only 23, with a brief that effectively made him an assistant manager out on the field.

He was all that a manager dreams of, possessing that quintessential English quality of determination within a range of abilities that made him ball-winner, schemer and scorer. Injuries to McFarland, Bell, Beattie and Francis, and Todd's reluctance to play internationally, robbed the controversial Revie of half a team.

There was about Francis, born within earshot of Loftus Road and, as a boy, watching his father, Roy, playing for Brentford, the same natural leadership on the field that Alf Ramsey had seen in Bobby Moore, only more articulate. Francis made others play better; he knew it, and liked it.

It was equally natural that he would become an outstanding coach. Long ago he had observed: 'I feel players want to be guided, want to know their positions [tactically].' It is his base instinct, arriving at Tottenham amid tactical chaos, that the players need *organisation*, to be told where to *be* at different phases of the game.

For many years, Tottenham have had a miserable time playing at Anfield, where they go today, primarily because their style, and Liverpool's, has made it exceedingly difficult for Tottenham to win, and to keep, the ball. Correcting this will be at the forefront of the instructions from Tottenham's new manager to a side that this season would often have struggled to pin down a three-legged sheep. Poor positioning and marshmallow tackling in midfield and defence have left Tottenham horribly vulnerable; 24 matches without a clean sheet until Wednesday night.

'It's a tough one, there's a huge amount to do,' Francis admits with heavy understatement, inheriting from Osvaldo Ardiles, mid-season, a club with no money to spend, unless he sells, and with one win in the last nine matches; fourth from bottom of the table if penalised by six points as decreed by the Football Association.

Francis flowered as a young player at Rangers under the management of Gordon Jago, who admired most his ability to win the ball. It was the era of contrast: the eloquent Bowles (a Rangers colleague), Hudson, Bell and Currie on the one hand, the expedient Storey, Hunter and Tommy Smith on the other. Francis sees their interdependence: 'Neither a Gascoigne nor a Stiles will win you anything alone. You need passers, savers [goalkeepers], tacklers, leaders, scorers. You need a squad that is complete to win anything.'

His pride is that, in his three seasons with Rangers, they finished eleventh, fifth and ninth, always above Tottenham, never mind that he was obliged successively to sell Parker, Wegerle and Sinton, unable to compete financially with the big clubs. Transfers out, £10 million; transfers in, £2 million. The year they were fifth, he spent only £160,000. Only Blackburn Rovers (with Jack Walker's money), Newcastle United and Nottingham Forest, he considers, can come close in terms of resources to challenging the Big Six: Liverpool, Everton, Manchester United, Arsenal, Tottenham and Aston Villa.

Francis does not need the game, having financial independence from private business, but is driven by his love for it. During his giddy four years as manager of Bristol Rovers – he loaned them money to buy players, and in 1991 they won the third division title and reached the Leyland DAF Cup final – he had regular fish and chip Saturday suppers with the players, to whom he is 'Gerry', not 'boss'.

Now 42, he has an almost academic appetite for teaching, the true manager-coach. His private thrill is to have rescued Les Ferdinand from obscurity and turned him into a multi-million-pound target for rich rivals; to have enticed Nigel Martyn from a £100-per-week factory job in Cornwall – 'I'll give you £105' – to Rovers, and them made him the first £1 million goalkeeper sold to Crystal Palace.

Having gone from cleaning boots and sweeping terraces as an apprentice to captaining England, he likes to say, matter-of-fact: 'There is nothing any player can do that I have not experienced.' On or off the field, his man-of-the-world manner applies. He was something of a playboy of the Seventies, a gift to prying photographers, and remained a bachelor until he was 38. He did not believe in marriage; from his observed experience it was too often a shackle on young players, a restriction on both man and woman.

'I was into a round of parties, heavy drinking, and hitting the sack with various birds,' he told an interviewer in 1977. 'My football suffered a lot. I began to realise the price you pay for being in the public eye.'

While continuing with the game, on which he was hooked, and fighting off injury, he built a series of businesses together with a girlfriend with whom he lived for 14 years, including antique furniture. This venture was sold when he joined his present partner, of the past five years, with whom he has an 18-month-old son, Adam. His private life may be unconventional yet, in its way, is steady, sensible, logical. Modern, you might say.

He is, indeed, an unusual mixture. A former star player, yet a born teacher who can still say: 'I'm learning every day.' A man of absolute certainty in his convictions, yet without undue boastfulness or self-promotion. Bold, yet cautious. A player who responded like an actor to the roar of Wembley or Hampden Park, yet back home in rural Surrey breeds racing pigeons.

On the one hand, he can say of his time with Bristol Rovers: 'When I went there, they didn't think they could win. When I left, they didn't think they could lose.' There were 5,000 supporters' signatures pleading for him to stay, but he felt he could do no more, and pined for a return to his West London roots.

On the other hand, he has made it clear to Alan Sugar, Tottenham's impulsive chairman who has no background in the game but who longs to ride publicly in a champions' celebration chariot, that it is Sugar as much as he who is now on trial. 'If I'm not happy next June, who knows?' Francis says, enigmatically.

Clearly he is not to be pushed around. The Rangers owner has just learnt that, Francis regarding his proposed appointment of Rodney Marsh, as chief executive, as intolerable. 'It didn't matter if it was Rodney Marsh or Donald Duck [as my superior],' Francis said, when quitting, before his appointment at Tottenham. 'You have to live by certain principles. I just hope the club will not suffer.'

Nor is he hungering, some day, for the England job now held by his mentor when he was a previous Rangers manager, Terry Venables. Contemplating the vacancy, after Graham Taylor's dismissal, Francis was ambivalent. 'I'm very patriotic and I'd love to see us do well again internationally,' he said, 'but there are many things about the present England set-up that would have to change before I would consider the job.' Francis does not like to gamble. That is why the Tottenham team gives him the shivers: as likely to lose 4-3, as it did to Villa last week, as to win 5-4. Perhaps it is also why he does not believe in marriage, and why he is, basically, still in two minds about management, as opposed to coaching. Coaching he enjoys, like training his pigeons.

'I don't really enjoy management,' he says candidly. 'It will never replace playing.' You can be sure, however, that he will give Tottenham everything, just as he used to do on the field.

PYTHAGORAS IN BOOTS

Johan Cruyff's intellect on and off the field

6 December 1994

It could be said that Johan Cruyff, in his prime, was superior even to Pelé: not as an individualist, but in the capacity to extract the most from other players around him. If Pelé was a sorcerer with his feet, Cruyff, like Di Stefano before him, was Pythagoras in boots.

The geometric complexities that illuminated Cruyff's play have been applied as coach of Barcelona with stunning success, not least against Manchester United recently in the European Cup Champions' League. The intelligence with which Cruyff applied a rare talent, for Ajax, Holland and, later, Barcelona, separated him from all but a handful of players in my lifetime. Few have been able to exact, both physically and mentally, such mesmeric control on a match from one penalty area to another. Di Stefano, almost judicial in his authority, often did for Real Madrid, so did the sleek Suarez for Barcelona and then Internazionale, though with less physical bravura.

Of the many occasions when Cruyff was awesome, during the three consecutive European Cup victories of Ajax in the early Seventies, or in partnership with Rep, Krol, Neeskens, Haan – all Ajax players – and van Hanegem for Holland, the match I recall best was the destruction of Argentina during the 1974 World Cup finals. Two electric thunderstorms struck Dortmund that night; the more severe befell Argentina on the field.

Scoring one goal and creating two others, Cruyff, for 90 minutes, was untouchable. You never knew what would come next out of the magician's hat. With his extraordinary capacity to read the way a move would develop, or to make it develop, gliding about the field like an ice hockey puck, he was impossible to mark.

It is not often the great players become outstanding managers or coaches. Di Stefano and Suarez had undistinguished records. Great players like Matthews or Bobby Charlton exist, even within a team game, in a kind of mental isolation that divides them from lesser men's conflicts; stresses with which they have difficulty relating. Raich Carter, though I was too young to see him at his pre-war peak, was said by contemporaries to have been in Cruyff's class, yet Carter as a manager was impatient with lesser players.

Cruyff's distinction as coach is a continuation of the system applied by Ajax, the Total Football in which all players are expected to operate the same principles in all parts of the field, principles based on movement and accurate passing; often, passing designed not to find space but to prevent the opposition filling that space.

To this end, Barcelona's training, other than for physical fitness, is almost entirely confined to playing six-against-four, two touch, in an area half the size of the penalty area, about 20 yards by 20.

Cruyff explains: 'In a small area, the movement is necessarily fast and the passes must be pinpoint. Two of the "six", playing wide, repeatedly change "team" whenever the "four" gain possession . . . so it is always six with the ball against four trying to retrieve it. This possession principle should operate in any area of the normal field of play. So our training is intense and is the basis of our game. Also, it is not widely realised that you can close down space more effectively by accurate passing, when you have the ball [forcing opponents into certain positions], then you can by man-marking without the ball.'

Thus Barcelona's apparent absence of defensive formations: the measure of success of their training is evident in the degree to which their play is attack-orientated. Consider, too, if you have watched them regularly, how often a receiving player successfully turns away from or past a marker.

'This ability is controlled not by the receiver but by the passer,' Cruyff says. 'If the receiver has his back to goal, the passer sends the ball to the foot on the side where the receiver should turn, reducing the arc through which he must control the ball to move. The passer can see the field in a way the receiver cannot. Often, of course, it's the receiver determining the direction of pass by his initial movement without the ball.'

Most people recall the 15 consecutive passes made by Holland preceding the goal in the first minute of the 1974 World Cup final against West Germany. That was an example of closing down space. German players were kept in forward positions, 'closed down' without the ball, leaving space behind them to attack.

'Coaches talk about "pass-and-go", but go where?' Cruyff asks. 'If you pass repeatedly in a small area, as in our training, you are closing down opponents in one area. A larger, unoccupied area is then empty if you beat an opponent one-against-one.'

Although Pallister and Bruce were left covering Romario, it was still effectively one-against-one, Romario against Pallister, because Bruce was not between Romario and the goal as cover, but wide on his right [Romario's left].' Romario and Stoichkov ran riot.

A further product of Barcelona's training system is the use of a sweeper in front of the central defenders, aimed at interception of passes on the ground and closer contact with midfield.

'The great strength of the English, which worries all foreigners,' Cruyff says, 'is the pace of their game, the quick movement of the ball forward; but so long as you allow yourself to be outnumbered in midfield, you will not exploit this advantage.'

Cruyff spends many hours working at the natural inabilities of players: simple techniques such as right-foot/handed players having more difficulty heading left-to-right, as opposed to the instinctive right-to-left; and being at a disadvantage when meeting a cross from the left and needing to head at goal, to their right. Yet, as a former nonpareil, Cruyff is acutely conscious of how a coach can harm rather than help a player, how the 'fit' of a player is often wholly dependent on the coach. He points to the way Bergkamp, of Holland, fails to fit into the system at Inter.

Cruyff emphasises that the time for deciding whether to keep young players schooled in junior Barcelona teams arrives when they are only 12. 'At that age, you know whether or not a boy is going to be a player. There are fundamental skills which you have or don't have, which cannot be taught after that age.'

Barcelona set demanding standards. This season, they are as yet falling short of those, though they need only draw at home to IFK Gothenberg, leaders of their group, to eliminate Manchester United from the Champions' League, even if United defeat the Turks of Galatasaray tomorrow.

'We were tired even before the European Cup final against Milan,' Cruyff says. 'From February, we had a fantastic run of 15 games, from which we took 28 points to win the league in the last stride. The moment we did that, I knew, inside, that we wouldn't win in Athens [the final], that we were empty and couldn't do anything. That's not an excuse; it's reality. Our president, for all his hopes, fully understood.'

This season, he feels Barcelona are still suffering from the added stress of the World Cup finals, in which they had 12 of their squad involved. 'They are not only tired, but getting injured,' he says. 'It's not to be surprised they're not 100 per cent.'

That was not how it felt to Manchester United.

SYMBOLIC OF THE BEAUTY OF THE GAME

Stanley Matthews, a sorcerer beyond description

1 February 1995

Johnny Carey, the former captain of Manchester United and Ireland, once said: 'Playing Stanley is like playing against a ghost.' Today, the ghost is 80, still spry and lean and wondering, with that strange, detached modesty, what all the fuss was about. Stanley Matthews, the only footballer ever likely to be knighted while still playing, never properly understood his fame, nor the affection in which he was held throughout the land and far abroad.

From Brazil to Belgium, from South Africa to Sweden, the greetings have been flowing in from foreign federations, dignitaries and fellow players for whom he remains a phenomenon without equal. More than 700 guests are attending a gala dinner in his home town of Stoke tonight, among them the inimitable Ferenc Puskas, from Hungary and Real Madrid, Ladislav Kubala, from Barcelona, and Branko Stankovic, from Yugoslavia, former foes and life-long admirers.

This celebration of a unique life, of a player who took the bus to the ground together with his followers, who was never cautioned, stands in contrast to a game today besieged by violence, greed and withered sportsmanship.

Across three decades, Matthews brought to football an aura of unprecedented glamour, yet he himself, in the words of Arthur Hopcraft, the celebrated author, 'was the opposite of glamorous, brought up among thrift and the threat of dole and debt'. The unqualified devotion of the British public, which flocked to see him, before the age of television, in tens of thousands, lay in his seeming frailty and his magician's spell over the opposing full back.

This unassuming genius brought a sense of freedom and adventure, satisfying a common public yearning for simple pleasure. At his best, he was unplayable by fair means. Such was the esteem in which he was held by opponents that few descended into the expedient fouling that intimidated the genius of later players such as Best and Maradona.

Sir Walter Winterbottom, the first England team manager, said Matthews was 'without parallel, the matador goading and provoking . . . it was extraordinary how he could get the ball to float'. Stanley

Mortensen, Matthews's acclaimed partner at Blackpool, eulogised his qualities: 'Fitness, balance, confidence, pace over ten yards, body-swerve, instantaneous control, two-footed, marvellous temperament.'

Geoffrey Green, the former football correspondent of *The Times*, who witnessed the golden international eras before and after the Second World War through to the Seventies, called Matthews 'the greatest dribbler, the most superb ball-manipulator in the history of the game' – and Green had seen them all. Jimmy Seed, the manager of Charlton Athletic's FA Cup Final teams of 1946 and 1947, said: 'His feet are the greatest entertainment that football has known.'

Matthews transcended ordinary football in a way none has ever done, not even Di Stefano, Pelé, Cruyff or Maradona. A mythology grew around him. Many of the record attendances in Britian were established when he was present: 84,569 at Maine Road, Manchester; 149,547 at Hampden Park. The week before he returned to Stoke City from Blackpool, in 1961, *aged 46*, the attendance had been 8,400. For his reappearance, against Huddersfield Town, it jumped to 35,000.

In his message of goodwill today, João Havelange, the president of Fifa, the world governing body, says: 'Within the exulted company of elite personalities regarded on a plane superior to all others, foremost among these, for his ability and sportsmanship, shall always be Sir Stanley Matthews.'

Matthews had not one career, but three: prewar – probably his peak – war-time and post-war, the last the more astonishing because of his age. He first played for England at 19, against Wales in 1934, the last time against Denmark in a World Cup qualifier, aged 42, in 1957. Repeatedly discarded by vacillating selectors, his 54 caps – plus 30 wartime – should have been 154. Tom Finney, his friend and rival, said he ought to have been included in the squad for the 1958 World Cup finals.

The trance in which he could hold opposing full backs was bewitching. The *Daily Mirror* reported, of his performance against Wales in 1937, that the crowd 'were laughing when they were not gasping in amazement'. In 1954, when England beat West Germany, then the recent World Cup winners, at Wembley, Matthews so mesmerised Kohlmeyer that the crowd of 80,000 repeatedly laughed out loud. Like many before, Kohlmeyer's confidence was destroyed and he never played for Germany again.

Two years later, aged 41, Matthews dismantled Nilton Santos, the Brazil captain and regarded as the world's best left back, in a dazzling 4–2 victory at Wembley.

It was not uncommon for some moment of wizardry, resulting in a colleague's goal, to be openly applauded by the opposition, as when England beat Scotland 8–0 in 1943 – 'our best team', Bill Shankly said – and Belgium 5–3 in 1947. For the maestro, there was little pleasure in scoring goals, only in making them. As Nat Lofthouse, the Bolton Wanderers and England centre forward, observed: 'He nearly always went to the line, so you were never offside.'

When Matthews, at his third attempt, won an FA Cup winner's medal in Blackpool's 4–3 defeat of Bolton, in 1953, Lofthouse reflected on the final dramatic minutes: 'I spent the time just watching Stanley. He stood there, toes turned inwards, looking like a little old man – until he moved. In that final spell he could do it, and he *knew* he could do it.'

After eventual retirement, having played his last match for Stoke at 50 – 'too early', he thought – he devoted himself to coaching. Briefly, he was manager at Port Vale, and in the Seventies, revered for his work in Soweto, he took the first all-black South African team on tour to Brazil.

The inscription on the statue by Colin Melbourne erected in Hanley in 1987 reflects the legacy from Sir Stanley Matthews to all sport: 'His name is symbolic of the beauty of the game, his fame timeless and international, his sportsmanship and modesty universally acclaimed. A magical player, of the people, for the people.'

AS REFINED AS A MANTEL CLOCK

Why the Boat Race is Different

27 February 1995

To suggest that rowing is no more than repetitively shifting a blade-full of water is about as accurate as saying that a sculptor merely chips away the marble he does not want. Rowing at its peak is as refined as a mantel clock.

For those rowing in the Boat Race, supposedly one of the year's social events, the occasion is no more social than running a marathon, and as emotionally serious, for seven months beforehand, as getting married.

We all understand the complexity of skill of a Matthew Le Tissier or a Steve Davis because we have all tried to kick a football at some time or other or to sink the black over the length of the snooker table. Rowing is, physically, an utter contradiction: threading a needle with sledgehammer force. Some 600 times in the Boat Race.

The race won last year by Cambridge – according to pundits, one of the most outstanding crews of all time – ranked eighteenth among the year's largest sporting television audiences. Yet not one viewer in 10,000 would have had the slightest conception of the technical triumph being enacted by both crews.

So fine is the margin among eight huge oxen, and their tame parrot calling the shots from the stern, that, when the two crews are announced today for the race on April 1, the respective coaches will be delighted if, during the six months of training so far, their boat has touched perfection even once for a dozen strokes.

Consider, for instance, one fact. Say you are Laird Reed, the 25-year-old American in the engine-room of the Oxford boat, a politics and economics postgraduate from Princeton, a former world junior eights gold medal-winner and 1992 Olympic trialist, 6ft 4in and 15 stone. If you apply your immense power a fraction too soon as your blade enters the water, you will kick your boat *backwards*.

'The start of the stroke, at the moment of entry, needs the greatest dexterity,' Robin Williams, the Cambridge chief coach, said. 'And relaxation. There is this daunting contradiction: at the moment of maximum stress, you need the maximum relaxation, if the boat is to have rhythm and synchronisation.'

Such is the stress on individual oarsmen that the months of training are necessary to refine details until they become second nature. A week ago, Williams reports, the Cambridge boat showed flashes of 1994 form, and certainly something superior to 1993, when Oxford's almost humiliating run of ten successive victories was finally ended. 'If all goes well, we could be looking as good as last year in a month's time,' he said, cautiously.

Cambridge's recent victories were greeted by Oxford with the sort of incredulity that some Battle of Britain veterans reserved for the RAF's first qualified woman Tornado pilot. It drove Oxford to summon Dan Topolski, the coaching guru who presided over their years of glory.

He came reluctantly. Topolski rowed for Oxford in 1967 and 1968, represented Great Britain in the European championships the following year, and won a lightweight eight world championship gold medal in 1977. He was Oxford's chief coach from 1972 to 1987, by which time he was no longer enjoying it.

'Our system was falling into disrepair,' Topolski said. 'The first loss came in spite of having two Olympic gold medalists in the boat, including Mathew Pinsent. There was no foundation below the peak of the pyramid. Isis, our second crew, had won only once since 1987, and I was asked to supervise the reconstruction, on a three-year part-time contract.'

He finds it, nonetheless, difficult not to get sucked in, so absorbing is the ambiance. The Boat Race, he rightly says, is a unique event not just in rowing but in the world of sport. 'One race. One opponent. Maybe one chance in a rowing career. No heats, no subsequent regattas for revenge, no medals for second place. An immensely difficult, tidal course. An endurance test over nearly five miles, not two kilometres. So public, such hype. Terrifying. Often raced in conditions where world championships would be abandoned. We race until we sink. A test of nerve and courage of Everest proportions.'

Topolski dwells on the complexity of the attempt to achieve unison to which Williams refers; the fact that 'timing' is less with colleagues in the boat than effort in the water, where there is a relatively long 'gate' within which the power can be delivered, early or late. It is possible to be out of time with colleagues yet still in time.

More than anything, however, Topolski has tried to give the Oxford squad an understanding of selection procedure. Of seat-racing, the performance measurement of individuals acquired by swapping one oarsman at a time between two competing four-oar boats, which was abandoned last year; of acclimatising them to Tideway conditions, winds and bends and rough water, by sending them out in sculls.

'As the stress of the event mounts, with the approach of race day,' Topolski said, 'you have to reduce the information input.' Ultimately, as in all sports, refinement is as much mental as technical.

This perception is echoed by Richard Phelps, president (skipper in colloquial terms) of the Cambridge boat, and a member of the Britain Olympic and world championship eight for the past three years. 'In the first couple of months of training, you reach 98 per cent of your boat potential,' he said. 'It takes the next four months to find the other two per cent.'

It should again be a formidable Cambridge crew including, as it does, besides Phelps at No 4, Roger Taylor at bow and Matthew Parish at No 2 from last year's British eight; Dirk Bangert, of Germany, from the 1993 crew, and Marko Banovic at No 7, from last year's Croatian coxless pairs that finished fifth in the world championship.

Rowing is, outstandingly, the one Oxbridge sport that has fully kept pace with world standards. In the eight years since Beefeater became the race sponsors, 11 Boat Race oarsmen have been in winning crews at Henley; 12 have represented Great Britain; 15 have represented their country at the Olympic Games; and 29 have appeared in world championships. So unique is the race and its hold upon an international public that last year there were 250 million television viewers in 160 nations.

The practice on the Tideway yesterday between Cambridge and a powerful Dutch crew would seem to have determined the place at cox in favour of Russell Slatford, the Hughes Hall postgraduate controversially discarded shortly before the race last year. His rival, Mark Davies, from Christ's, the son of Barry Davies, the BBC television commentator, yesterday steered the Dutch but Cambridge's confident performance meant that a side-by-side duel, which would have tested their nerve, did not materialise.

Davies, who steered the Goldie crew to victory in 1992, has perhaps more Tideway experience than Slatford, whose composure under stress was last year doubted at the last minute, even though he had demonstrated his quality during training at Ely. Cambridge are intent on avoiding any uncertainty this year. Last night the two men were anxiously awaiting the call that would say they were in today's selection.

KLINSMANN'S OPPORTUNIST MASTER-STROKE

Spurs steal victory in classic cup-tie

13 March 1995

A cracking game, Roy Evans called it, remaining magnanimous in defeat. I thought this FA Cup quarter-final, in which Jürgen Klinsmann gave Tottenham victory over Liverpool in the closing minutes, was among the best dozen matches between English clubs I have witnessed in more than 40 years – as fine a contest as you could see.

During a first half of exceptional skill, one could not glance at one's programme for fear of missing a vital, split-second incident. For those 45 minutes, Gary Mabbutt was the impenetrable barrier upon whom Liverpool's attacks foundered. Just when Robbie Fowler's header seemed to have given Liverpool the advantage they deserved, Tottenham answered on the stroke of half-time with Teddy Sheringham's stunningly struck shot from 20 yards.

And just when we were all relishing the thought of a replay at White Hart Lane, between these teams so splendidly re-fashioned in a short time by new managers, Klinsmann stole victory with a master-stroke of opportunism. As the final whistle signalled Liverpool's abrupt defeat, it was reassuring, amid so many problems within the game, to witness the spontaneous appreciation from the Kop towards Tottenham's exhausted but joyful players.

Evans and Gerry Francis, his opposite number, each attempted to expose one flank of the other's defence: Austin at right back for Tottenham and Bjornebye, Francis had supposed, on Liverpool's left. In the event, though, Bjornebye was omitted as a result of Evans's ploy of including Walters against Austin.

The outcome thus presented fascinating tactical stresses within the overall struggle. Walters, an amiable dribbler who has a willowy sidestep that even he knows little about, established enough dominance over Austin to have turned the result.

Sadly for him, as Evans would later lament, the final pass was missing for all but Fowler's goal. Thus Evans had considered the substitution of Bjornebye, eventually made after 75 minutes, even during the first half.

On the same side of the field, Barmby, switched by Francis to the right, was exploiting the 'hole' behind Walters to such an extent that Babb was continuously harassed. This meant that Scales and Ruddock were more than usually stretched apart. So, two marvellously fluent teams were operating at permanent breaking point. And what a treat it was.

Of the many enduring memories – the opposing authority of Mabbutt and Ruddock, the wiles of McManaman, Redknapp and Barnes, Fowler's pace, Howells's dependability in midfield – none is stronger than the stamina and application of Anderton, in central midfield in place of Popescu instead of his usual role on the flank.

I admit to doubts about Anderton as an England player, at times thinking him frail and irresolute. How wrong. He now seemed to run ten miles, covering the ground the way Colin Bell once did. When, in the second half, Liverpool began to run out of ideas and to lose their legs, one of the reasons was the performance of Anderton.

Tottenham had one or two serious openings in that blistering first half, Liverpool half a dozen or more, yet Walker in Tottenham's goal was another of the afternoon's impeccable performers, alert to every threat. Strangely, two of Liverpool's sharpest moments came from Scales when he moved into attack. Their passing, with six- and seven-man moves, was a constant delight, though the goal after 38 minutes was less than clinical.

Barmby slipped, conceding possession; away went Walters, drawing three men to Tottenham's right, and just when he seemed to have no options, he turned to cross the ball onto Fowler's head.

There were demands for a penalty when Calderwood brought down Fowler moments later, but then Howells accurately found Klinsmann lurking on the edge of the penalty area. Intelligently scorning the chance of a difficult shot, Klinsmann rolled the ball square for Sheringham to bend his shot cleverly round James.

The second half was level, equally tense and mutually frustrating as the teams counteracted each other, Tottenham ably forcing Liverpool increasingly to play across the face of their defence. Now there was the sneaking feeling that Tottenham were becoming the more likely to score. After 70 minutes Sheringham had a falling, diving header that beat James and spluttered just wide. Six minutes from the end, Calderwood's header from a corner flew a couple of yards wide.

With a minute to go, Tottenham attacked from a throw on the left,

Sheringham glanced the ball behind Scales, and Klinsmann, with the experience of all those years at the top, slid his shot past James.

Francis spoke afterwards of his long-time admiration for Liverpool's style and the wish to emulate them. The change he had effected in 22 matches with Tottenham was, he suggested, built on fitness. 'The fitter you are, the longer you keep your skill level and your concentration,' he said.

No, he did not think he would be signing a contract at the end of the season, always supposing he stayed at White Hart Lane. He likes freedom for his players and for himself.

LIVERPOOL (3–4–3): D James; J Scales; N Ruddock, P Babb; R Jones; S McManaman; J Redknapp; J Barnes; (sub: M Thomas, 75min), R Fowler; I Rush; M Walters; (sub: S Bjornebye, 75min).

TOTTENHAM HOTSPUR (4–4–2): I Walker; D Austin; C Calderwood; G Mabbutt; J Edinburgh; N Barmby; D Anderton; D Howells; R Rosenthal; E Sheringham; J Klinsmann.

Referee: M Bodenham.

CARLING COMES OF AGE

Jack Rowell's chain of command

18 March 1995

Rugby Union is probably the most tactically complex team game there is: more so than cricket, a team game of individuals, and certainly more than Rugby League. If England are playing well, it must therefore follow that Will Carling is doing a highly competent job as captain.

The former Sedbergh schoolboy is 29 and is in his seventh year as captain. At times, there have been criticisms that he did not exert sufficient influence; that, on the field, England had captaincy by committee; that the forwards or stand-off half were too much the decision-makers; that Carling was captain by osmosis. Had not two grand slam opportunities gone begging, the critics asked?

Yet the achievement of a grand slam – winning all four five nations' championship matches – is, in some ways, a confined and even arbitrary way of judging a captain's influence. England could lose today and still win the World Cup. Bill Beaumont, for example, famously won a grand slam, but, in the technicalities of captaincy, is said to have had less than catalytic influence. The reality of Carling's impact has only fully emerged under Jack Rowell's management. As Rowell observed: 'Now is the time that Carling should be at his best as captain – and he's doing well. Is it a coincidence that he's *playing* well?'

Few at Twickenham today will have any idea of the complexity, and flexibility, of spontaneous command that is running through the England team from moment to moment.

Before Rowell's arrival, England tended on any day to have a fixed intention: plan A or plan B. Now, Rowell has the whole team thinking and adapting on the hoof. 'He's very good, particularly at the broad picture,' Carling said. 'He's hands-off, yet quick to say 'Hey!' if it's not happening. There's a lot more info on the field among us. Previously, plan A had to be made to work, there was less flexibility. We had the best set-pieces in the world [with the forwards] and saw no reason to change. Jack doesn't have as structured a look [as Geoff Cooke].'*

Rowell's approach to rugby management is similar to business efficiency: to facilitate delegation, to establish and achieve self-reliance on the field. Captaincy, he insists, is not a matter of saying do this, this and this.

'That's old hat,' Rowell said. 'The captain shouldn't have to go and pick up the ball every time there's a penalty kick. He needs sub-managers. In rugby, there are a lot of moving parts, so the players must be physically, mentally and technically fit enough to take their own decisions in split seconds. The captain has to be a good player, playing well, and have the man-management ability to keep the team going in the right direction, and that must be about winning.'

In any organisation, Rowell says, there are power groups, or sub-teams. The pack must have its leaders (in the present instance, Moore, the hooker, and Richards at No 8). 'The captain shouldn't necessarily be in the pack,' he said. 'Inside centre is a good position – not under pressure at the coalface, having the wider view. The team's potential is dependent on the captain.'

While Carling relies on verbal communication from Moore or Richards, Rowell expects him to have the knowledge, and authority, to change things if he senses that they are not working; to switch, say, from rucking to mauling, or vice versa.

'You can go only so far with a team by *telling* them,' Carling said. 'To win the World Cup, we shall need leaders throughout the side. That's not captaincy by committee, but co-ordination'.

Rowell's management sets out to be non-interventionist by match day, an attempt to ensure that, ultimately, the team is run *by* the team. He cites, as an illustration of what he wants to avoid, the response of a Harlequins player when asked why they had lost a cup match to Bath – 'we're going to ask the coach'.

Halfway through the final team talk the night before any match, when Rowell has given his analysis, the remainder of the discussion is handled by Carling. For the last 30 minutes in the dressing-room before kick-off, there is no coach present, not even Rowell.

'I want the mood where there can be no backsliding, where they know they are responsible, self-reliant,' Rowell said. 'I'm leading from the back. I want the captain leading at the front.'

In the chain of command-improvisation that runs from Moore and Richards through Bracken and Andrew to Carling and back again, there are predetermined codes to relay which player is intended to make the break at the next scrum or lineout, so that the back row can be sure to arrive simultaneously to create second-phase possession.

'It's imperative the forwards play well, so there's got to be a leader,' Moore said. 'Dean [Richards] is a voice of wisdom. He cuts through the verbiage. If we don't win the ball, we can't win matches. Mine's a primary job, as hooker. Weill's is the overview. But both of us rely on Numbers 8, 9 and 10 for practicalities. They – Dean, Kyran and Rob – have to adapt, not attempt things that are not on. They direct the way in which first-phase [possession] becomes second-phase.'

Carling is revelling in the team's development. He acknowledges that he was too young to be captain at 22, but then he did not ask for it. 'Now, I don't have to spend time thinking about every aspect of play, which is a big help to my own game,' he said. 'I can get on and play.'

Winning the World Cup, Carling thinks, will depend much on the ability to assess quickly breakdown situations; to break free from obsession with old, conventional English virtues such as the rolling maul, which brought the first try in Cardiff. To play what Jeremy Guscott has called 'sharp, reactive rugby'.

'If we push out our limits, our ambitions, we can do it,' Carling said. 'If we resort to our former restrictive game, we won't.'

* Memorably defeating Australia with a drop goal by Andrew, England were hammered by New Zealand in the semi-final.

NEGATIVE EQUITY

Scotland's cynical cheating brings no reward

20 March 1995

If World Cup victory by England is to depend on the last-ditch tackling by Mike Catt, at full back, that kept out Scotland on Saturday, heaven help the nation's nerves. England may be bland slam champions, but the odds of success in South Africa will have lengthened after this less than storming performance. All that got slammed on Saturday were the laws of the game.

Jack Rowell, the England manager, has warned often enough that kicks ahead behind the opposition defence that do not find touch – as opposed to up-and-unders – invite instant, dangerous counter-attack, especially on South Africa's firm grounds. England were several times guilty of this; among them, Andrew, the match-winner. Australia, New Zealand or South Africa would exact a harsher penalty for such errors.

A shallow kick ahead that is retrieved, especially by a runner as threatening as Gavin Hastings, can catch the kicker's entire team spread across the pitch, disorganised and not knowing where to expect the point of counter-attack. Momentarily, there is no wall of resistance such as England famously have at set pieces. England now had to be thankful that Scotland were so average, even if they were dismayed at what amounted to Scotland's persistent cheating.

Rugby union is a strange game. Euphemisms dominate. The leading international countries are to all effect professional, yet the administrators, head in sand, continue to pretend that the game is amateur. One player lacerates the face of another with his studs, and people are reluctant to say outright who was the guilty man, when everybody knows. Scotland bent the laws until they were almost back to front and nobody, except, it seems, Brian Moore, the England hooker, is willing to spell it out publicly.

Moore said that Scotland wrecked the game. They did. Traditionalists are appalled by his attitude, by his honesty. He has dared to say, like Danny Kaye: 'The king is in the altogether'. Decent chaps do not say that kind of thing. I say good for Moore. Pretending that things are not the way they are, in rugby, is even worse, in my opinion, than simply ignoring the way things are, as in football.

Scotland were deliberate and cynical in their attitude. Five years ago, to frustrate England at Murrayfield, they had set about collapsing the scrum as often as possible. The referee did almost nothing. On Saturday, at Twickenham, they were offside in loose play continuously throughout the match. Brian Stirling, the Irish referee, could have given Andrew another ten penalty kicks, several of them directly under the posts. In a properly controlled match, Scotland would have been humiliated as the price of their own forlorn expediency.

Frankly, the match as a match was not worth bothering about. If the result had not been all-important, if there had not been a fortnight of expectation and World Cup prognostication hanging on the outcome, you would have been forgiven for walking out before the end. All the talk is of brave Scotland hearts giving the game everything, when all they gave it was a chloroform pad.

We have seen this negative mentality in football for the past 30 years. In no time, the mentality will have gripped rugby union. Unless referees have the courage, and the backing, to stamp on the practice now, to give cards and penalty tries for persistent fouling, rugby can never again be the sport that some people were fooling themselves, at 4.30pm on Satuday, it still is. That belief is wilful self-deception.

TRAVESTY OF JUSTICE IN LAS VEGAS

Foreman reprieved by judges' disgraceful verdict

24 April 1995 Las Vegas

Axel Schulz, from eastern Germany, genuinely and convincingly claimed the International Boxing Federation heavyweight title during 12 rounds of thrilling combination punching on Saturday night. They were dancing in the streets of Frankfurt an der Oder at European sunrise as Schulz punched the air at the final bell.

The shame, sadly also all too genuine, is that three Nevada judges, overcome by sentiment, myopia or bald-faced bias, gave the verdict to G F: grandfather George Foreman, the defender. Those celebrating Germany's triumph were stunned when the sickening decision was announced. Jeering and whistling flooded the arena here.

In this capital of avarice, boxing and the commendable upstart Schulz suffered one of the most disgraceful verdicts in the history of the ring. While the moneymen – Bob Arum, the promoter, and the sleek presidents of HBO Television and the hosting MGM Hotel – squawked like the Queen of Hearts about 'a great fight, a great fight, a great night for boxing', honest men hung their heads in dismay or even shook their fists in fury.

'Axel was robbed,' Johnny Tocco, the veteran Las Vegas trainer-manager, who had advised Schulz, said. 'He scored the points. The decision makes America look so bad.'

On this evidence, even a rusty Mike Tyson would make a fool of the ancient Foreman in their widely projected $100 million (£66 million) clash. A sensible Tyson, ignoring Foreman's jibes of 'avoiding me', will, however, be advised to have a couple of sharpeners before meeting anyone with a big punch.

Boxing, in contrast to its sleazy administration, is and always will be a noble art for some of the truest sportsmen you can meet. Schulz, throwing two hands for every minute of the bout, and the dogged Foreman, leaning on instinct and summoning the bravery that once made him a great boxer, had produced a worthy, dignified bout.

Schulz had routed every American forecaster. When Foreman turned towards his corner at the conclusion, his left eye almost closed by a tomato-sized swelling, his hefty frame was limp in mute acknowledgement of the other man's victory. Schulz modestly raised his arms in recognition of a supposed victory both tactical and physical.

Incredibly, the three judges conclusively awarded the bout to the bruised, dazed defender, whose wrinkled old man's legs had all too evidently gone by the seventh round. Yet the majority of experienced American commentators, never mind their ill-judged pre-bout dismissal of Schulz, gave the verdict to the German by anything from a two to four-round margin.

On my count, Foreman won only the second, fifth and eleventh, with the first even. His brave last charge in the eleventh, lumbering at Schulz like a wounded old buffalo, was an emotional sight even for a neutral. The oldest champion in history weathered Schulz's stinging left lead and counter-punching, himself swinging lefts and rights in the knowledge that he had to knock down his man if he were to win.

Afterwards, Foreman paid tribute to the momentum given to him by the crowd's chanting of 'USA, USA' during the interval before the eleventh. 'I'll never forget it – it pulled me through,' he said, peering at the audience through dark glasses that barely concealed the damage inflicted upon his still handsome face.

The suspicion must be that the judges were among those chanting. Two of them gave the bout to Foreman by seven rounds to five, the third marked them even, though that was almost as laughable.

Yet from the third onwards Schulz – a product of the meticulous former Communist training system within which he developed until the regime collapsed and he turned openly professional – had the champion blinking.

Out of sheer pride, Foreman had refused to take to his stool between rounds, leaning on the ropes in the corner while the veteran Angelo Dundee, rising barely to Foreman's chest, tried to talk his man past trouble. Foreman was seriously in bother by the fifth and sixth, swinging and missing, forced to clinch for the first time. Trouble worsened in the seventh when Schulz, now starting to throw his painful rights to the body, also caught Foreman high on the temple with a right hook which raised the bruise over his eye. Now, it was Foreman backing off, halted in his tracks by two more rights to the body in the eighth.

By the tenth, Schulz knew that the bout was his if he stayed calm. He began to open out, going for his combinations of left lead and right uppercut, left and right hooks. A worried Foreman was increasingly convinced that he had only three rounds to find the one punch that would protect his $50 million share of the Tyson bonus. He never found it, but the judges gave him a reprieve.

Perhaps they gave it for such courage at his age, which was indeed exceptional. While the bout revealed that Schulz has become an accomplished boxer, it also proved that maybe he has not the punch to put down a big opponent.

Schulz was sanguine in his comments. 'Our strategy worked,' he said. 'I scored the points, but I also had to fight the referee and the judges.'

Foreman alleged that a challenger needs to come at his opponent more than Schulz, that Schulz backed off too much. Schulz rejected the criticism. 'I think the main objective in boxing is to avoid punches, and I stuck to that plan,' he said. It was a plan that worked. Or should have.

INSPIRATIONAL SKIPPER LOSES FAVOUR AT HOME

A new storm to weather for Dennis Conner

6 May 1995 San Diego

Is Dennis Conner, one of the finest match-racers in yachting history, no worse than a loveable ogre, nasty but nice, or is he a straightforward involuntary boor? His more loyal friends say he is working to improve his bruised public image, yet the truth is that even some Americans hope the man who has won the America's Cup four times will now lose it for the second time.

In the land of the compulsive winning mentality, something must be seriously amiss to cause such loss of public sympathy. There is more to it than the manipulation of the race regulations that has seen Conner win a defenders' final series from which he had already been eliminated, and then switch to a rival boat to contest the challenge round against *Black Magic*, the New Zealand challenger. This campaign has witnessed the best and worst of the famed sporting streetfighter.

While his dogged, occasionally inspired leadership has extracted the maximum from *Stars & Stripes*, the slowest of three United States hulls in the series, his onshore behaviour has often been surly or loutish. Despite all the hyperbole about American solidarity, when Conner's

crew were allowed to jump ship onto *Young America*, the rival maintenance team engraved teardrops on the face of the mermaid that decorates
Young America's bow.

Throughout the series, Conner consistently ignored the women's crew
of *Mighty Mary*, never speaking to Leslie Egnot, their soft-voiced but
resolute helmswoman, and condoning sexist insults by the crew during
close-range manoeuvres at sea. At a cocktail party, Conner asked *Mighty
Mary's* navigator, Annie Nelson, the wife of *Young America's* designer,
Bruce Nelson, a former crew colleague of his, what it was like being with
a bunch of lesbians. She threw a full glass over him, obliging him to return
home. An embarrassed Bill Koch, owner of *Mighty Mary*, lamely
attempted to excuse the 'locker-room jest'.

This is the man who, some years ago, tried to prevent Paul Cayard,
now his helmsman, from becoming a member of the San Diego Yacht
Club. Cayard was then the protégé of Tom Blackaller, Conner's arch-
rival. Cayard, generously, has forgiven him.

'In the Eighties, Dennis was single-minded and didn't care about anything except winning,' Cayard has said. 'If he was rude, it didn't matter
to him. Now, at 52, he's more concerned about what he is perceived to
be.'

Not always. At the final media conference before the challenge round,
Conner stomped irritably out of the meeting at the finish, refusing to
answer a simple question on his emotional mood going into his seventh
final. 'John can answer that,' he snapped.

John Marshall, the head of the *Young America* syndicate, has done a
rapid somersault. Three weeks ago, he was proclaiming 'the end of the
Conner era'. Now, suddenly, once more in harmony, Conner is worthy
of support.

If they gave British-style international caps for America's Cup races,
Conner would probably wear his in bed. There is the suspicion that
without the separation from more normal life when aboard a yacht under
sail, or the insularity of a loyal, similarly obsessive crew, he feels insecure,
even inferior.

Off the water, he is like a lion-tamer without his lion. His voice carries
a hesitancy. Failure, even the possibility of failure, bothers him. Hence,
perhaps, his evasive response to the question on his mood when facing a
Kiwi boat that has won 37 of its 38 races in the series. For a man who has
achieved all he has, not winning an Olympic gold medal nags him.

The defeat at Newport, Rhode Island, by *Australia II* in 1983 is
scorched on his soul. I remember, as if it were yesterday, him shouldering his way through the milling crowds of joyous Australian supporters
to attend the post-race conference, having inexplicably surrendered a
winning lead in the seventh and last race. This was the master tactician
who never usually made an error, whose first biography was entitled *No
Excuse to Lose*.

He was alone and close to tears. The shell-shocked New York Yacht

Club committee, who had stood frozen in disbelief on the deck of their committee boat, in defeat now abandoned the hick 'loser' from California. 'We sailed well, I'm proud of *Liberty's* crew,' Conner said, before hastening out into darkness, knowing they had excelled against the innovative Australian boat. In that moment, you felt for him. There is a defiance in him that is noble. It was there when, eyes bloodshot and skin parched by the southern sun, he regained the cup in 1987. It has been there throughout this campaign, considering that his under-funded *Stars & Stripes* was the slowest boat. He has refused to concede, whatever the odds.

It is this which makes Tom Whidden, his ever-loyal tactician, say: 'I feel his [bad] image is ridiculous. He's a nice guy.'

That Conner's emotions are close to the surface was apparent after *Stars & Stripes* came from four minutes behind to qualify as the United States defender, *Mighty Mary* having sailed into a windless hole on the final leg. Barely across the finishing line, Conner stated: 'Anybody in touch with reality would not be looking forward to defending the cup with this boat.'

Later, some time after midnight, neighbours at Conner's rented house were awakened by shouting in the street. Conner was loudly arguing with Daintry, his young second wife. 'You can't go out again, it's not safe [at this time of night],' she was insisting. Conner, clearly weary from celebrations, was proclaiming: 'I beat them all today . . . and I need to find a faster boat!'

Such is Conner's reputation among contemporaries that Gary Jobson, a former cup skipper and now commentator, has forecast an American victory over the formidable opponents discreetly led by Peter Blake. Jobson reasons that *Young America* is the fastest defender and has been tested by more close races than *Black Magic*, and that no New Zealander has previously sailed in the final.

Yet the charge of manipulation hangs heavily over Conner; not least that, having switched boats, he has also been permitted by the race committee to transfer *Stars & Stripes'* allowance of new sails, less expended than *Young America's* because of budget shortage.

Conner defends the changes, saying that the regulations allowed alteration 'by mutual consent of the three participating defenders' and that there has been no complaint from Bill Koch. The New Zealanders may sense sharp practice; yet their own publicity brochure, published four months ago, specifically made the point that Conner could conceivably change boats.

Expediency has lived side by side with Conner a long while. During lengthy court battles between the Sail America Foundation and Michael Fay's ill-fated New Zealand challenger, San Diego Yacht Club's brief to arbitrators stated: 'It is repugnant to any sense of fair play and sportsmanlike competition, as well as to the Deed of Gift [of the cup], for the syndicate of Sail America to have the opportunity to manipulate the rules, trials, defender selection and site of the next America's Cup races, in order to favour its own yacht and its own skipper.'

When the opening gun fires today at 21.15 BST, Conner is fighting not just a slick rival seeking New Zealand's first win in four attempts, but for his own credibility.

MASTERS VICTORY, PUPIL'S HOMAGE

Crenshaw's win is charged with emotion

11 April 1995 Augusta

When the last putt sank, so did he. The public expression of private sorrow can occasionally be embarrassing, but not now. As gentle Ben Crenshaw became Masters champion for the second time, at 43, everyone clustered around Augusta National's 18th green understood in that moment the winner's feeling for Harvey Penick, his coach and mentor, whom he buried the day before the tournament began.

Crenshaw was shaking as he bent and dropped his head in his hands, joy overcome by deeper emotions. Slowly across the green came the burly black figure of Carl Jackson, former butler of Jack Stephens, the club chairman, and Crenshaw's caddie these last 19 years. There has never been a cross word between him and the Texan, and now he consolingly put his arm around him. *They* had done it.

Traditionally, the final nine holes of the final day hold the drama of the Masters. Seldom has there been a more fluctuating, engrossing tale, invoking eruptions from the huge galleries as Davis Love III, another pupil of Penick's, Greg Norman, Jay Haas and Fred Couples, all playing out ahead of Crenshaw, made their bids on a scorching late afternoon of fiery greens.

Indeed, as Crenshaw's seven-iron pitch at the notorious short 12th was bunkered in front of the green, threatening his 12-under par lead, Norman and Love each simultaneously birdied the 15th to distant roars of acclaim. This pulled Norman level with Crenshaw and put Love ahead at 13 under.

One of Penick's maxims, a lesson in life as much as in golf, was 'take dead aim'. It is the oldest of military principles: maintenance of the objective. After the first round, Crenshaw had been 16th; after the second he was fourth; and he jointly led on the final day with Brian Henninger. As he observed afterwards, somewhere there was a hand on his shoulder. He had not looked at the leader board until the 15th, when he saw that Love, a close friend, was already home in 13-under, on 275.

If magic did pass from the benevolent Penick, it started at the 9th. From the bottom of the hill, Crenshaw struck a sand wedge some 120 yards which spun back to within a foot, giving him a birdie for 12-under.

Down the other side of the hill, they moved to the formidable par-four 10th, known as the Cathedral hole because of its austere surrounding of a hundred towering pines. A silver half-moon hung in a cloudless sky. The dappled shadows on the sloping green made the line difficult to read; Crenshaw's birdie putt grazed the hole, as it did again at the 11th.

The greeting as he mounted the 12th tee was one of warm friendship rather than mere respect, and a sigh followed him into the trap. A perfect splash-out to within five feet rescued him and he sank the putt. 'Crucial,' he would later say. This, and the next five holes, made him champion.

At the dog-leg, par-five 13th, he pulled his five-iron second shot onto the slope at the back of the green, almost into the azaleas. With the pin at the front, sitting just above the creek, he had a nigh impossible shot. An excruciating bump-and-run feather chip saw the ball halt 16ft short: an equally alarming downhill putt remained. He holed, to go 13-under. Norman had just bogeyed the 17th.

Love, too, had bogeyed the 16th to fall back to 12-under. Crenshaw hit a cunning low-trajectory seven-iron to run up the slope on the 14th, to hold par; and then spent an age considering his second shot to the 15th. Lay up short of the water, or go for the green and an eagle or birdie?

He did an Arnold Palmer: made sure of length with a four-wood, over-hit so much – 'like a bullet' – that it might have run 70 yards further but for being buffered by the gallery. From among their stools and hampers, he had a 20-yard chip back on the green, and two putts for par.

Now came a memorable pitch from tee to 16th green, the ball running a beguiling semi-circle on the sloping skid-pan before coming to rest seven feet from the hole. Another birdie: 14-under.

If that was a fine putt from the man who was without a three-putt green throughout four days, nothing could surpass that at the 17th where he pitched nicely to 16 feet.

As the evening sun cast its long shadow, not a whisper could be heard among the gallery. Crenshaw measured the borrow, remembered Penick's words – never let the head of the club pass the hands – and sank it.

He had five shots to play with on the par-four last hole if he were to put the seal on his gratitude to Penick and on our memory of him. As he said afterwards, 'just another golfer who loves the game'.

MANDELA UNITES A GRATEFUL NATION

Euphoria and symbolism at climax of rugby's World Cup

26 June 1995 Johannesburg

For any other head of state, from Africa or wherever, to have appeared at a Rugby World Cup final wearing a player's No 6 shirt and symbolic cap would have been at best inelegant, at worst histrionic and opportunist. For Nelson Mandela, it was a touch of genius.

To take hold of the very colours of your historic enemy, of your cultural, social and political oppresser, and to raise them aloft as a symbol of brotherhood, was more powerful than a million words. With a mere green-and-yellow cloth on his back, instead of resorting to guns and bombs, this unique statesman's gesture had overturned a former hated bastille of racist privilege and created, instead, a talismanic club of equality.

That this statesman should, coincidentally, be granted the euphoric climax of the narrowest South Africa victory, in extra time, was beyond expectation and served to intensify the impact. What might be achieved elsewhere in the world's most troubled regions by such magnanimity, by such demonstrative respect towards a political rival's most cherished and precious institution?

While sport was officially the name of the game, and the game itself produced one of the most intense afternoons of physical endeavour and emotion that any of those present are ever likely to witness, the wider watching world is entitled to be open-mouthed in admiration for Mandela's spontaneous stage management of this unique moment in his nation's evolutionary crisis. The man is truly blessed with that simultaneous gift of humility and inate leadership. At this finale of five weeks' sporting festivities, blacks and *bokke* saluted him with equal fervour.

Within minutes, literally, of Francois Pienaar, the South African captain, raising the trophy aloft at Ellis Park, the surrounding streets of downtown Johannesburg were grid-locked with wildly celebrating pedestrians and joyriders. It is needless, yet also necessary, to say that 99.9 per cent of them were black. It was hard to believe what one saw as an invisible emotional lid was lifted.

Here, in a city that fundamentally had always cared only for football – though the rugby phenomenon is, and has been, nationwide in recent days – blacks were celebrating a triumph that was *theirs*. They were celebrating South Africa's international identity, they were enjoying the newly-discovered envy of the rest of the world. There are few intoxicants more pleasurable. Mandela and their boys had done it: it was incidental that all but one of their boys was white. Mandela had thus pulled the political magician's trick of all time: to have allowed his rivals the most precious of all prizes they could ever have wished and – *swish* – with one sweep of the cloak, re-presented the prize unchanged, yet suddenly belonging not to the minority but to the majority.

Ask my taxi driver. I am not sure which was the older, he or the vehicle. For 20 minutes, he blew his reedy horn at anybody and anything. He had watched the first half of the match on television and then, back on the road, listened to every kick of the remainder on his rickety radio. It was, undoubtedly, the greatest day of his entire life.

The measure of Mandela's achievement is that, only a year ago, at the time of England's first international tour here for 20 years, his African National Congress colleagues were still ardently anti-Springbok. Within sport, they were busy insisting on the abolition of the reviled Springbok emblem, its replacement by the Protea flower and the categoric substitution of *Die Stem* (The Voice) as national anthem by *Nkosi Sikelele Afrika* (God Bless Africa).

Recognising, from his all too personal and painful experiences, that you can never achieve unity by the moral subjugation of one side, Mandela encouraged, in pursuit of 'one team, one nation', the maintenance of the Springbok emblem – by visible, personal proclamation – and two anthems in parallel.

The unaccompanied rendition by a black choir, at the closing ceremony that proceeded the final, of *Die Stem*, after its own anthem, on a cloudless winter afternoon within a packed stadium, was one of the most moving occasions I have known; lyrical yet nerve-shredding as the hearts of a nation stood still in expectation.

What agonies there were in store. In a final of Herculean commitment, the infantry forces of both packs ground each other in near-neutrality, seldom allowing the cavalry of either side to break into the gallop for which we neutrals longed. Whenever New Zealand did manage to fling the ball out to the towering Lomu on the wing, he was regularly pitchpoled by the heroic kamikaze low tackling of James Small and others. How the cheers echoed.

While South Africa's victory owed much to the mental tenacity and fortitude that, for so long, has been the traditional quality of the *bokke*, tactically and technically it was a duel between two of the lightest men on the field, Joel Stransky and Andrew Mehrtens, the stand-off halves. Gradually, they nudged us towards the prospect, worse by far than the

Brazil v Italy shootout in football's World Cup final in Los Angeles last year, of a South African defeat by the retro-active dismissal of James Dalton against Canada in a pool match.

Then Stransky let fly a second, glorious dropped goal. Minutes later, one nation, blacks and *bokke*, was heaving in ecstasy, the president included. May the significance of the day never be lost.

PISTOL PETE CALLS THE SHOTS

Sampras wins respect, Becker the hearts

10 July 1995

Being a winner and being loved by the public do not necessarily go hand in hand. This may puzzle Pete Sampras, who was yesterday described by Boris Becker as by far the most accomplished of the four men who have defeated him in a Wimbledon singles finals. 'He doesn't give you a chance,' Becker sighed.

Excellence, even fame itself, requires charm to capture affection. Off the court, Sampras is the most gracious of men, but the public remains unaware of this. They see only an untidy figure who looks as if he has fallen out of a tumble dryer, interminably plucking at the strings of his racket between shots.

Sampras yesterday won the Wimbledon title for the third time in succession, yet the crowd's heart remained emphatically with Becker, in spite of the fact that the German, fatigued from his epic semi-final against Agassi, had played short of his best. Sampras held aloft the trophy, but it was Becker whom the crowd wanted to run a lap of honour with his loser's plate. If Sampras is looking for an explanation, it is not far away.

Great champions, of which he undoubtedly is one, usually look as if they enjoy being champion. But Sampras looks about as happy on court as if he were shifting bags of cement in a Panamanian warehouse without the benefit of air conditioning. So the public admires him, but finds it difficult to love him.

Yesterday this irritated Sampras. Having lost the first set, unexpectedly, he then had Becker trailing 40–0 on his own service at 1–1 in the second, as Becker hit a weak volley and then Sampras a fine backhand pass. The crowd, which had enthusiastically greeted Becker's tie-break triumph, considered this change of fortune in near silence.

As Becker prepared to serve again, Sampras gestured at the rows of spectators near to him, invoking some response to this turn of the tide. It did him no good. All the way to the finish, anti-climax though this may have been, the crowd was aching for a Becker revival. It will be a shame if they come to appreciate Sampras only when he is past his best.

There were those who said Bjorn Borg, Wimbledon champion five times in succession, was boring. Yet Borg's geometric mastery of the tennis court, and of all opponents whether grass-court or hard-court specialists, was a marvel. Only the casual, vicarious spectator could not have appreciated him.

Sampras, who joins Fred Perry as the only other man besides Borg since the First World War to win three successive titles, is similar to Borg: his personality is expressed by his racket rather than by facial illumination, intellect or humour.

Becker, who is a close friend of Sampras off the court, was generous in his appreciation of the man. The game being played by Sampras, Becker said, was altogether different from that of Lendl, McEnroe and Edberg, the dominant figures when Becker himself emerged. 'They gave you a chance on their service,' he recalled, 'but, when Sampras hits those bombs at you, you just hope for rain.'

Never mind the lack of public response, Becker said, the fact is that Sampras 'is a role model who behaves well on the court and doesn't have a bad shot in him'. His three successive victories, Becker said, were 'an amazing feat', especially because this year he had struggled in some of his matches.

It was particularly difficult, Becker reflected, because Sampras was such a good front-runner once he had gained the lead. 'When he broke my service in the second set, he went up another level, and there was nothing I could do,' he said.

Sampras was so modest afterwards, so undemonstrative, that it was almost as though he had not yet appreciated the magnitude of his achievement. He had not even begun to think about emulating Borg's five in a row. Even three was 'a kind of a blur'. He did recall with affection how, six years ago in Philadelphia, when he was 17, Perry had told him he would win Wimbledon one day. Like all of us, he regretted the loss of Perry's magnetism, humour and good advice from the dressing-rooms these days.

It was pleasing that, on two consecutive days, Wimbledon should have such amiable and rational losers as Sánchez Vicario and then Becker. It is the quality of the loser that is fundamental to the quality of the winner, and it is imperative that Wimbledon, among the great traditional sporting events, should retain this quality.

With its ever-expanding commercial development, Wimbledon becomes increasingly like Gatwick airport: as much about eating and shopping as about flying/tennis. The players themselves must be attentive to preserving the essence of sport, which Wimbledon represents, if eating and shopping are not to become all that matters.

That first service break at 1–1 in the second set, when Sampras appealed to the crowd, was unquestionably the turning point of the match. From then on, Becker's prospects were ever in decline as the relentless Sampras – 'Pistol', to his friends – shot his legs from under him. Becker's 15 double faults did not help.

FORMER RENEGADE BECOMES A TRUE CHAMPION

Daly's Open victory is a fitting reward

24 July 1995

The buffeting wind and gusting showers that galloped across the Old Course yesterday afternoon had marginally relented as John Daly strode towards the Open Championship title, just as the fires within his soul have eased over the past two years.

For nearly 4½ hours, Daly, the wild one, had been a picture of composure and control as he overhauled the overnight leaders to place himself within reach of a second major title to add to his US PGA victory in 1991. The dream began to slip after the 14th hole where, between putts, he allowed himself a furtive glance at the leader-board.

At that point, he had three shots in hand over Michael Campbell, and four over Costantino Rocca. The crowd from the start had given him every encouragement. True to that streak in human nature, the appeal created by the whiff of anarchy and vulnerability in a public sports performer had gathered momentum in recent days, and now there could have been no more popular a winner.

It is his golf, rather than the man, which is handsome. The potter's thumb slipped when the clay for Daly was on the wheel, but as compensation for his ungainly features and erratic temperament, he was granted the gift of remarkable flair with golf clubs. Yesterday, he gave exemplary proof of that for 14 holes.

It was then merciless misfortune when, at the par-five 15th, having pitched to some 30 feet or more to the right of the pin, his first putt hit the back of the hole and bounced out. A birdie there, to add to those at the 4th, 7th and 8th, and the title would have been his outright.

Had the ball not hit the hole, he admitted later, it would have run several feet past. 'So I was glad to hit it.'

Jack Nicklaus had said before the round that, despite Daly's marvellous touch around the greens and his immaculate short game – superb yesterday – his huge distances off the tee would make it more difficult to control the ball in the fearsome crosswinds. Yet seldom had Daly been in trouble until he came to the 16th.

Here, he pitched short and was left in a hollow at the front of the green, overhit his first putt from 70 feet to five yards past the hole, and missed the one back, downhill. Having begun five under and moved to eight under, he had dropped a shot. 'That was the only bad thing I did,' he said.

The formidable 17th still awaited him. He had hooked a couple of earlier drives, but only onto the adjacent fairway. Now he was wretchedly placed out of sight of the green, behind the temporary stand at the back of the 1st tee, and his blind pitch landed in the Road bunker, side by side with his partner, Ernie Els, whose prospects had disintegrated around the Loop.

Daly splashed out well to the left of the flag, leaving him with a longish uphill putt. A huge welcome from the crowd will have helped to steady his nerve, and he rolled his putt to within two feet, but another shot had been dropped. His approach to the 18th was 25 feet from the hole. He two-putted, and thus had the agony of waiting to see whether Rocca, now only one shot behind, could birdie the final hole to force a play-off. Rocca's spectacular uphill putt, following his appalling fluffed chip, was one of the great moments of golf.

It had been a harrowing climax for Daly. After the third round, he had said that he had no idea how he would react if he found himself placed to win the Open, never having been in the position before. It has to be said that he faltered, but none could suggest that over those last three holes he was a quitter. The renegade of the past became a true champion in the four-hole play-off.

His battle against his private weaknesses, his rehabilitation from alcoholism and for being, off the course, a loose cannon, has been resolute. If now he remains vulnerable to eating excesses and to gambling, the latter as a means of relaxation, these problems serve to generate an affection among those who admire the power and electric quality he exhibits around the course.

None could have set about closing his hands around the trophy with more application. The first three holes were put away with faultless par. At the 4th, left with a 30-foot uphill putt, he sank it, and the challenge was on. At the long 5th his drive was in a nasty hollow in the rough, but he recovered well on to the fairway, pitched to within 50 feet, and two-putted.

As he and Els set off down the dog-leg 7th, the rain was driving into their backs, and the wind accelerated by compression from the low clouds. Holing from eight feet for a birdie, Daly gained another shot, and did so again when holing from 12 feet at the short 8th. Suddenly, the sun was shining again on the huge gathering at St Andrews, and on none more than the blond American.

He hooked his tee-shot into rough on the 9th, but saved par with a critical putt from eight feet, then two-putted into a headwind that was almost strong enough to blow the ball back at him at the 10th. At the short 11th, his birdie putt was two inches wide.

Now they turned for home, with the wind pushing to the favoured left side. That was no problem with a hook from the tee at the long 14th, but would prove a nightmare at the 17th. 'That bunker shot at 17 was do or die,' Daly said. 'I had nowhere to go. I just took my chance.'

The demonstration of control for most of the day was confirmed when he said: 'It's the first time I've not attacked the course. I got nervous after 15. I felt my knees shaking, and my whole body. I've never felt that before.'

Whatever the inner anxieties, or the brief moment of dismay when Rocca's ball dropped to create a tie, Daly was equal to the occasion. He was on the putting green, to re-focus his concentration almost before Rocca had climbed back to his feet on the 18th having collapsed in joy. It surprised few that he should win the play-off so comprehensively, for on this day he had been a man, not a maverick.

CONTRADICTIONS OF AN UNFULFILLED CHAMPION

Christie still erratic off the track

5 August 1995 Gothenburg

Linford Christie stands once again on the threshold of success in a significant athletics event. Great Britain hopes that he will retain his 100 metres title at the World Championships, which begin here today. He has fulfilled every ounce of his potential on the track, but has he met his own expectations off it?

Five years ago, at the European Championships in Split, Christie expressed ambition, in a lengthy interview with *The Times*, to help in the sporting education of athletic youngsters. In the interim, he has advanced spectacularly as a sprinter.

'I could help bridge the gap, the sport can be better run,' Christie said at the time, suggesting that he would welcome the opportunity of an administrative post to encourage the development and appointment of, particularly, more black coaches and officials by the then British board. At the time, he was working for the Milk Marketing Board, lecturing at schools on the role and responsibility of the international athlete.

What has happended since Split is that he has famously become Olympic, World and Commonwealth champion, in the fastest of times against the swiftest of opponents, including Carl Lewis, but, some would say, his sprinting success has not been matched by his conduct in relations with officialdom. He has been criticised for the extent of his financial demands, he has recently shown scant regard for normal competition regulations at the domestic championships and he has become erratic and emotional in his public statements.

This is regrettable. Athletics – and particularly black athletes – needs responsible, mature voices and leaders in Britain, where equality still falls short on the racial front. Instead of acquiring more authority through his immense success, Christie now has less.

It is normal for sporting champions from all parts of the world to find difficulty in adjusting to public acclaim. At an untidy, commercially origentated sponsor's press conference yesterday, Christie said: 'I can't get more famous than I am now . . . you don't need to sing my praises . . . I've got everything to lose.'

Quite apart from it not being his prerogative to evaluate the extent of his fame, he seems not to understand the nature of genuine fame, which survives defeat in the normal advance of years. He is so full of contradiction. His dedication to the interests of the British team is, on the one hand, unwavering. He has insisted on living here in sweltering Gothenburg in the less than adequate athletes' accommodation. He stressed yesterday the pity that Colin Jackson was absent because the Americans 'look vulnerable in the relay'.

On the other hand, he can show scant respect for colleagues, such as that he showed Braithwaite when manipulating the AAA championships, or when ostentatiously signing autographs alongside the track at Crystal Palace simultaneously with events under way. Uniquely for a champion, he was booed by the crowd at the trials, which sensed instinctively his unethical attitude. Yet this is the man who could dedicate a gold medal to the late Ron Pickering, the president and inspiration of the Haringey club, mecca of black competitors.

Christie is articulate, amusing and relaxed when so minded, but it is clear that he has, like many, found public exposure and prestige simultaneously intoxicating and confusing. Nuff Respect, the marketing agency built around himself and Jackson, while seeking legitimate financial opportunities, has conspicuously failed in public relations. Demands for £50,000 appearance money from the British Athletic Federation (BAF) were provocative in a sport confronted by declining sponsorship and audience interest in the post Ovett/Coe/Cram era, never mind that Jackson could, last year, draw an 11 million-strong television audience for his Commonwelath Games hurdles final. Christie even contemplated joining Jackson in the recent Padua appearance-money trip that conflicted with the AAA championships.

'There has been nobody prepared to stand up to him,' a member of the BAF management said yesterday; at least, not until Peter Radford, the executive chairman, resisted Christie's demands in a public row earlier this season that damaged credibility all round.

Christie oscillates under the pressure of tabloid media attention, for which he deserves sympathy but lacks advice. 'I'm so fed up I could walk out any day,' he said during one outburst. 'I used to love it, but it doesn't mean much any more.'

Yet here he was yesterday saying that it fills him with pleasure every time 'they play *God Save The Queen* for me rather than the *Stars and Stripes.*' He is a miserable hero one moment, defiant again the next. He feels somehow persecuted, yet the British public has given him unrestrained applause, and reward, for his glory.*

Everyone hopes he will retain his title tomorrow, but he urgently needs to recognise that British athletics acutely needs new champions.

Christie has, in every sense, put a lot in the bank. He should now consider how best to utilise his credit, for the benefit of the sport as well as himself in the second half of his life. Those who continue to market their fame when achievement has ceased, such as Arnold Palmer, Mohammed Ali and Henry Cooper, have done so because of their charm, not by exhibiting resentment.

* Christie pulled a muscle in the semi-final and was sixth in the final.

BRITISH TRIPLE JUMPER DOES MORE THAN WIN

The world warms to modest Edwards

9 August 1995 Gothenburg

Despite what American sporting culture attempts to teach us about the importance of winning, much of the world still admires good losers. Even more, there is instinctive admiration for winners who are gracious rather than assertive. The difference in appeal between a Connors and an Ashe does not require explanation.

The Swedish crowd here, and an international audience of millions, responded to the astonishing performance of Jonathan Edwards, in leaping 60 feet, with unrestrained pleasure because they spontaneously recognised what they saw: a man without any assumption in his moment of greatness. When an extraordinary champion behaves in such an ordinary way, it is so much easier to share his joy.

Too many champions nowadays, in all sports, *demand* acclaim. It is, they seem to think, a reward they should receive as of right. It is as though the fame of achievement is more important than the achievement itself. Edwards looked as much bemused as overjoyed. He did not suddenly cast away the boundaries of perspective. 'It's only jumping into a sandpit,' he said. Almost disparagingly, he reflected: 'If I had had to choose an event [originally], I probably wouldn't have done the triple jump.'

Yet the applause that greeted Edwards when the Queen of Sweden placed the gold medal around his neck lasted longer than for any other winner of these championships so far. There was a particular warmth, and it was accorded as much to the man as to what he had just done. The Swedes are a dignified and restrained people, and here was someone with whom they could identify.

The appreciation was by no means limited to Scandinavians and the British. As the *International Herald Tribune* reported, when he rose from the sand after his second record jump, 'he stared down at his impression in the sand as if it wasn't his impression at all. The jump had been beyond his imagination'.

'He is an echo of *Chariots of Fire*,' Juan Antonio Samaranch, President of the International Olympic Committee said, 'not because of his religious faith [like that of Eric Liddell, who ran in the 1924 Olympic Games] but in his manner.'

The quality of modesty is not exclusively a British phenomenon, and there were those who found Harold Abrahams, Liddell's 100 metres rival, less than modest. Yet a strange twist of perception regarding Britain has occurred within international sport in recent years. The tradition of British modesty, the so-called Corinthian spirit, has become to be seen as a failing, even by some of the British.

An American history of the decathlon, for instance, refers to sportsmanship as 'an invention of the British in the nineteenth century', as though this attitude was obsolete in this commerical, winning-is-everything era. The irony of that comment, of course, is that of all athletic events, the decathlon is consistently demonstrative of a true sporting ambience among rival competitors.

A sense of sportsmanship is as natural to the human mind as that of right and wrong, never mind that it may be corrupted every day. Edwards's sportsmanship is such that, to a degree, he found it uncomfortable to be in the victor's chair when being interviewed afterwards.

Sympathising with the deposed doyen of triple jumping, Mike Conley, Edwards said: 'Suddenly, a skinny-looking, ordinary guy comes along and decimates the event.' Self-confessedly shy and uncertain at university, he cannot believe he left home in Devon 'with no job to go to in Newcastle, to try to be an athlete jumping 15 or 16 metres.'

Edwards is a champion as modest as Mary Peters or Dave Moorcroft, while his performance has left his peers in awe. Now he must find an agent – 'an area that is funny to me' – because he has the potential to make £500,000 from performances and endorsements in the next few years. His secret, as such, is speed plus control. Look at most triple jumpers and on the 'step', switching from one leg to the other, their upper body, shoulders and arms are usually off the horizontal line and out of equilibrium. Edwards, by comparison, looks as if he is cast in bronze.

I suspect, however, that his real secret, which neither he nor any coach or sporting psychologist can define, lies in his head. His faith, he says, is the basis of his whole life.

GLORIOUS THEATRE PRODUCES NO LOSERS

Ryder Cup again proves flagship to rest of sporting world

26 September 1995

Triumph and disaster, Kipling's twin imposters, have seldom been so conspicuously side by side on stage as they were on the 18th green at the Oak Hill Country Club on Sunday. There, together, as though in the same room, stood horror and joy: two groups of people divided by no more than the whim of a golf ball around a hole, behaving as though alternately experiencing bereavement and a birth.

It was truly an extraordinary sight: although the contrasting emotions were justified, they were overwhelmingly exaggerated. The beauty of the 31st Ryder Cup, which Europe won by one point, was not the result, but the magnificence of the contest: a theatrical, six-hour cavalcade of 12 separate acts in which the united outcome remained in doubt until the final agonies of two of the last three matches.

These people, Americans and Europeans, are, after all, usually friends. When their shaking limbs, their minds anaesthetised by anxiety, have returned to normal, it must be hoped that the bond between the sides will hold a lifetime's shared significance of equal pride.

In a professional sporting world wrecked by greed and exploitation, the Ryder Cup, devoid of material incentives, remains a flagship of competition for honour and friendship. There was no dishonour in so narrowly losing such a momentous event, any more than there was when Langer missed his putt four years ago.

Some of the fleeting but enduring memories are Jacobsen's embrace of Clark when the latter holed in one at the 11th on Sunday; Rocca putting his arm around Woosnam's shoulders in reassurance during the Saturday four-ball, having just birdied the 11th and 12th to restore their lead over Love and Crenshaw; and Mickelson's forlorn embrace of Johansson, his former Arizona college companion, after winning the last but, by then, irrelevant singles.

'We'll stay friends, whoever wins the Cup,' they had vowed beforehand, never supposing that they would be cast against each other carrying the last torch of each side.

Yet, at the conclusion of a glorious autumn day among the towering oaks and firs of Oak Hill, the United States team filed into the interview room, in their Fifth Avenue grey checked jackets, like a row of ghosts, hollow-eyed and expressionless. Such is the expectation now mounted around the outcome, since Europe's first victory in 1985, that the pain of defeat has become intolerable. That ought not to be so.

The outcome of any Ryder Cup is the gradual building of a pile of imponderables – holes in one by Rocca and Clark, holed chips from off the green by Pavin, Haas and Ballesteros, missed putts from four feet – so that the drama of the whole is an amalgam of unrelated individual incidents that defy conclusive analysis.

The Americans did not capitulate. Lehman was resolute against the waywardly brilliant but fading Ballesteros; Couples fought valiantly for his half with Woosnam; Love's excellence subdued Rocca, who had become one of Europe's foremost players; Pavin, with his four victories in five matches, including that devastating chip from off the final green against Faldo and Langer on Saturday afternoon, now emphatically beat Langer.

Yet, who would have forecast the victories by Clark over Jacobsen, James over Maggert, Walton over Haas? If there was one indisputable element in the last analysis, it is that the Americans were over-confident. That confidence was audible over three days in the television commentary of Paul Azinger. He simply did not believe that they could lose, especially from two up after two days; and nor, I suspect, did Lanny Wadkins, the captain. 'I really thought we had them in the bag,' Faxon, beaten by the unruffled Gilford, said.

Thus, as the pressure began to mount inexorably thoughout Sunday, the Americans were less ready to accelerate in response. It is the oldest lesson in sport, and a bunch of Americans learnt it in the most painful way.

The pressures are, of course, indescribable; the more so when, as the Cup reaches a climax, players know that their colleagues are around the green, silently moving every muscle and nerve in tune with theirs. 'There was someone else's legs standing out there,' Walton half-whispered as he recalled his short wedge on the 18th, which cleared the rough's rim by only six inches, and then his putt for the Cup.

If any one shot can be said to have won the Cup, it was Faldo's 90-yard pitch on the 18th to within four feet. 'Everything was shaking except the putter,' he said.

Rocca, whose three points were critical, especially coming from a seemingly vulnerable player, emerged as probable pillar of the future. Affection for this finest of sportsmen, so indefatigably good-natured, is equal among colleagues, opponents and public. 'I lost today,' he said, 'but I have 11 friends more.'

COMFORTABLE IN THE HOT SEAT

Atherton maturing as batsman and captain

20 October 1995

There is nobody in English sport more exposed, in performance, character and leadership, than the captain of the Test team. Ian Chappell, foremost among Australia cricket captains, said when commentating on the Melbourne Test last winter: 'These are the field placings of a captain who has lost faith in his bowlers.'

Michael Atherton's captaincy survived a disappointing, much criticised tour: just. He was initially reappointed, some thought insultingly, only for the opening three matches of the summer. By September, he had confirmed that he is becoming one of the outstanding England captains in post-war cricket.

For his resolution at the crease and leadership against West Indies, he is certainly more worthy of being the sports personality of the year than the BBC's usual run of snooker players, motor racing drivers or self-preoccupied runners.

During a period of substantial change in personnel and constant frustration from injuries, Atherton has held the reins for 24 of his 50 Tests, winning seven and losing ten. He is only 27. On England's first official visit to South Africa for 31 years, he has the chance to consilidate a position that could remain his to the turn of the century.

For a Lancastrian, he has a Yorkshire streak of obstinacy that is invaluable both as opening batsman and captain. Like a panel of walnut wood, the colours of his personality have become more apparent with maturity. He is pleasingly without assumptions.

'I haven't changed much in style,' he says, 'just become more experienced, so that I'm able to do better because I'm dealing with things for the second or third time. I'm more positive, though that's not to say I was previously negative.

'Maybe my demeanour, the field placings [in Australia], betrayed we were on the back foot, that we needed more kidology. After the defeat in Brisbane, it was difficult.'

He feels he has been consistent, true to himself, straightforward with the team. 'Those who play under me know that I'm not image-conscious, that what they see is what they get. It's very simple. I demand the basics from them. If they don't give that, I'm entitled to feel upset; if they do, I'm understanding of their [individual] failings.' Like the best in any field, he leads by example.

Atherton played for England first under David Gower, briefly in 1989, then Graham Gooch; for Lancashire, under David Hughes, Neil Fairbrother and Mike Watkinson. He learnt by observation rather than discussion. 'I do talk to people, but there's no one I ring once a week. I did go out of my way to talk to Ian Chappell, the best of the modern Australians, and I've been lucky to have had Keith Fletcher and Raymond Illingworth [as managers] because they're so well-regarded.'

Cannily, he never considers how long he might continue, always thinking in the short term, aware that reversal lurks around every corner. 'I've been around long enough to know that if you're coasting, the game can come back at you,' he said, remembering his back injury four years ago.

Atherton has found the relentless pressure of public scrutiny and expectation, and the demanding calendar, has served to harden his resolve to find a winning team. The tabloid pack is not going to break this one.

'Playing the year round, you either lose your edge or become more determined. I feel more on top of it now, have proved I can handle the pressure of getting my due amount of runs at the top of the order – which is important as captain – and that tactically I've got a grip of things. I hope I'll improve.'

In his unassuming way, he is not sure if his reliability at the crease has come from need, the responsibility as captain, or simply from the aggregate of experience. He admits the captaincy can at times be a burden, but talks lightly of the requirement for 'a bit of equilibrium'. He smiles easily.

On his relationship with Illingworth, who has Field Marshal Montgomery's certainty of his own wisdom, Atherton is frank yet tactful. But the management structure is simpler and clearer, he says, with Illingworth as chairman and manager, and the captain in charge on the field, dealing with players first-hand.

'He's not an interferer,' Atherton says. 'He's happy to let me get on with things, but I like to have him in the dressing-room because he has a good presence, he's somebody I can fall back on, talk to at lunchtime and teatime if the need arises. He's not too distant, despite his age. He's a professional Yorkshireman, and there's not a game in which he took five for 100 that he doesn't recall off-hand. He leaves room for self-mockery, which contradicts the criticism. I think he prefers the dressing-room to the committee-room.'

Atherton insists he his happy with the extent of his input on selection, Illingworth having the casting vote, and that they are now finding the continuity of selection fundamental to success. 'If you chop and change you get nowhere.'

After the Old Trafford Test this summer, men from Manchester Grammar School were queueing up to congratulate their former colleague, yet Atherton, never mind his Cambridge University background, sits comfortably in John Major's classless society: shoulder-to-shoulder with his team, yet sufficiently apart, and severe, to be a respected captain.

The eye that can, and does, stare down Ambrose, when he follows through intimidatingly is one to avoid by any England player who might drift.

When Atherton came on the scene in 1989, the Test side had been through a period of free-wheeling: a clique of friends sure of a place, a good income, and a shade happy-go-lucky. Atherton wants men who are first for England. 'If there was any of that now, nice 'n' easy, they'd be out. We're getting there, the right type in the team, no bad eggs, nobody 'getting by'. There's enough competition for that to be long past.' Of the party for South Africa, the eight or nine 'certain picks' make a sound nucleus – a happier situation, the captain says, than having Stewart, Smith, Gough, Malcolm and Hick injured, as in recent experience.

'The established batsmen, myself, Stewart, Smith, Thorpe and Hick, are all in the right age group, all experienced, with Test hundreds behind them. That's a strong batting side. Malcolm, Gough and Cork have genuine pace and fire-power, Fraser and Martin less pace but steadiness, applying pressure through accuracy. So I'm hopeful. The key thing will be maintaining fitness.'

The No 3 in the batting order, he admits, is the debate. There was talk of taking another opener, but it was considered best for Nick Knight and Jason Gallian to go to Pakistan on the A tour. 'The chance is there for Ramprakash or Crawley to take.'

Atherton shrugs off South Africa's high-pitched, in-season preparation. 'That's an advantage, but we're the more experienced, and you soon get back the buzz. The first three Tests will decide the series – they're the "result" wickets.'

If the England batsmen master Allan Donald, Atherton should return home victorious.

KARATE CHAMPION TARGETS URBAN DESPAIR

Geoff Thompson's crusade against youth crime

24 November 1995

Youth crime today costs Great Britain £7 billion a year. In perhaps one of the most intense personal campaigns since William Wilberforce's for the abolition of slavery, the Youth Charter for Sport (YCS) was launched in Manchester yesterday.

The founder, inspiration and life-force of the YCS, a man who will talk you to the point of exhaustion in three hours, or less, given the chance, is Geoff Thompson. When Thompson was a violent, disorientated boy committed to unspecific vengeance on a society that he felt had disowned him, his mother forecast his lifestyle would find him dead by the age of 20.

Rescued from the streets of Hackney, east London, by the Sobell centre in Islington, taught the self-discipline of karate, which channelled his aggression, Thompson became the world champion five times. In astonishment and gratitude at the transformation in his life, and for his achievements, the hyperactive Thompson is attempting to create an institution that will rescue other youngsters from the streets, gangland and despair.

Yesterday, after a reception in Manchester hosted by the Duke of Westminster and attended by Manchester City Council leaders, corporate business and youth agencies, promises of funding in cash and kind were pouring into YCS coffers. The initiative is one that has drawn the attention not only of the Conservative Government, but also of government and youth agencies in gang-torn Los Angeles, in Cape Town and in Johannesburg. Thompson is a consultant in both those countries.

'If we could pocket the enthusiasm shown today, we could achieve so much,' Thompson said after the launch, which was attended also by Alex Ferguson, the Manchester United manager, never mind that the heart of Thompson's social renaissance lies in Moss Side, within a few hundred yards of Manchester City's Maine Road ground.

This was an area where, only a few years ago, city councillors dared not tread. Or journalists, for that matter. Murders were commonplace, vandalism rampant and unchecked. Even the supervisor at one leisure centre was kidnapped. Security guards at Nia Leisure Centre wore bulletproof vests; entrances had electronic metal detectors.

In barely two years, establishing an unprecedented relationship with local youth and schools, Thompson has transformed facilities such as Proctor Youth Centre, Hulme, the Nia Centre and the Moss Side Youth Centre.

For half a day, I toured with him the Moss Side streets. So derelict had the area been that the only occupation of older people was fear. Today, the centres are safe, busy, a thriving picture of racially-integrated social life. White, black and Asian children learn to swim side by side; mothers and teenagers work out at aerobics in the gymnasiums.

The Moss Side Youth Centre has 18 part-time staff, three volunteers and a participant turnover of 5,000 a week. Eighteen projects of the YCS have already raised £1 million. Thompson needs and seeks millions more.

'For a fraction of the cost of crime, we can steer a great many antisocial young people away from drugs and violence by giving them an opportunity to develop a life thorugh sport,' Thompson said. 'Many of Britain's top athletes have used sport to overcome social disadvantage, I'm one of them.'

The progress is visible, tangible and exciting. A football team, Moss Side Amateurs, drawn exclusively from gangland, lead the local league, yet for the time being they play on a pitch where there is no changing-room, no toilet. If someone would provide the cash, they would find the voluntary bricklayers, plasterers, carpenters and electricians.

South Africa, which wants to copy Thompson's initiative, has sent the first multicultural football side, an under-23 Olympic squad that will play Manchester United's youth side.

In 1993, shortly after the Los Angeles riots, a group of US youngsters visited Moss Side. The next year, against all advice, the YCS organised a return visit for 16 children in a party led by Dame Mary Glen Haig, a member of the International Olympic Committee, and organised by Thompson together with Billy Hughes and Pauline Weir, two youth leaders. The trip was a huge success.

'Today's launch has given us a national platform,' Thompson said yesterday, 'but all agencies concerned with youth and schools must work together. Without a collective national approach, we will not be able to redirect the violent way of life as seen in America.

'We need a response from the Home Office as much as the Department of Education. The YCS can perhaps produce a few sports winners, but the overall benefit is to the whole of society. I can't now do any more on my own.'